MW00989667

Grant Green

Rediscovering the Forgotten Genius of Jazz Guitar

SHARONY ANDREWS GREEN

San Francisco

Published by Miller Freeman Books
600 Harrison Street, San Francisco, CA 94107
Publishers of *Guitar Player, Bass Player,* and *Keyboard* magazines

Distributed to the book trade in the U.S. and Canada by Publishers Group West,
P.O. Box 8843, Emeryville, CA 94662

Distributed to the music trade in the U.S. and Canada by Hal Leonard Publishing,
P.O. Box 13819, Milwaukee, WI 53213

Design: Sandra Kelch
Copy Editor: Carolyn Keating
Production Editor: Jan Hughes

Library of Congress Cataloging in Publication Data:
Green, Sharony Andrews.
Grant Green : Rediscovering the Forgotten Genius of Jazz Guitar / by Sharony Green
p. cm.
Discography: p.
ISBN 0-87930-556-8
1. Green, Grant. 2. Guitarists—United States—Biography. 3. Jazz musicians—United States—Biography. I. Title.
ML419.G74G74 1999
787.87'165'092—dc21 98-43710
CIP
MN

Printed in the United States of America
99 00 01 02 03 04 5 4 3 2 1

Photo previous page by Francis Wolff, courtesy of Mosaic Images.

Cover photo by Francis Wolff, courtesy of Mosaic Images.

Back cover albums courtesy of Blue Note Records, a division of Capitol Records.

In special memory of
Joe Charles and Oliver Francis Matheus

...ask Jah to cool my tempest so that I may write safely and accomplish my mission.

—Peter Tosh

Earl Buchanan Presents
JAZZ GREATS
Volume 1
SUNDAY, APRIL 7 8 P.M.
Get Your Tickets NOW!
★ HORACE SILVER
★ GLORIA LYNNE
★ GRANT GREEN
Plus extra added attraction
The "ELECRIFYING"
★ EDDIE HARRIS
EDDIE HARRIS
HORACE SILVER
GRANT GREEN
GLORIA LYNNE
MASONIC
AUDITORIUM - Temple at Cass
Tickets: $5.50, $4.50, $3.50, Avail. all Hudson's & Grinnell's,
White's Record Shop & Vaughn's Book Store
ADDED FEATURE
Frederick of Berkower's Fur Shoppe
FUR FASHIONS '6
CLUB
FENKELL at NORTHLAWN
MOZAMBIQ
GRANT GREEN
Coming FRI. DEC. 28
BRO. JACK McDUFF
APPEA
Thru S
DEC. 2

Table of Contents

Foreword

Japanese jazz fans have had a bad habit of relying completely on magazines and newspaper ratings of artists. Whenever a well-known critic writes, "Listen to this great artist," that record sells. After having bought the record, people are often disappointed when they actually hear the music. The listeners of jazz must be able to trust their own ears. I find it very regrettable that many listeners have been missing out on great artists whose music deserves to be heard.

In Japan, we do not have and never have had jazz music constantly flowing out of FM radio as it does in the States. Instead we have a great place called the "jazz coffee shop," where you can indulge in jazz records all day long for the price of a cup of coffee (a slightly expensive coffee, about three dollars). More than twenty years ago when I was a student, these places only played the so-called "upright" jazz that was recommended by the critics. It was in a shop run by a somewhat cranky owner that I came across music by Grant Green. In those days critics always spoke highly of Wes Montgomery and Kenny Burrell, but Grant Green was not exactly who they had in mind. They said that he "lacked in artistic quality," but when I first listened to Grant Green, something else rang true. "This is jazz," I thought, and that is when I began to trust my ears.

Two years after getting *Feelin' the Spirit,* which was the first Grant Green record that I bought, I had the complete selection of his Blue Note albums released under the Blue Note label. Even though most of them were not even pressed in Japan and were not easy for a student to spend money on, I am proud to say that they have now become my personal treasures.

From 1977 to 1983, as the A&R person at King Records in charge of the Blue Note label, I reissued the LPs of Grant Green as part of a license deal with United Artists Records. I also released, in collaboration with Michael Cuscuna, his unreissued masters on LP. All my efforts have been very fruitful.

I have often said that the guitarists who represent the '60s are Wes, Kenny, and Grant Green. And that one can never talk about jazz guitar without listening to Grant Green. In the past this has brought me ridicule by many critics. But today I feel very proud when I hear the young listeners, who now carry Grant Green's music in a Walkman, praising him just as I did. Trust your ears. Trust Grant Green. He is what we call jazz.

—Yoichi Nakao, Tokyo, Japan

Preface

I was born in 1967, four years after Grant Green recorded his *Idle Moments* album for Blue Note. In December 1994, that album ranked No. 9 on *Rolling Stone* magazine's Alternative chart—more than thirty years after it was recorded. This chart reflects the music being played on college radio stations across the United States. Its primary audience is college students, at the time Gen-Xers, who were dismissed as an unfocused bunch by the Boomer experts. But they have never received full credit for the revival of something pretty intelligent—jazz.

For too long, jazz was overly intellectualized. Its most urgent need was to speak to a young audience. Instead it had become the kind of music featured on late-night radio by the geriatric set, who rattled off names, dates, and sessions without offering context. Hip-hop changed that in the late 1980s. Rappers began to "sample," or digitally fuse, tracks by R&B artists from the funk era of the 1960s and early 1970s. Thousands of James Brown and George Clinton tracks were swiped. But the trend managed to revive the career of these two funk masters and others, including old-school jazz musicians, who were smart enough to participate the first time around—musicians like Grant Green.

Critics often dismissed the bulk of Grant's work from the late 1960s and 1970s as a lame effort to pay the rent. Truth is, it was the laid-back funky jazz tracks that he and others like Lou Donaldson and Horace Silver recorded that hooked rappers and deejays in what became known as the "acid jazz" movement. The most telling example of Grant Green's appeal was the smooth coup by the London-based hip-hop group Us3, who lifted riffs of Grant Green's "Sookie, Sookie" tune from a bootlegged tape and ended up with a contract with Blue Note Records. Their 1993 *Hands on the Torch* album featured songs from Blue Note artists like Grant Green and sold millions of copies worldwide, making the group the most successful to come out of London in a good long while.

Today, acid jazz has evolved into something pretty indeterminable. At best, there are signs that it created a renewed appreciation for jazz and the instruments used to play it. Witness jungle music, and all its hybrids, like drum and bass. Or Erykah Bàdu cooing, *Don't want no snare, don't want no snare* on her 1996 tune "Rim Shot." Witness today's young deejays who are multirhythmic and prone to improvising on turntables the way musicians improvise on instruments. A few weeks back I was in New York, kicking it in the Liquid Sound Lounge. It's located in the basement of a club in the village called the Knitting Factory. There, words like *mixologist* and *wordologist* reign, and the lineup of deejays are listed on promos according to their specialty—bass, contra bass, or drums. It's all about the beat. And even more. (The R&B market is even co-opting vocal cords.) Who reinvented himself better than Ronald Isley when he hooked up with R. Kelly, not once but twice this decade?

Today the record companies are reissuing music like bats out of hell, and original vinyls by Grant Green and his contemporaries command high prices on the collectors' market. This tardy triumph just may be giving Grant a reason to do a James Brown hack in his grave. Say it loud.

That this book is being published on the twentieth anniversary of his death, and the sixtieth anniversary of Blue Note Records, the label on which he got his start, is fitting. With his stinging single-note lines, Grant helped change the way guitar is played forever. Everyone from Carlos Santana and Stevie Ray Vaughan to George Benson has credited him for influencing their work.

Some folks like to focus on Grant's nasty groove. Others zero in on how he could make the guitar sing like a horn. He called it all the blues, but that is not to say "his playing [was] simplistic," explains Adrian Ingram, a British guitar professor who wrote the biography on Grant's leading peer, Wes Montgomery. "It's just that he always had that feel whenever he played, whether it was a ballad like 'Old Folks' or whether it was one of the R&B-type blues. He retained that earthy feel, which I think is important to good jazz. Charlie Parker, Coltrane, and Billie Holiday, all of the great jazzers had that feel."

A little over a year ago, I was in a Tower Records store in Ann Arbor, where I purchased a copy of Grant's 1965 *I Want to Hold Your Hand.* I would later learn that it was among the Top 25 albums Tower was selling that month. By the time this book is published, Grant Green fans will have no doubt seen the release of other reissues and tribute albums. A documentary on his life is in the works. A web site in his honor yields letters from Sweden, Spain, Pittsburgh, and the Netherlands. He is without question steadily making moves into the mainstream. For awhile, his song "Sookie, Sookie" was a theme song on HBO. And I once heard his music playing under a Meg Ryan film. I asked Greg Green, Grant's oldest son, what his father would make of it all. What would he make of how far music and technology have come as we close the millennium? What would he think about how a musician can now make a CD on his own computer if he wanted? Greg laughed and told me about the time his father struggled with even the wah-wah pedal. "I said, 'Dad, just give it here,'" he laughs.

Grant Green is said to have been at his best on *Idle Moments.* Let the scholars debate. I have found great pleasure in Grant's *Visions* date. Originally released in 1971 during Grant's supposed artistic slump, the album was a hit and featured instrumentals from some Jackson 5 songs and other pop tunes of the late 1960s and early 1970s. It speaks directly to my snotty-nose, Saturday morning *Schoolhouse Rock* days. So I hear you, Grant. And while giving a nod to Robert Lamm, I have never heard a freer rendition of "Does Anybody Really Know What Time It Is" than the one that appears on *Visions.* I say it might be past time Grant Green got his name right and proper in the annals of America's jazz history.

—S.A.G.

Introduction (re)Discovering a Forgotten Genius

"Where's your father's guitar?"

I never felt like I could own up to the challenge of telling Grant Green's story. I'm the daughter of a Pentecostal preacher, and the "devil's music" was not to be heard in my father's house. And such was jazz, I suppose, if my daddy had anything to do with it. But anyone with good sense knows Pentecostals can jam for Jesus even if Daddy called our music by another name. We had a drum set in our church, an organ, and a red wooden tambourine folks used to pass up and down the aisle so anybody who felt like it could get into the groove come Sunday. If we went to a tent revival meeting, there was likely to be a guitar player up on the stage putting his two cents in. And on cue, between swatting mosquitoes, I was clapping like a good preacher girl was supposed to.

As I grew older, the jazz greats I heard about had names like Bird, Miles, and Diz—those who had managed to meander through the mainstream. On the sidelines, still in the currents, were musicians like Grant Green, who bopped around every bend as good as the best who stroked down the middle. But for whatever reason—and we'll get into that later—they got caught up in a wave and went under a little too soon. And the history books ain't said bleep.

Preacher girls like what ain't good for them, and I liked Grant Green—the son. We first met in 1992, when I was a reporter for *The Miami Herald.* He and two of his friends had just opened a little sandwich shop on 22nd Avenue in Liberty City. Liberty City is a predominantly black section of Miami, typically written off as a ghetto. In the early 1990s, the neighborhood got a certain amount of flak when a German tourist was pulled from her car and murdered in front of her family. At the time I met Grant Jr., some local rappers had penned a tune about tourists, or them folks with "the map on the dashboard." On the heels of that attack and the media coverage

Grant Green, pictured here in a 1961 Blue Note session, helped change forever what people could expect from a guitar, but never received the commercial acclaim he desperately sought. Photo by Francis Wolff, courtesy of Mosaic Images.

that followed, tourists were directed away from the area with a funny new symbol—a bright orange sun. State officials ordered that these suns be pasted on every highway sign leading from the airport. Forget the yellow brick road. The smart hid their maps and followed those bright orange suns to Miami Beach. Never 22nd Avenue. (Before I continue, the Grant Green Jr. of whom I speak now and throughout the rest of this book should not be mistaken for his older brother, Gregory, the guitarist in New York who has played professionally under the name Grant Green Jr.)

Since the days of Jackie Gleason, Miami Beach has been a mecca for those looking for sun and fun. In the 1940s and '50s, black entertainers like Duke Ellington, Josephine Baker, and others filled the city's ballrooms, concert halls, and nightclubs. They packed hotels they themselves could not stay in because of the Jim Crow laws, which forced them back over the causeway to Overtown, then a prosperous hub of black life with restaurants, hotels, barber shops, and other businesses, most of them black-owned.

Ironically, both Liberty City and Miami Beach suffered a decline for a myriad of reasons in the 1960s and '70s. But in the 1990s, Miami Beach—or more specifically South Beach, its southernmost point—managed to make a comeback. When New York became passé, South Beach became a favorite roosting spot for everyone from the late Gianni Versace to Madonna. From Latin America and Europe, they came in droves. Few folks ever went back over the causeway except to get to Miami International Airport.

While South Beach was doing well, black neighborhoods like Overtown and Liberty City continued to fall. In time, local officials found the perfect opportunity to right their wrong. The impetus was a visit by Nelson Mandela. When the South African leader was released after twenty-seven years in prison and began a tour of the U.S., he got red carpet treatment nearly everywhere. Everywhere, that is, but Miami. The Cubans called him a Commie and local officials refused to give him a key to the city. Outraged black leaders led a national boycott and asked black sororities, fraternities, and other organizations to not hold their conventions in the city. Hundreds of thousands of dollars went to Dallas and Detroit and other cities. It wasn't long before state officials wanted the green back home.

Part of their apology came in the form of seed money for minorities to start their own businesses in the tourism field. Grant Green Jr. and his business partners, Mac Cox and Rodney Martin, were among those who benefited. They were three smooth brothers with strong resumes that included jobs at some of Miami's finer restaurants. With the help of public dollars, they quit their jobs to open a little sandwich shop in the inner city. I was the reporter sent to cover the story.

Grant and his friends named their shop Underground Subs. Sometimes it was just called the Underground. It was a fitting name, given the political backdrop of the time. It became a neighborhood hangout where characters with names like "Hometeam," "Bruh," "Deck," and "Dred" came by. And Grant and his friends became neighborhood heroes to school teachers, school kids, and drug dealers alike. Black folks were still mad about Mandela. But these three entrepreneurs were making a difference legally. Before the grand opening, they worked until the late hours of the night, building their own counters and making sure the plumbing and electricity were right. That the *Herald* wanted to talk to them was a special coup. That is, everyone seemed to think so but Grant. He didn't care for the establishment and all but kicked me out of their shop the minute I stepped foot in the door.

"We don't want to be in *The Miami Herald,*" he said from behind the counter. He was tall and thin, a little on the rugged side, but cute enough. And arrogant. Yet the indifference with which I was met was mutual. The name Grant Green was just another scribble in my note pad.

Not one to be easily chased away, I surveyed their little shop. On one wall was a blackboard where news stories about black people were tacked up. This became especially clever when I learned they actually called it The Blackboard. Shellacked to the ceiling were still more black stories. And on a rack not far from the blackboard were black newspapers from around the country, positioned for customers to read as they waited for their sandwiches. An eatery with a militant bent. I smiled. And did not leave.

Finally, Grant decided that I could do my story, but I could not talk to him. After a few minutes, my interview with his two business partners became a friendly conversation that Grant not only joined, but took over. He told me about his "dope soufflé" and the crepe shop they intended to open some day, maybe on South Beach.

I got the story. And the Underground got the Local section. Front and center.

The next time I went by the shop, Grant was there alone and in better spirits. He made me a roast beef sandwich and came from behind the counter and ate half of it. Within one week, he had kissed the Establishment. In two weeks, he moved into her apartment. In three months, he asked her to marry him. And still the name Grant Green had no particular significance to me.

The author sitting beside Grant's youngest son and namesake, Grant Green Jr., in Oakland, California, in 1995.

In time he took me home to meet his mother. Back then, she lived in an apartment near West Palm Beach, not far from his sister, Kim. West Palm Beach is about an hour north of Miami, so this was a quick trek. After introductions and dinner, everyone took to playing cards, something I'd never done well, so I decided to be the deejay for the evening. I sat on the floor and sifted through a pile of CDs until I noticed one had my new beau's name on it. The words "Grant Green" were on the album cover, offset by a moody black and white photograph of a man holding a guitar.

"Oh, honey, this man has your name," I said, picking up the CD.

"He's my dad," Grant replied, not looking up from his card game.

"You're lying," I giggled.

A hush fell. Who was the bimbo Junior had brought home, I was sure they were thinking. Or maybe it was just one of those lulls in card games when folks try to outsmart one another. In any case, not knowing who his father was called for a talk in the kitchen. Grant excused himself and summoned me for the necessary discussion. He quickly gave me the headline: his dad, the elder Grant Green, was a world-famous jazz guitarist who had influenced a lot of music and a lot of people. The end.

"When can I meet him?" I asked, hoping to make good with the man himself.

"You can't," Grant said, returning to his game. "He's dead."

On the way home, he told me a little more, although he never seemed entirely comfortable talking about his father. I only got snippets here and there that blended into a scant testimony of the man whose contributions to jazz guitar, while phenomenal, remained an enigma for many, even jazz guitar students.

Known mostly for his playing with Blue Note Records, Grant's output in the 1960s and the 1970s was huge, but he was severely overshadowed by other guitarists, most notably Wes Montgomery and later, George Benson. To date, Grant Green's story has been told mainly through the voices of critics who wrote the liner notes for his many albums. Here is the story they tell:

Born in St. Louis on June 6, 1935, Grant Green came up in a time when boogie-woogie and big band were the popular jazz styles of the day. His earliest exposure to music came by way of his father and uncle, who played "old Muddy Water–type blues" on their guitars. A young Grant wanted to play too, and it wasn't long before his father bought him an old Harmony guitar and an amplifier. (Grant would later say the amp looked like "an old-timey radio.") His primary influences were both named Charlie. One was the god of horn, Charlie Parker. The other was Charlie Christian, a pioneer of the electric guitar.

Historically, the guitar had typically been a prop, a means of filling out the sound of the other instruments on the stage. In the notes for the 1960 *Grant's First Stand* album, Robert Levin wrote:

"Prior to the middle twenties, Lonnie Johnson and Eddie Lang, the function of the guitar (or its, at that time prevailing predecessor, the banjo) was, apart from its use in the hands of blues singers, primarily rhythmic. Lang, particularly, was the first to successfully demonstrate both the guitar's hardly realized harmonic possibilities and its capacities as a solo voice. He developed a single-string style that was later to be most fruitfully explored and extended in the work of Charlie Christian.

"Of course, not all pre-Christian guitarists remained ignorant of the guitar's solo potential. George Van Eps, Dick McDonough, and Carl Kress were prominent early disciples and popularizers of Lang's approach. Django Reinhardt brought his own indigenous folk tradition, that of the gypsy."

But Christian, who hailed from a ghetto in Oklahoma and went on to play with Benny Goodman, was among the first to electrically amplify the guitar and give it a volume to equal the other instruments on the bandstand. In discussions about jazz guitar, references to "before Charlie Christian" or "after Charlie Christian" are often made. Christian was a pioneer in bringing the guitar to the forefront and made it the instrument around which a band was built. But he would not live to see the maturation of his genius. In 1942, at the age of 25, Christian died of tuberculosis, but jazz guitar evolved rapidly after World War II, and Grant Green, approaching his teen years, was right on time. The guitar became an instrument that was welcomed by the public because it blended well with blues, jazz, country, rock 'n' roll, and even Negro spirituals.

It was Leonard Feather who took the audacious step of implying it was Grant who took the baton from Christian in the liner notes for Grant's 1961 *Green Street* album:

"It is accurate, though somehow not adequate, to hail him as a vital new link in the six-stringed lifeline from Charlie Christian through Barney Kessel to Kenny Burrell and Wes Montgomery. But the degree of maturity already discernible in Grant Green indicates that it would be an injustice to him to make the usual comparisons with his predecessors or toss some of the conventional and overworked adjectives his way...Christian, let us not forget, was barely out of his teens when he joined Benny Goodman; Kessel was twenty when he made the Norman Granz film *Jammin' the Blues.* Bearing this in mind, one should not find it totally unbelievable that in his thirtieth year Grant Green has accomplished at least as much as had his important precursors when they first came to prominence."

Feather added: "...Though it may seem heretical, I would venture the opinion that Green has extended jazz guitar playing far beyond [where]...Christian had taken it....If a Grant Green had come along in 1938, playing exactly as he plays on this LP, the arrival of Charlie Christian the following year would have seemed anticlimactic. But this is hardly a valid hypothetical case, since there could have been no Green without a Christian, a Bird, and a Miles." (Feather, like many chroniclers, was a little off on the dates. Grant was born in 1935, not 1931.)

Grant's role in the evolution of the jazz guitar's solo possibilities has been well documented. He was among the few guitar players aware of its hornlike potential. He learned by studying Charlie Christian records, but mostly by listening to horn players, particularly Charlie Parker. "Listening to Charlie was like hearing a different man play every night," Grant said. "I used to sit up all night copying Charlie Parker solos note by note."

By 1948 at age 13, Grant was playing professionally in local churches. As bebop hailed the onset of modern jazz in the 1950s, he made a name for himself performing in rhythm and blues and jazz combos. He played with St. Louis groups led by Joe Murphy, Harry Edison, Sam Lazar, and Jimmy Forrest.

In 1959, a saxophonist named Lou Donaldson spotted Grant playing in a club in East St. Louis. (East St. Louis is actually a city across the Mississippi River in the state of Illinois, not Missouri. This is the town near where Miles Davis grew up on his daddy's hog farm, and the town where night crawlers headed after last calls were made in St. Louis's bars.) The 24-year-old Grant was certainly beyond what one would call a new talent when Lou saw him. Impressed by his work, Lou invited Grant to New York to audition for Blue Note Records, one of the premier jazz labels in the country. Founded in 1939, Blue Note had committed itself to the recording of New Orleans and Chicago-styled jazz, boogie-woogie, piano and small group swing, and later, soul and gospel-like jazz. Lou introduced Grant to Francis Wolff and Alfred Lion, the founders of the label. Grant would later acknowledge the two men as "gods of jazz who knew music and loved the business." They must have seen something in Grant, too, as they quickly hired him as a staff guitarist. His first Blue Note record date was on Lou Donaldson's *Here 'Tis* album, which was recorded on January 23, 1961.

Grant performing a tune from his 1961 Green Street *album in Englewood Cliffs, New Jersey. Photo by Francis Wolff, courtesy of Mosaic Images.*

Just five days later, Grant was given his first date as a lead player, and the album was appropriately named *Grant's First Stand.* These Blue Note albums, however, were not his first. He had participated in a December 10, 1959, Delmark date with Jimmy Forrest and in a June 1, 1960, date with Sam Lazar on the Argo label.

Many of Grant's early sessions were combo dates, where there was little room to cloak. Often there would simply be guitar, bass, and drums, or guitar, organ, and drums. (Speaking to Grant's abilities in this context, Feather points out that Charlie Christian was never confronted with this challenge.) Grant delivered an unheard-of eight sessions as a leader or sideman in 1961 alone. His quick start was reflective of Blue Note's most fertile period: the 1960s.

Grant quickly became known as a musician who could play widely varying styles. From 1959, when he first began to make his mark in jazz, until his death in 1979, and even posthumously twenty years later, Grant Green was involved in all genres of jazz. Though he would later be criticized for becoming too commercial, it is a fact that even from the starting gate Grant Green was a musician who played for the audience. He was an entertainer. He played standards. He played Top 40. He played what the people wanted to hear. Though the music changed, his intentions did not. In the 1960s it might have been a Bacharach or a Rodgers and Hammerstein tune. Years later, it might have been a James Brown or a Jackson 5 song. "It's all music," Grant would say again and again.

Grant was also known for being a performer who looked unusually relaxed when he played, which is rare in jazz. "He is seldom tricky or flashy where it is uncalled for, preferring to state his message simply and with power. [His work was]...the kind of music one might hear in a small club at night when the musicians are playing primarily for themselves," Joe Goldberg wrote on the liner notes for Grant's 1963 album, *Am I Blue.*

This "deceptive simplicity," as another critic put it, might have counted against Grant as he came on the scene when the more technical Wes Montgomery was making his own mark on the instrument. But his "style owed nothing to the genius from Indianapolis," Mark Gardner wrote on the notes for Grant's 1961 *Reaching Out.* There were obvious differences between the two: Wes played octaves. Grant was a single-note line player. Wes used his thumb. Grant used a pick. And Wes was part of a smooth marketing machine—his contributions to the jazz guitar were documented in *Time* and *Newsweek*—while Grant's name recognition rarely went beyond jazz's inner circle.

By 1966, Grant had grown frustrated with the small financial returns on his music. He left Blue Note and formed his own band. In 1968, Wes Montgomery suffered a heart attack and died at the age of 43, but Grant, though celebrated, still had not received the public acclaim he sought. In time, he returned to Blue Note.

Along with working for that label, Grant recorded for other labels, including Cobblestone, Verve, Prestige, CTI, and Versatile. Beyond his woes with music, he had long fought a drug habit that, coupled with the disillusionment of his uneven career and failed relationships, began to take a toll on his body. Grant's health began to decline in the mid-1970s, sending warning signals for him to take it easy. Ironically, his last album offered the same suggestion in its title—*Easy.* Grant went into the studio to record this session in April 1978. Though little regarded, the album was a tragic ode to his own mortality.

By the fall of that year, Grant suffered a minor stroke that left him temporarily paralyzed on his left side. As *Easy* crept up the *Billboard* charts, disregarding medical advice, Grant made a long road trip across the country to a gig in California. On the long haul back to New York, he collapsed in his green Cadillac, the victim of a heart attack. Grant died en route to Harlem Hospital. Like Wes Montgomery, he was 43.

That is the story the liner notes tell.

What they do not reveal is how a playful Grant Green used to taunt his grade school teacher by plucking the strings on a ukulele he snuck into class. Or how he used to shake his roommate out of bed every morning to make him listen to "this cat named James Brown." Or how Grant, the gentleman, took the arm of an undiscerning young woman who'd stumbled onto the upper floor of a nightclub—where musicians were shooting up dope—and showed her the way out. Or how Grant, in trying to cope with the questionable business dealings in the music industry and the unglorious times in black America, had found value in a Muslim faith. Or how Grant dealt with the fact that the premier black jazz guitarist slot was never opened up to him, even after Wes Montgomery's death.

I wanted to know more about the man. The results are this book. Journalists are naturally curious. We want to save the underdog, expose the unexposed, uncover the covered. Grant Green fit the mold perfectly. He was without question a man who missed his celebrity. He was a straightahead jazz man turned funk-wizard who pioneered a sound that was at once crisp and lyrical.

But he was eclipsed by Wes and later George Benson, who, ironically, admired the hell out of his playing. (George has told just about everyone the story of how he snuck into a bar where Grant was playing, taking care to tuck himself near the back, only to bump into Wes, who was also there to partake and learn.) After Wes's death, George unleashed the ultimate whammy the following decade. He revealed that he not only could he play, but he could also sing. He took the music to the mainstream. He took it to an audience who couldn't tell a single-note line from a chord, and didn't care to. They liked the music. They liked George.

But the licks they heard on George's Grammy Award–winning albums had roots somewhere. They had their roots, in part, in a guitar player from St. Louis, Missouri, named Grant Green. He was a country boy who wore green suits and drove a green Cadillac. And he was woefully infatuated with word play, faithfully delivering a slew of songs and album titles playing on his name—*Grant's First Stand, Grantstand, Green Is Beautiful, A Wee Bit o' Green, Green's Greenery,* and *Green Jeans,* among others. From 1961 to 1965, Grant recorded more songs than any other musician at Blue Note.

Grant easily incorporated all styles into his music: bop, bebop, soul and gospel, Latin, country-western, and funk. He did the Beatles. He did Mozart. He did the Commodores. But he never strayed far from his roots in the blues. The most widely circulated Green discography lists around ninety albums. It would be over a hundred if other artists' samples of his work were included. Producer Bob Porter once wrote, "If [Grant] Green had never recorded as a leader, his contributions as a Blue Note sideman in the 1960s would be enough to make him one of the greatest guitarists in jazz history."

The magnitude of Grant Green's legacy became real for me when his son and I moved to Detroit in December 1992. I had taken a job as a reporter with *The Detroit Free Press.* I quickly saw that Detroit was a city with a strong musical history that went beyond the Four Tops and the Supremes. The hometown of many famous jazz musicians, for one decade, it was also Grant Sr.'s home base. In between his gigs around the country, he charmed Detroiters in the local clubs. Even after his untimely death in 1979, the city never forgot him. Wherever we went, after hearing his son's name or seeing it on a check or driver's license, people would say, "I knew a great guitarist..."

In the beginning, my husband rarely told them that he was the son of the guitar legend. He was clearly conflicted about his legacy. Most times he pushed it away. I remember the day he finally warmed up to the idea. We were sitting in a drug store waiting for a prescription. The clerk called, "Grant Green, your prescription is ready." As he got up from his seat, two gray-haired men sitting near him turned to each other.

"Hey, man. You remember that guitarist named Grant Green who used to play over at the Mozambique?"

"Yeah, the cat was always cookin'."

Overhearing them, Grant said, "He was my dad." The two men fell silent. Then they reached out to touch him. He obliged them with a firm handshake and a smile.

On a 1995 trip to California, Grant Green Jr. stands in front of the famous intersection in San Fransico bearing his father's name. Photo by Sharony A. Green.

Shortly after the move to Michigan, I drove out to Ann Arbor. I drove out to Ann Arbor because college towns always have the best book stores and record stores. I drove to Ann Arbor because I did not yet know the streets of Detroit. I drove out to Ann Arbor because the signs on Interstate 94 led the way.

I went into Schoolkids Records, where I quickly spotted Grant Green's name among a sea of white plastic name plates for other jazz greats. I grabbed the Grant Green CDs—there were just five in the store at the time—and took them home. At the time, we were living in a loft in Greektown, above Niki's Pizza. I put them in the CD player and played them one by one, over and over again. Night fell and I was still listening. It was close to midnight when my husband came home from a long day at work. He was back working as a chef. When he heard the music—which song, I don't remember—

Grant's signature uncluttered lines and seemingly relaxed approach to playing is very evident on the 1961 album **Grantstand**, *his third session for Blue Note. Courtesy of Blue Note Records, a division of Capitol Records.*

he stopped in midstep. He went over to the stereo, looked around, and noticed the CDs.

"Where'd you get all this from?" he said, almost whispering.

"Ann Arbor," I said.

He got a glass of wine, took off his sneakers and began to sip and listen. "Honey, don't wait up for me," he said.

About three or four in the morning I heard the erratic notes from a Grant Green tune cutting through the darkness where he sat, listening.

In late 1993, I took a trip with some friends to New York. While I was there, I decided a visit to the Library of Performing Arts at Lincoln Center was in order. Maybe I could dig up something on my husband's dad. I was quickly overwhelmed by the books, the music, and the information available on everyone. Everyone *but* Grant Green. I found his obituary in *Down Beat* and a few other newspapers along with a few articles in some back issues of guitar magazines and other music publications. Then I headed for the jazz stacks.

"You looking for Grant Green on that shelf?" said a man in the section who looked like a regular. "Humph. Good luck. I ain't seen none of his stuff in here in a long time." I later learned that some of Grant Green's music had been checked out of the library and never returned.

A couple of months later, I was back in New York on business and I decided to see what else I could find on my husband's dad. I headed for Tower Records in the Village and went searching through the jazz department. I found nothing. I was stunned.

I walked over to a store clerk and asked him what was up. Where were the Grant Green CDs, I asked.

"What? You a rapper?" he asked.

I told him I was doing some research and he quickly informed me that he couldn't keep Grant Green's music on the shelves because the rappers were really into it, but he could order some imports for me if I wanted.

I hit the streets of Harlem, where I found a man selling old albums from some crates on a sidewalk. I stooped down and began to flip through a few and sure enough, there was an old vinyl of Stanley Turrentine's *Rough 'n' Tumble* with Grant Green assisting on guitar. I bargained it down to $9 and promised to stay in touch with the sidewalk dealer, who regularly got old albums at estate sales.

I went to the Hard Rock Cafe, pissed that everyone's guitar—Elvis, Jimi, Wes, and others—was hanging on the walls, everyone but Grant Green's.

"Where is your dad's guitar?" I asked Grant when I returned to Detroit.

"I dunno, Greg might have it," he answered, referring to his brother.

The reply bothered me. Why was there so little energy put into keeping Grant Green's name alive, particularly by his own family? Was he that forgettable? Who was Grant Green, anyway? Trying to answer this question on the twentieth anniversary of his death yields evidence that could suggest he was nobody special, for you can pick up a jazz encyclopedia or a jazz guitar book today and not see his name in the index. But you can also look at the vast amount of his music being reissued by record companies and the homages paid to him nowadays on tribute albums, calendars, and everywhere else and be certain that forgetting him would be a travesty.

Telling the Story

"Look, he was never a guy who stopped playing jazz. Okay?"

In a thirty-year career that began inside of a holiness church in St. Louis, Grant Green brought something to jazz guitar no one had seen before or has seen since. He had a tonality and rhythm that was wholly original and adored even by the men whose careers eclipsed his own.

"People were always all over Grant. He was an icon, you know," George Benson once told me. "Guitar players were trying to learn what his secret was, and there were people in general who just loved his groove. Grant made the guitar come alive and sing. It was his talent alone. Only he could do it like that. Nobody else I ever knew could make the guitar talk like that or speak like that."

But how to define his genius? I asked four people, "What was it about Grant Green that made his work innovative and essential to any serious discussion of jazz guitar?"

The first person I posed the question to was Nat Hentoff, a respected music critic. Nat and I had met by accident at a Miami book fair in 1997. I was still living in Detroit. I had taken a leave from journalism and was at the fair promoting my first book, *Cuttin' the Rug under the Moonlit Sky: Stories and Drawings about a Bunch of Women Named Mae.* As I sat down to recover in the author hospitality room, in walked a short, distinguished-looking gentleman. Very much the author type. Very New York. He wore a plaid jacket, if I remember correctly. Proper etiquette suggested that we introduce ourselves, so I stood up (even though I had observed Jamaica Kincaid, quite the veteran, who seemed to support my original stance, which was to sit down, suffer through it all and speak only when spoken to because the only thing most of us really wanted was to do the reading, go back home, and hope people bought the book).

Grant Green assisting in John Patton's 1964 The Way I Feel *session. Photo by Francis Wolff, courtesy of Mosaic Images.*

But there was something about this man in the plaid jacket. I walked over and decided to introduce myself to him. "Sharony Green," I said. "Nat Hentoff," he said, and extended his hand warmly. I couldn't believe it. That very week I had been making a mental note to call him because I needed to go over some things in this book with him. He was at the fair promoting his book, *Speaking Freely,* about forty years of his life as a journalist. We chatted briefly and he suggested that we talk more when we both returned to our respective home bases.

And we did. I was happy to call Nat. I like him. I like his liner notes, and I don't like most liner notes. Maybe it's jealousy. Critics have power—too much power. I tell Nat this right off the bat. He understands. He has heard it all. But he feels the critic's job is a necessary one, for the listener and for the musician.

"I know a lot of musicians don't like it," said Nat about album reviews. "It's one of the few natural things that critics do. They act like listeners. And listeners say, 'Well, I dig this guy more than that guy,' or 'I like what he did better.'"

And thus a career is made or ruined. I get to the heart of matters: Where exactly did Grant Green stand in the history of jazz guitar, particularly in the 1960s? Is it true that he was overshadowed by Wes Montgomery?

"He may have been overshadowed," Nat began. "But, to me then and now, I much preferred listening to him than to Wes Montgomery because one of the virtues of Grant's playing was that he was very melodic. He always told the story, whereas a number of musicians—and I think Wes Montgomery is among them—they are so technically skilled that much of their playing is to show you how skilled they are, and they do it by very sophisticated harmony or rhythms, and the clear melody is often not apparent, is not immediate, whereas with Grant Green's...he was like *talking* to you and to me. That's always the best indication of a musician's quality, that it's conversational."

What Nat said was something I would hear over and over again. That there was a quality to Grant's playing that was unmistakable. There was something that made those in the know say, "Grant Green!" upon first listen.

"When I was coming up," Nat continues, "what struck me

Grant Green Jr., Grant Green's son

To me there are several Grant Greens. There was a Grant Green [who] had a drug habit. And there's the Grant Green in the '60s, this new shining star that came out of nowhere. That's the Grant Green I never knew because I was too young to understand it anyway. When I meet people and say, "My name is Grant Green Jr.," and they say, "I know this guitarist who was outrageous named Grant Green," and I'd say, "He's my dad,"...they would like freak and go, "Oh, no stop kidding me." It's like I never knew the impact of my dad's music or his legacy until I met people who listened to his works and said, "This man was a great musician," and it made me feel like, "That's great. My dad was awesome, you know." It always makes me think of him in a better way, and I know that he's resting in peace everytime someone calls his name or plays his music or buys his music. I know he's resting in peace more. I think about him in spurts when I see things, when I hear certain songs. Different things give me memories of him. Sometimes I sit up at night and talk to him, and ask him, "I wonder what you're doing now and I still love you."

about the players [was] that they seemed to be larger than life size. They had such presence in their music and, in fact, off the stand as well. Most of them had an immediate identity, so that if you were listening to the radio at home or put on a record and didn't know who was playing, you could tell who the key ones were by the first couple of bars. I think that was true of Grant Green, too. Whereas now we've got very efficient technical players. Some of whom play with considerable feeling, but it's hard to tell them apart. Benny Carter, who usually says nothing ill about anybody—he's a true gentleman—went to Texas State College years ago. I'd been there before. That's where they train jazz musicians. I don't know where they go afterwards, and he had the same impression I did. He said on National Public Radio, 'My goodness. Those young players can cut anything. They can read. They can play. There's only one problem. I can't tell one from the other.' And then there's a kind of self-consciousness among some—not all—of the younger players."

Nat pauses and surprises me with something I had again heard before, but which was clearly taboo. It was something people in the music business didn't say too loud.

"I am not a fan of Wynton Marsalis."

I smile as he goes on. "I think he's been very valuable over the years in inculcating younger players with the need [to play jazz] and he has the information as well to understand where this music came from, but his own playing...it's studied somehow," he says. "I don't get this. When Lester Young played, I knew that there would be a lot of surprises."

But Nat has hope. He believes that someone will come along like Louis Armstrong did way back, and John Coltrane did later, and turn jazz upside down. "Maybe the next one will be some Bulgarian guitarist. It may not be in the United States," he speculates.

"Wouldn't that be something?" I say. "But, how do we bring all of this back to Grant Green?"

Nat replies that his digression about Bulgaria is merely that—a digression—for he truly believes "to reach that kind of individuality and depth of the music you have got to have some experience as an American," he says, "especially like Grant Green—I'm thinking of him again—some real knowledge of the blues."

Playing the devil's advocate, I say, "But certainly pain is universal."

"Well, that's it. Pain is universal," he agrees. "There have been white players with great inventiveness. One of my favorites is Stevie Russell. But by and large, when you think of the players who have really either originated a whole line of musical endeavor or are in the first rank of players, most of them are black. And many of them—and this goes for Charles Mingus as well as other people—came out of a background of church music. I remember when the West Coast jazz thing was getting very popular, and it was largely white, and they were getting a lot of money and selling a lot of records, and I went to the first rehearsal of Art Blakey's Jazz Messengers, with Horace Silver and Blakey. They were very annoyed [and] angry at the fact that they were being ignored. Blakey said, 'We're going to play some stuff that they can't play because they never was there!'"

Indeed, the struggle inspired the work. And Grant Green's work was no exception. But I was still trying to determine what it was about his playing that was so damn special.

I called Michael Cuscuna at Mosaic Records, one of the giants in the jazz reissue business. Like others, Michael spoke about Grant's brilliance in relation to Wes. "Both of them had very, very distinctive styles that were unlike anyone else that had come before them—styles that were different from each other. And they were very much rooted in the blues. They were both very soulful players, and they sort of had parallel careers, although I think Wes Montgomery's pop records pushed him onto another level where historically he kind of overshadowed Grant Green. But they were equally original and equally soulful and equally important in terms of jazz guitar. Grant had a very stingy, kinda clear single-note, kinda sound when he was improvising. Wes Montgomery used to pick with his thumb and play octaves a lot, and that sort of became his trademark. It was a thicker and rounder sound."

Though it may have appeared otherwise, Grant and Wes were never real rivals. Still, Grant wanted his share of the pie like any other guy. It seems guitar players are especially competitive. I once asked my brother-in-law, Greg, what it was about the guitar that made players go head to head.

"It's just that way," he answered with a cagey smile.

Greg told me how he was really looking forward to a tribute gig for his dad with Mark Whitfield, Peter Bernstein, Ed Cherry, Russell Malone, and Dave Stryker. The three had already performed on a tribute album to Grant that was released in Japan and the United States. On a sunny day in 1996, each guitarist showed up and took a seat in a recording booth in New York City. Idris Muhammad and Larry Goldings held down the rhythm section. Each guitarist was asked to play an original Grant Green composition. They were friendly enough, but an unspoken rivalry seemed to linger two years later. "I'm gon' tear them up!" Greg said with a laugh of the upcoming gig.

But guitarists aren't the only competitive ones. I remember hearing how the St. Louis that Grant left in 1959 was a drummer's town. Every cat tried to outplay the next. And then there's the scene in *Mo' Better Blues* where Denzel Washington and

Wesley Snipes's characters go head to head on the bandstand. Two bad-ass horn players trying to see who was the baddest. It's very human to just want to be better. To be the best. And Grant was very human. He tried everything. His album titles say it all: *Feelin' the Spirit, The Latin Bit, I Want to Hold Your Hand, Goin' West.* I wondered whether consistency was his genius?

"If he hadn't been a guitar player, he could've easily been a model," producer Michael Cuscuna says of Grant's ease in front of Francis Wolff's camera. He's pictured here during his 1962 **Feelin' the Spirit** *session. Photo by Francis Wolff, courtesy of Mosaic Images.*

I called Bob Porter. Bob has been in the music business for a while, having written for *Down Beat* and other publications. For the past seventeen years, he has hosted a nationally syndicated blues radio show on WBGO out of Newark. When I reached him by phone, he began our conversation by talking about Grant's place in the jazz world in the late 1960s. Following Wes's death, Grant was no longer the starry-eyed kid who was just happy to be at Blue Note, the one who could shoot out seven lead sessions in one year alone. It had been a couple of years since he'd left the label, and by 1969 he had a lot on his mind, including a failing marriage to his first wife, Ann. The music business had fractured his spirit and his family. So he made some decisions. He wasn't

Of all the albums his father recorded, during his childhood Grant Jr. was most drawn to the cover of the one with his father "sitting on the floor with the hat on his head." Courtesy of Blue Note Records, a division of Capitol Records.

going to play just straightahead jazz anymore. He was going to do the funk thing. Bob asked him to sign with Prestige Records.

"I had been a fan of his for many years," Bob says. "We had lunch and a long conversation and I really got to enjoy the guy. He had the biggest hands I'd ever seen on somebody who wasn't a basketball player. He just had huge hands. He was a very down-home kind of guy. I don't think he had a great deal of education. But he was warm, y'know, the kind of person you would expect if you listened to the way he played. He was interested in James Brown. He was interested in that sort of thing, that sort of rhythm. That's what he wanted to play when I met him. He saw it as the best way to make a success out of his career.

"Look," Bob continues, "He was never a guy who stopped playing jazz. Okay? You could go to see him and hear him play the funk all night long, and he'd simply sit back and play impressions of something and knock everybody on their ass. Okay? And that was what he did. And in fact, I think many of us would rather have heard him play jazz after the comeback, but he didn't. I didn't have the money available that he wanted."

How much was Grant asking for?

"$1,500, and Bob Weinstock wasn't going to pay that much," Bob replies. "This was 1968 wages."

Grant eventually agreed to work as a sideman for Prestige.

Over the next couple of years Grant would work with Sonny Stitt, Rusty Bryant, Houston Person, Charles Kynard, and Don Patterson between attempts to re-establish his relationship with Blue Note.

"He always contributed more than he had to, which is one of the things that makes a sideman valuable," Bob says. "You get stars who frequently will just show up and think that's all they need to do, but he was always willing to contribute and add whatever he could to make the music better, which is the kind of thing that producers truly appreciate."

Grant Green was simply "at the top of the heap. [He] brought something really unique in the sense of his sound. His tonal quality on guitar was something nobody had approached before or since. It was immediately identifiable, and I think in a large measure that was his great contribution...and he also had a very good rhythm feel. It's unusual to find modern jazz players with really good rhythm feel. He was one of them."

So Nat, Michael, and Bob were all in agreement that Grant's music was identifiable. It had a lively and clear tone. It spoke to listeners. It was not necessarily technical. It was lushly poetic, perfectly and imperfectly paced, and largely unheard before his arrival.

Still, something more needed to be said beyond the adjectives to make his life relevant to anyone.

I call Bob Belden, who is believed by industry types to be the biggest Grant Green fan in the whole world. When I tell him this, Belden responds with a chuckle, "There are probably a hundred other people who would challenge that. " Still he hastens to point out that he has every Grant Green album with the exception of a German Argo record with Sam Lazar.

I ask him why he digs Grant so much. Why this lust for the man and his music?

Belden responds, "I liked him more than I liked anyone else. I think he was an enigma to most people. Everybody who gets hipped to Grant, really gets into that sound. Who he was? He's probably for modern jazz guitar...the finest. Just pure music. He was every horn player's favorite guitarist because they had [a] spiritual connection."

A spiritual connection? While I think on this, Belden, who has done some impressive work for Blue Note over the years as well as produced others including the Artist Formerly Known as Prince, surprises me. "Hey, I have something I want to read to you," he says.

Belden has the liner notes he'd been asked to write for the reissue of Grant's 1972 *Live at the Lighthouse* date. I listen as he reads his notes. In them, he hits on the changes taking place in America's musical landscape at the time the album was released. Everybody from Isaac Hayes, Marvin Gaye, and Stevie Wonder to Earth Wind and Fire was trying to make adjustments. The 1960s had turned music upside down in nearly every field—jazz, rock 'n' roll, rhythm and blues, country, and even gospel. Who could top Motown, the Beatles, Janis, or Jimi? Most entertainers went commercial. Only a few, like George Benson, had a formula that worked in the coming decades. Quincy Jones and Herbie Hancock also come to mind. Some died trying to find the formula. Grant was one. Belden sums up Grant's career by saying that he died in 1979 pretty much an "unresolved legacy."

Eureka. That was it.

Grant was phenomenal, even without the accolades. But he died with a lot unresolved. Perhaps we all will.

But how to piece it all together? I needed more, maybe from the horse's mouth. Help came from a woman named Patricia Sweeting, who works at one of Detroit's leading AM radio stations. She came up to me after a book reading in Dearborn, Michigan. "Hi," she said. "I heard you mention your father-in-law, and I have a tape of an interview I did with him in 1970-something, back when I was in college. Would you like to hear it?"

So little written information, let alone visual and audio information, about Grant was available. Was she kidding? "Let me give you my address," I replied.

A copy of the cassette soon arrived in my mailbox. On it I heard an articulate college student interviewing a mature Grant Green backstage at Watt's Club Mozambique in Detroit. Though Patricia was young and not yet with a news organization, Grant was very warm and open to being interviewed about his life. By then, he had left New York and was living in Detroit. He was a prominent personality with a who's who list of friends in the community. Among them was the late Coleman Young, then a middle-aged revolutionary with a dirty mouth who'd sent white folks scrambling to Eight Mile Road when he was elected the city's first black mayor. To get folks to his fund-raisers though, ole Coleman had to have good music. Grant Green stepped up to help his friend. By then, he was making a comeback with his *Visions* album. It was more poppy than the stuff he had done a decade earlier on Blue Note, but the album was just the ticket to kick start his stalled career. With a Jackson 5 hit holding down the package, he had a winner that was played over and over on WJZZ, the city's premier jazz station. Grant Green was a star in every sense of the word, at least in Detroit, and kept the Mozambique, one of the city's most popular jazz spots, jam-packed.

A young Patricia found herself backstage interviewing the man. Maybe it was a comfortable naiveté, but Patricia coolly rattled off her questions and barely digested his answers. For example, when asked how he went about picking songs for each show, Grant said in his lumbering drawl, "Well, I play according to the house. I can feel the pulse of the house, and we look at the head-shakes out there and what gets them going...and if they liked this tune, the next song has to coincide with what they liked the first time, and then it has to be slower...we give them something fast and then we give them something slow. Fast and slow and it's in motion. You know?"

"I guess," she answered. Next question.

"A lot of musicians say that hard times and, I guess, poverty sometimes motivated them—"

Before she could finish setting up her question, Grant began to chuckle. Then he began to laugh. Then he began to howl. "All black people...all black people has hard times!" he laughed. "That's *nothing* unusual!"

Still laughing, he explained how hard it was when he got started: "I had an old beat-up guitar that my father bought. It was...I guess it cost about $20 and then I had an amp that was about $15. It was a $35–40 hookup. And that was the best you could do."

Patricia asked him whether there was a time when he had doubts. A more serious Grant settled down and said thoughtfully, "I've had some moments like that years ago...It was when I first started out. It was in the early stages. I really got discouraged.

People were talking to me and they told me I should continue, that I shouldn't give up. That things *would* get better."

Things did get better, but they also got worse. Grant reached for various crutches to help him get through the tough times. Those crutches included drugs and his little-known membership in the Nation of Islam. Some say both proved to be serious stumbling blocks. But in the end, Grant knew his own strength. He knew where he stood. He just got tired.

Tell the story.

This is a saying that goes way back. A musician could be up on a bandstand playing his heart out on an instrument and someone out in the audience who had been touched in some way by a particular note or phrase might call out, "Tell the story! Tell it!"

I was determined to tell Grant Green's story. Finally, a task delegated by no one. No news agency. No family member. It was just a certain knowing that something needed to be done, even with the unseen challenges ahead. I grew impatient with my own surface knowledge of the music. Why was jazz, long called the only true American music form, not taught in any of my public school music classes? It is illegal for a child to walk inside 90 percent of the places where jazz is played. Yet, Bach and Beethoven continue to be a part of school curriculums. The years. The loss. The many, like me, trying to catch up.

In the course of my research, I saw how my husband had much in common with his father. He had a love for music. A love for the black race. A certain culinary pickiness, a real temper, but an equally disarming charm—just like his dad. How many times did I think, "I see where you *got* that from." Recognition is a *motha'*. Or a father, evidently.

I interviewed the family members who were willing to talk, along with friends, scholars, nightclub hosts, critics, and musicians who knew the man or who knew his music. Many of the musicians seemed bitter about not getting their own accolades. Why wasn't I doing a book on *them*? But all were happy to see Grant Green finally getting his due.

In relaying his story, many of them focused on the 1960s, a difficult period in America. Jazz was the music to dance to, to cry to. Across overseas phone lines, over the din of music in dark clubs, and on the floor of surprisingly modest living spaces (for years jazzmen were at the bottom of the music business food chain), I heard the familiar voices of black men who had made it through the evils of the business. The evil of the times. Racism was rampant. But these men spoke eloquently, fully informed after a life of playing music they loved on stages around the world. Most were sharp dressers—jazz cats always could dress. Certainly everyone from Blue Note could dress. Just look at the album covers. These fellows had a taste that came from a life on the road, a life of being exposed to different cultures, different people, different places. But the good thing was that each and every one of these musicians, though gray-haired or on medication, was still playing. They were still alive. Doing their thing. They had made it through the changes in the music, even the audience. And now, they were willing to speak for someone who had not. Grant Green.

Some of the best stories I received came when the tape recorder wasn't on, though. I once overheard my husband on the phone with his brother Greg, laughing about the time their father fell down the stairs while chasing the family dog, Satan. Satan had done something or other and Grant went after him, only to trip and land upside down on his head, much to the delight of his sons, Greg, John, and Grant Jr. The tumble was so tremendous their daddy was afraid that he had broken one of his pick fingers.

"I done broke my pickin' finger! I done broke my pickin' finger!" he said. The finger was in fact intact, making his boys laugh even harder.

Sometimes digging up information on Grant posed unique challenges. As a reporter, I was trained to be detached from my subject, to straddle the fence. Sometimes I forgot that the information I came running home with from a good interview involved a man whose blood ran through the veins of the man I shared a bed with every night. Some of the things I would learn about Grant, particularly his drug habit, were not easy for his son to hear. What hurt more was that many of the musicians I interviewed had seen more of his father than he ever did. Or ever would.

2 Li'l Boy, Li'l Boy! The 1940s

"He would hit maybe one or two little notes on that ukulele, just enough to annoy Miss Stokes."

On June 6, 1935, a petite woman with deep dark skin gave birth to a son in St. Louis, Missouri. Her name was Martha Green. She was thirty-five. John Green, her husband, was thirty-eight. They named their son Grant. He would be their only child.

John and Martha were both born in Ripley, Tennessee, a small town just northeast of Memphis. How Miss Martha and Mister Johnny, as they were called by family members, made their way to St. Louis is uncertain. Perhaps they were on the forefront of the Great Migration of black people who left the South in search of better housing and jobs farther north.

But in terms of culture and even geography, St. Louis is not even a minute from the South, and so Johnny and Martha were in many ways simple, working-class, country people who, while never being rich, had a comfortable life in their later years. Grant Green's birth certificate lists his mother's occupation as a homemaker and his father's occupation as a laborer. His father would go to work as a police officer in the city of St. Louis. (However, there is one relative who likes to kid that John Green just pretended to be a police officer and was in fact a security guard who carried a gun and hung out in front of the police station.) In later years, Mister Johnny did own some parking lots that he guarded with the gun he always carried.

My brother-in-law, Greg, had the richest memories of his grandparents. This is partly because he was the oldest and could remember the most. But more to the point, Greg remembers so much about his grandparents because he was born in 1955, a time when his father was slowly making headway in local clubs.

While his parents were away at gigs around the city, Greg was looked after by his grandparents. The extent of his mother's absence is evident in that Greg calls Miss Martha "Ma."

My interview with Greg took place when he was still living in New Jersey. While there, I saw evidence of his legacy: tons of CDs stacked on a tall rack, DAT cassettes of his latest Sony session, and unopened packages of TDK cassettes scattered about the living room. On the walls were photos of Greg and George Benson, his godfather, as well as photos of him and other musicians who knew or had played with his dad. Music was the one thing he loved, besides maybe his plants. They were green and healthy, but he admitted a neighbor looked after them.

We sat down on his deco-like white leather furniture and ate dinner, some take-out Cuban food. Afterwards, I took out my tape recorder and we began to talk. Greg talked about what it was like walking in his dad's footsteps being raised by Miss Martha and Mister Johnny. His memories of them are sweet, although he knows little about any extended relatives on his father's side. He related the well-circulated story of an uncle who, along with his grandfather, taught his father how to play old Muddy Waters–type tunes on a guitar in the early 1940s. Around the same time—in 1939 to be exact—a German named Alfred Lion was starting a record company called Blue Note Records. The independent label would have a significant impact on the evolution of jazz, a word first used in the 1920s to describe a music that was beginning to have a pervasive influence on America. Years down the road, Greg's father would stake his claim to its history.

Greg's grandparents were in all likelihood the children of enslaved people. The biggest indicator: Mister Johnny's eyes. Miss Martha's hair. "My grandfather had light blue eyes. Look like they were blue-gray or something like that," Greg says. Miss Martha had long, shockingly straight jet-black hair. (It is widely known that many enslaved black women were made pregnant by their white owners, and so the eye color and hair texture of each succeeding generation was noticeably different from what was the norm for people of African ancestry.) Not only was Miss Martha's hair straight, she was stunningly beautiful and seemed to have Native American features. "There was definitely some Indian in her," Greg says. He told me that she suffered in later years from a

While he has played professionally under the name Grant Green Jr., Grant's eldest son is actually named Gregory. Photo by Sharony A. Green.

skin condition, maybe eczema, that made her already dark skin even darker.

It was in the house on La Salle that Greg lived with his grandparents. This was also the house in which Grant Green spent his early years. "We were all like one big family, so we ended up at their grandparents' houses as much as they did," recalls Ann Moody, Greg's first cousin, who still lives in St. Louis. She remembers the days when Grant's four children—Greg, Kim, John, and Grant Jr.—lived in the city. Most relatives readily admit that the four children were shuffled between their maternal grandparents' home on Clara St. and their paternal grandparents' home on La Salle. Unlike the house on Clara, a once-beautiful, three-story home with wood floors, the house on La Salle was very tiny. "This was a very small house," says Ann. "The bathroom was tiny. Even for kids, it was a tiny, tiny bathroom. I don't even remember where the bathtub was. That's how small the bathroom was. There was a screened-in porch at the front of the house, but we very rarely used that entrance. We would always

Gregory Green, Grant Green's son, guitarist

I'll tell ya what I think for me was the hippest—to do a record with Idris Muhummad. I really dug that. It was like a full circle almost. As a kid I would go into the studio and watch Idris play with my dad, and then now to do a record with him to me was great. Idris just told me that he loved my dad and he loved working with my dad, and said I had a big head like my dad. When I'm playing...the people who have seen my dad play, are freaked out a little bit. I guess we have some of the same mannerisms, but that's probably by me sitting and watching him for all of those years. When George [Benson] came over and heard my tracks over at the studio, it kinda freaked him out 'cause he said, "Omigod, man, you sound just like your father. I'm so proud of you." In a way my dad and I are a whole lot alike because he was my idol. He was the person I wanted to be like. I'll tell you something, this is going to sound so weird to you, but when I was doing that instrumental track that I did in the studio [he is referring to a track he did for a solo album]—me and my girlfriend had just broken up, and my head was all messed up, and it was just playing havoc with my mind. I couldn't play, and I'd start thinking about her and you know, and all of a sudden—boom, I just nailed this track. And when we listened back to this track, it freaked me out because it sounded so much like my old man. I was like, "Wow, I phrased that shit like my old man would phrase it," and it might sound silly to you, but I think that may be spiritual, like he was there or something, because he knew I couldn't do it and he was there to help pull me through. That probably sounds stupid. But I know it was definitely a spiritual thing.

go around to the side through the kitchen. But if you were to go inside from the screened-in front porch, you would enter the living room, which was very small, and there was a doorway that led to a middle room, which was the bedroom, and between these rooms, they hung a curtain. The house had a vinyl floor, and if I remember right, the floor was kind of yellow. In the front room, there was a big, pullout sofa bed. It was really only three rooms, so when we spent the night, me and Kim stayed in the front room with Miss Martha, who slept on a cot. Mister Johnny would stay in the middle room, which was really the bedroom with the boys."

The home was decorated with good furniture that lasted a lifetime, for Mister Johnny was the kind of guy who "would buy something in his house and it would be there for the rest of his life," my husband says. "It was like you could see a chair that my dad sat on and the same chair would be there even after my dad grew up. His house never changed. They never changed nothing in the house."

Because Grant was an only child, Mister Johnny and Miss Martha doted on him, but there were some limits to their love. "Like a lot of blacks, they were not able to show overt affection to their children," Ardis Moody Hansberry, Grant Green's sister-in-law, says. "[But] they would compensate in later years by showing much affection for their grandchildren."

Mister Johnny always insisted that they stay inside the fence around the house. When the grandchildren were disobedient, he

Grant Green's childhood house on La Salle Street in St. Louis, Missouri. Photo by Sharony A. Green.

sent them to a peach tree in the yard, where they were asked to pick a branch. "We had to pick off the leaves and he would whip us," my husband says, laughing. "He was very protective."

John Green's grandchildren didn't always need a whupping to stay in line. Sometimes all they had to do was take a good look at him. Mister Johnny was about six foot two inches in height and weighed about 220 pounds. He was big man who intimidated many. "Greg looks a lot like him, brawn and built," his aunt Ardis says. "Mister Johnny was the typical black man of his age in that he had this need to sorta build himself up, to have people respect him and look up to him. He clearly dominated Miss Martha. As they got older, I really felt he was somewhat abusive to Miss Martha, and because of her personality she went along with that."

Greg agrees that his grandmother was a very patient woman. "I used to always get hurt and cut up and she was always taking me to the hospital. She was very gentle."

"Mister Johnny," says Ann, "had the greatest laugh. It was like, 'Heh, heh, heh, heh,'" she says, issuing up an Eddie Murphy–like laugh up from the bottom of her throat.

In 1978, Miss Martha died, followed by Mister Johnny in 1980. Eerily sandwiched between their two funerals was a third funeral, one for their only child, Grant. "In a matter of three years, one side of my family was just wiped away," my husband has said many times.

But during their lifetime, Mister Johnny and Miss Martha gave Grant and his music their full support. After his father showed him a few licks on his own guitar, the story goes, Grant asked him to get him one of his own. Mister Johnny complied and continued to teach his son how to play. "My father played guitar—blues and folk mostly," Grant once told an interviewer. "He taught me a few things, but I learned mostly from listening to records of Charlie Christian and to Charlie Parker. I heard Christian with Benny Goodman's big band and with the Sextet. I heard just about everything he recorded. I wasn't playing electric guitar at that time, but I didn't find it too hard to learn his lines."

It is unclear at what age Grant began to listen to these records, but there is evidence that by the fifth grade, he had a serious interest in music. One woman had the most lucid memories of Grant's childhood years in St. Louis. Her name was Sylvia Shabazz. We first connected when she read an appeal I had posted in a black St. Louis newspaper to people with Grant Green stories and photographs. She called me and told me she had attended Johnson School with Grant. We talked for the better part of an hour.

Some months later, my husband and I went down to St. Louis and met Sylvia. Her home had smells and objects that were familiar, the kind that might be found in the home of my own grandma—trinkets, a Bible, closets full of clothes and other old goodies. With her hair wrapped in a scarf, Sylvia invited us into her bedroom, sat on her bed, and made space for us. Then she began to recount her memories of a young Grant Green, who used to sneak a little toy ukulele into class and plink and plank on it much to the dismay of their teacher, Miss Stokes. "I was eleven years old. I think Grant may have been maybe a year or two older. A year at the most," says Sylvia, whose last name had been Fulton in the 1940s when she and Grant were in grade school. Because her class was seated alphabetically, she sat next to Grant. They became good friends, and worse, the class clowns. It didn't help that Sylvia was adept on the piano and that Miss Stokes was the school's music teacher.

"Whenever Miss Stokes left the room, I got on the piano and I [played] the boogie-woogie," says Sylvia. "Everybody liked for me to play the boogie-woogie. I was playing the boogie-woogie and Grant was plunking on the guitar. We had a lookout on the door because if she went to the principal's office, we could see all the way to his door. When she got ready to come back, someone would give the signal and we would jump back into our seats. A lot of times she could hear the music because we had it going on! But by the time she got back, everybody was in their seats and she never caught us. At recess time, we'd play together out in the yard, but mostly it was in that classroom that we had a ball. And Grant was the leader. Grant and myself and two other friends, Odessa Adams and Winifred Taylor. As for the males, there were the twins, Booker and Oscar Snodgrass, Rodell Johnson, Charles Foster, and Edward Alexander. There were about eight or nine of us and we all sat near the back of the room.

"Miss Stokes was a very religious lady and kind of on the nervous side," she continues. "And we played on that. Sometimes when she was out of the room, I'm talking no holds barred for the foolishness. We would throw spitballs. We had eraser fights. And Miss Stokes, she'd go to praying over us. And Grant could just really needle her. She'd always say to him, 'Li'l boy! Li'l boy!' And he'd say, 'What? What did I do?' And everybody would start snickering. He was always drumming on the desk."

Sylvia says Grant went on to play drums for the school's Drum and Bugle Corps. He also sang in the choir, but caused Miss Stokes anguish even there. He wanted to sing bass with his buddies, but she insisted that he sing with the tenors. "She had a li'l tenor section lined up, and before she knew anything, Grant would be done disappeared," laughs Sylvia. "He would jump down and go all the way to the back there with the bass boys so he could sing bass, and she'd be, 'Grant! Grant!' And by that

Sylvia (Fulton) Shabazz, Grant's grade school classmate, says that Grant showed a love for music early on and was quite a prankster. Photo by Sharony A. Green.

time, Grant would have tried to ease back up to the tenors. She had him come up to the front and she'd do the scales and he'd pretend to have a sore throat. 'I can't sing. I-I-I,' he'd say. 'C'mon, you can,' she'd say. And he'd, 'I-I-I,' and she'd say, 'Young man, you don't have a sore throat and you better sing this right now.' And he'd be just like a chicken, singing, 'I-I-I.' And man, we'd be crying, do you hear me?"

There was another instrument Grant liked to play: toy ukulele. "He would hit maybe one or two little notes on that ukulele, just enough to annoy Miss Stokes. She'd look up and want to know who it was. She got up and came to the back of the room, but the kids had passed it over to the far end. So wherever she thought she heard it, when she got there, naturally it was not there. So when she headed back to her desk, they'd pass it back to Grant. By the time she reached their desk, he might have hit maybe one or two little notes on it. Sometimes she would get aggravated enough and send him to the principal. Mr. Everett, who was our principal, was a very sweet guy. I think it was amusing to him that they were annoying her, but he'd make Grant sit out on the bench or let him run around to different rooms taking memorandums to the teachers and different things. If she would put him out of the room before morning recess, he would be back in by lunchtime."

Sylvia described Grant as being a very neat and well-dressed kid. "He was kinda tall and thin. He had a fairly nice grade of hair, about my complexion, [a] dark brown-skinned guy. Dressed very nice. People dressed very nice then. Khakis and blue jeans were in. Most of the guys wore the jeans, but Grant wore the khakis. Sometimes he just wore plain dress slacks. And always a sweater and a shirt. I remember Grant wearing those sweaters. And he wore whatever the style shoes the boys wore, but they were always shined. Most of the guys wore their hair to the front. Some also wore what we called the box cut, a low kind of crew cut. It was after the war so it was around '48, '49, somewhere around in there."

And Grant had one more gift, Sylvia says. He could draw. "Grant was an artist. Oh, he could draw," she says. "All the guys who were part of our little clique were some artists extraordinaire. They decorated the doors at Christmas time. They painted the

Nativity scenes on the windows and the doors and put on displays in the rooms."

At the time Grant attended Johnson School, Jim Crow laws were still in effect. The city's schools were segregated, but Mr. Everett, the school principal, loved to present his students to the community, especially white administrators from the district office, says Sylvia. "He was always inviting someone who was white from the board to put us on display," she says. "Johnson Elementary was the exception of the elementary schools in that our principal always wanted and tried to get more for us. We were the only elementary school that had a public address system, and he could sit in the office and talk to each room. We had some very nice activities. We had choir at Johnson. We had a Glee Club. The last thing he did before we graduated was to get the Drum and Bugle Corps. The PTA and all the teachers worked together. They raised the money for whatever it was he [said] we needed. During that time, we did not have tape recorders. We had the wire recorders. He [said] he wanted us to have tape recorders. They raised money for the recorders. We had a spring festival that came right after Easter. We'd have a fashion show, a play, and talent show. The kids were all very talented. We had all types of vocalists and instrumentalists and then the Drum and Bugle Corps performed. The girls wore white pleated gabardine skirts and a white satin blouse with the great big balloon sleeves. They were real pretty."

Johnson was located in the Mill Creek area of St. Louis, a neighborhood not too far from downtown and the Mississippi River. It was a thriving community filled with black-owned businesses. "The race stuff here was just like Mississippi. It was no different," says Sylvia "There were places you couldn't go downtown. There were areas you couldn't go in and places we couldn't eat in. A lot of the salespeople in the department stores didn't want to wait on you. I tell everybody that St. Louis was Up-South."

During our visit, Sylvia asks us if we would like a tour of the area. As we drove to the neighborhood once known as Mill Creek, we could feel the St. Louis in which Grant Green lived. But many changes had taken place during his absence, however. Houses were condemned in the late 1950s and razed, making

Sylvia Shabazz, Grant's grade-school classmate during his St. Louis days in the 1940s

I have an album of Grant. It's got his picture on it, with him standing with his leg raised on something. It's the only album I have by him. I got it from a Muslim brother named Brother Abraham. Brother Abraham operated a book and record store down on Grand where we black Muslims had our businesses. I would always go through there when I'd get paid or had some money looking for records. I liked jazz. In fact, I like music, period. Brother Abraham was into jazz and I was into jazz. I was there going through the records one day and he said, "I've got a record here. I don't know if you're familiar with this brother, but when he comes to St. Louis, he always comes to the mosque." And he whipped out this album and said, "Are you familiar with this brother?" I told him, "Am I ever! I went to school with him! We go way back." He said, "You know Brother Grant?" I said, "Yes, I do know Brother Grant." It was the only album he had, and I ended up buying it. He said, "I'll sell it to you because I can always get another one. But I'm going to sell it to you simply because you know him." Brother Abraham was just so outdone that I knew him. And then Brother Abraham called to tell me that Grant had passed. And I tell you I just almost went through the floor. It hurt me so bad because I really was looking forward to seeing him. And he was looking forward to seeing me, because we just talked about some of everything. He remembered all our classmates, Edward and the Snodgrass brothers, and all of them. He had just called me long distance to tell me that he was coming back. He was coming to see his father, because when he was here before he didn't spend too much time with him and he had promised to come back. He was going to spend more time with him. I never knew he had been sick. He sounded like the same Grant that I left at Johnson School.

way for industrial and new commercial businesses. Hundreds of thousands of black families were displaced in the process. "The buyouts actually started taking place around about '59 and by then, a lot of people had already moved out," Sylvia says, sweeping her hand through the air. "A lot of the houses had started being leveled. The purpose was to rebuild the area, to destroy the slum properties and to build modern homes, they claimed. But it ended up being all commercial. They lied and told us that the people that lived there would be able to come back and have first priority to come back in the area. But none of that ever took place. Once they got the people out of there, and they had the land, that was it. It was a kiss-off. I think they'd found some of the biggest rats they'd ever seen during the demolition. The workmen had on display the rats that they'd killed. The workmen were going down with loaded pistols. They were shooting them because as they tore those houses down, they ran into the rats. The Housing Authority took pictures, and they had those pictures on display in the lobby to show. At one time, the city was almost infested with rats. On the billboards they were trying to tell people how to keep the trash and stuff down. We had trash pits, and the rats lived in those trash pits. But all of the houses in Mill Creek were not in a deteriorated state. Some of those houses were very sound. But the city had designated it a slum area. It had more to do with the designation than it actually being a slum. There were some very nice, well-kept properties in that area. But once the whole area was termed 'blighted,' that meant everything had to go.

"All this was houses," says Sylvia with another sweep of her hand as my husband drove through the area. "Kids would walk straight down this street, and Grant and them lived back over there. Blacks in those days—which the city didn't know until they got ready to do the buyout—owned a lot of that property. Black businesses flourished. There were good black businesses in everything, real estate, accounting, and photography. Mill Creek had hundreds of blocks. They realized that we would control a key voting block, and just as we were waking up to that fact, they came in and had a black man help sell us out. We used to have a saying here, 'Urban renewal means black folks' removal.' That's what they did. From this side of Martin Luther King all the way to the railroad tracks, this was Mill Creek. Houses came all the way down to 23rd Street."

She pauses and then says, "We're scattered throughout the city now, in South St. Louis, in the county, in North St. Louis. It was about the power of that vote. They realized we had a city within the city, see?"

After she and Grant graduated from Johnson, years passed before Sylvia heard of her classmate again. It was 1959, the year before he left for Blue Note Records in New York. At the time, Sylvia was in her mid-twenties. "I was dating this guy named Jimmy, and one night Jimmy came home telling me about how jammed packed this place was where a guitar player was playing. Turns out it was Grant. He was making an appearance at the El Patio with this group the Quartet Trés Bien. So the next night, which would have been that Saturday, Jimmy took me up, but the place was so jammed, people were all coming out the door. I never got to see him," she says.

Some two decades later, they finally connected. A security guard who worked in a laundromat near her house was the link. His name: Mister Johnny. "I ended up moving into the John Cochran housing project in '63. And it was through Grant's father, who worked as a security guard at the laundromat across the street, that I later became reacquainted with Grant," she says.

Unbeknownst to her as she poured her detergent and washed and dried her clothes in the machines, the man standing guard over the laundromat was someone with a distinct connection to her past. She would see him time and time again. When she left the projects and purchased a home, she and her kids returned to the neighborhood to see their friends. She waved at Mister Johnny, thinking that he was a nice guy, but no one special. "He always looked out for the kids coming over there to wash for their parents," Sylvia recalls. "And he would help to see them back and forth across the street. Well, one day he told my children that he had a son that played guitar professionally. My son came home and says, 'Mama, what grade school did you go to?' I says, 'Johnson.' He says, 'You probably knew Mr. Green's son.' I says, 'Mr. Green?' He says, 'You know, Mr. Green, the guard down at the laundromat in Cochran.' I says, 'Yeah.' He says, 'Because he says his son went to school in...what was that area called then?' I says, 'Mill Creek.' He says, 'Yeah, that's what he says.'

"So I says, 'I'll tell you what. Tell him to call me because more than likely I did go to school with him.' So Mr. Green called me and we got to talking. He says, 'What grade school did you go to?' I says, 'Johnson.' He says, 'Well my son went there.' I says, 'Who was your son?' And he says, 'Grant Green.' And when he says it, I just started screaming. I says, 'Grant was your son!? Grant? That was my buddy!' He says, 'Well, that was my son.' So then we got to rehashing and I was telling him about how Grant used to cut up in school. And he says, 'Yeah, I remember.' He says sometimes Grant used to bring little notes home or maybe they might need [Mr. Green] to come up and talk with the teacher. Mr. Green asked me would I mind if he passed my number on to Grant, and I told him of course not. And Grant called me and we talked for a long time."

They had a lot to catch up on. Both had been married and divorced. Both had kids. And both had become Muslims. (Hence, Sylvia's name change to Shabazz.)

"When he called me he [said] he was in Detroit," Sylvia continues. "He told me about being in New York and [that he] had played with Wes Montgomery and all about where he had been. He mostly was telling me about his career. He seemed to be very happy. He told me he had children and wanted to know what I had been doing, and I told him about my having five kids. I did some of everything for a living. I cooked. I cleaned offices at night. I was a janitor for a children's clothing store. I worked [with a] private family some. Then I decided I wanted to go back to school and complete my education, get my GED."

As they continued talking, Sylvia heard something in his voice. Grant had something he needed to say. "He told me that he had had some problems and how he had to get a grip on himself," she says. "When he made that statement, I heard a change in his voice. It was a voice of some despair. Being street smart, I had an idea what he was talking about. I knew a lot of those musician guys use to smoke the 'pot,' as we call it now, and some of them did use the needle, but I didn't push it. I kinda picked up later that that's what he was trying to say, and I didn't want to go into something that would maybe make him depressed. I didn't want to get depressed. I was on such an upbeat just talking to him."

A few weeks passed and Grant called her again. He told her that he was planning on making a trip home to St. Louis and hoped to be there within a month. He didn't mention that his doctor had recommended a triple bypass. "He just [said] he was coming to see his father and there were some things he wanted to tie up, and he definitely wanted to see me and maybe have lunch or something," she says. "He wanted to know if I knew how to get in touch with any of the other crowd, and maybe we would just try to have a little mini-reunion. In the meantime, I had bought this album with his picture on the front of it and I told him, 'Listen Grant, you've got to autograph this album for me. After I told my kids about you and showed them the album and everything, they've been about to have a fit.' They were crazy about Mr. Green, his dad. I told them I went to school with Grant and how we used to cut up and how he had made a name for himself as a guitarist. I showed them the album cover and everything. They were looking forward to meeting him."

They would never get a chance to. Instead of staying in New York for his surgery, or going to St. Louis to see his dad, Grant went to California for what would be his last performance, at the Lighthouse. He died on the trip back.

The record she had purchased was his 1970 *Alive!* album. Before we left her house, Sylvia asked my husband to do the honors. He signed his father's name—which was, of course, his own.

3 Gigging in St. Louis The Early to Mid-1950s

"You could tell when a cat's got potential."

Grant's period at Johnson School appeared to be the only time he got consistent schooling. As he entered his preteens, music became his priority, and he started going to class less. In 1948, he began playing guitar for local churches. At the time he was just thirteen years old. Richard Henderson, a St. Louis jazz historian, has a vivid memory of seeing Grant play at one of his church gigs. "Why, it was the first time I had seen a guitarist playing in the church. The church where I saw him singing was kind of like a sanctified church. The church I went to was Baptist. So that—a guitar player in church—wasn't going on there," Rich chuckles.

The church gigs would have a lasting impact on Grant's work. Historically, the church has had a strong influence on jazz and all black music. "Jazz came out of the gospel," says Kenny Rice, a St. Louis drummer who played with Grant. "You can hear gospel while listening to Aretha Franklin. In New Orleans, they would play a gospel tune while taking bodies to the grave and come back playing, 'Just a Closer Walk with Thee' after the body had been buried. This was some of the earliest roots of jazz. They'd come back from the grave rejoicing and playing this music we now call jazz."

As Grant honed his craft in area churches, he began to look for other places where he could perform. He wanted in with the big guys, the ones who were already playing in clubs. But the older musicians didn't think he was ready and refused to allow him to participate in the informal jam sessions held in their homes. This didn't stop Grant.

Oliver Matheus was a concert promoter who spent much of his time with black musicians, including Grant. He was a care-free white man who wore sandals, big straw hats, and funky rings and bracelets; he adored black people. Of Grant's early days, Ollie, as he was called, says, "I remember once we were having a session inside a house and Grant was trying to play with the band from outside the window! He was outside, listening to the band under this window and playing with 'em."

Albert St. James, a drummer in the city, confirmed how important music had become to Grant during his teen years. Johnson School students went on to Vashawn High. Grant never made it. One day, the school's choir instructor needed a guitarist to play chords. Albert told her about Grant. "Although I hadn't heard him play a whole lot, I knew of him," Albert says. "So I told her and she got in touch with Grant's father. They brought Grant to Vashawn. By then, he could read the chords." Albert, who plays with Quartet Trés Bien, a popular St. Louis–based band, says their instructor was impressed. "Most guitar players at that time couldn't read chords. Grant knew all of the chords she wanted him to play, and she was wondering why he wasn't in school.

"I couldn't answer that," Albert says, laughing.

Former nightclub owner Ollie Matheus (right), pictured with Grant Green Jr. in 1995, was instrumental in helping the author find the musicians with whom Grant played during his early years in St. Louis. Photo by Sharony A. Green.

By the ninth grade, Grant had dropped out of school, and Mister Johnny and Miss Martha backed his decision. "I think his parents were taken aback by the fact that he was so talented musically," says Albert. "They didn't really appreciate his educational thing. He was musical and he was making money."

Grant studied guitar for a year with a local instructor named Mel Bay and, later, Forest Alcorn. "He wasn't a local yokel. And he didn't think like none," says Joe Charles, another St. Louis drummer. "You could tell when a cat's got potential. A lot of guys knew it. I knew it, Chauncey [Williams] knew it. Sam [Lazar] knew it. We all knew it.

Ardis Hansberry, Grant Green's sister-in-law

Grant played jazz, and so jazz musicians could appreciate him, but he always had a bluesy quality to his jazz, so even people who may not really have understood modern jazz could get with Grant's playing. I have good memories of Grant. He was very well-liked in St. Louis. I could get in places free because they knew [I was] Grant Green's sister-in-law.

"This has always been a drum town. And Grant loved drummers, especially when he got high. He played his ass off then. He'd get a funny look on his face, man. He was a natural. Self-taught! He knew a lot of music," says Joe.

Grant's first apprenticeship was with an accordionist named Joe Murphy. "Joe was a rarity and a novelty," Grant once told an interviewer. "You just didn't find any black people playing accordion then."

By the mid-1950s, Grant was making the rounds in local beer and wine gardens, playing everything from boogie-woogie and rock 'n' roll, to standard jazz tunes, the blues, and even country music. "Once we had a gig out at this hillbilly place, way out in the country. We played bluegrass and Grant was doggin' it! They loved him. They didn't want him to go. This one white girl out there was crazy about him! He was a sweet cat. Everybody loved Grant. He was bad with those girls. If we had gigs somewhere and he [saw] a girl he [wanted], we'd have a fifteen-minute intermission, which was enough time for him to get in the backseat and take care of business. He was terrible! I says, 'Good God A-mighty!' He'd drive the girls crazy, man. I'd say, 'Boy, what kind of tongue you got?' Grant was a terrible freak! All of them musicians was terrible freaks, Jimmy Forrest and all of them. Charlie Parker and all of 'em."

A certain young lady did catch his eye in a special way. Her name was Annie Maude Moody. She and Grant would have four kids. It was on the floor of her living room that I saw my first Grant Green CD. I'll always remember how she presented herself upon our first meeting.

"Call me Annie," she said in a smooth, coquettish voice that made me think of Della Reese, who, as I understand it, is one of her distant cousins. Annie Maude was Grant's first love. His Cantaloupe Woman. She inspired such tunes as "Blues in Maude's Flat" and "Miss Ann's Tempo."

Ardis Hansberry, Annie's sister, revealed a picture of this woman who was not only Grant's muse, but the mother of his four children. "She had a very, very, very nice shape, beautiful legs, and because she was tall, she had a kinda model figure," says Ardis, recalling the Annie that Grant met in the mid-1950s. "And she was always doing something with her hair. She had a friend named Lela Mae, and she and Lela Mae did everything to their hair. They dyed it. They cut it. I remember once they were trying to dye it and they were using peroxide, and their hair fell out. I remember another time when the style was short haircuts for women and one would shape the back with a razor or shaver. Well, Ann and Lela Mae made a V in the back of their hair and went up too high, so high that half of the back of their head [was] bald.

"But my best memories of her [are] probably when she was a senior in high school. She was going out a lot. They'd go to dances. And I was an avid reader always so I have memories of her taking me to the library. We'd go to the main public library. Every Saturday she would take me to the library. I remember when she graduated from high school. She had taken a secretarial course, and she got a job on the South Side, and I remember her wardrobe. She had a lot of suits, which was unusual for young women in those days...I was always impressed because she [wore] a suit to work. I remember visiting her in the office once. You could tell people really were impressed with her and had a lot of respect for her."

According to Ardis, Ann, as she was also called, may have met Grant at the Romer Room, a club on Finney just east of Vanderventer in St. Louis. Ann's family lived on Biddle Street in the first housing project built in St. Louis. Locals called the neighborhood Car Square Village, and it was not too far from Grant's own Mill Creek home. But while Ann had roots in the South—specifically, Mississippi—the tone of her home was somewhat different from what Grant was accustomed to.

"He was very country," says Ardis who also speaks in a sexy, solid voice like Ann. During our interview in the living room of her condo in Culver City, California, she coolly held a cigarette. She is the "wayward" one. The "intellectual" aunt who moved out west and worked for IBM.

"In fact, I think one of the things that Grant kind of admired about our family was that we were all sorta educated and somewhat cultured, especially my sister, Jewel, and I, because we both sang," she says. "We sang all through school. That was one of the places that we learned about so-called 'good' music. And we were Lutherans, and our church was almost like Germany. We sang a lot of Bach. My sister, Jewel, had an operatic voice. She could've been an opera singer if she wanted to, but she didn't have the discipline and that heart. And I think Grant really admired that."

But Ann's father, Mack Moody, had his own ideas about Grant. "My dad didn't like him because he was a musician. To him that was not a decent job. He thought all musicians were drug addicts. My dad was a truck driver and a Teamster for thirty years. No, my dad didn't care for him at all."

That didn't stop Ann, who was taken by Grant's charisma. They decided to get married. Ardis will never forget the day. "I remember the wedding primarily because of the dress I wore. I had just gotten it for my baccalaureate service. It was a black and white print dress, and this was in the '50s, so we were still wearing the wide-skirted dresses and skirts, and I had on these white patent leather shoes that had two little glass beads at the tie, and I had a black straw hat, and in those days you always wore gloves and a hat to church, and so I remember more about me and what I wore than I do about the wedding," she says. "They got married at Transfiguration Lutheran Church, our family's church. It was on 18th and Biddle, right up the street from our house. Ann had grown up in that church. She was confirmed in the church and there were a good number of people there because she had a lot of girlfriends. I cannot remember whether [Grant's] parents were there. Certainly his friends, all the musicians, [came]."

Not long after the wedding, Ardis decided to pay the newlyweds a visit. "Ann and Grant were living around the corner from his parents' house on La Salle, and one day I went over there and she was fixing Grant's hair," she says. "At the time, he wore his hair pressed and curled, and Ann was not a licensed beautician, but she had been fixing hair for years, and I went over there and they were in the kitchen and he was sitting between her legs—the same way I did when my mom did my hair when I was a little girl—getting his hair done. My family was like, 'What's his problem? What? Does he think he's Little Richard?' We laughed about it."

One thing they couldn't laugh about was his dedication to his music. "He was very into his music. It was very clear that his whole life was music. I mean, music came first," she says. "You could go to their house at any time and almost any time you would go in, Grant would be doing something with his guitar."

At the time Grant and Ann met, Ann already had a little boy named Gordon. "Gordon was actually the first grandbaby, and he was very spoiled. I remember, because Ann went out a lot with Grant," Ardis says. "I have memories of me and my dad babysitting because my mom was in a card group and most nights she played cards. I went to college on her card-playing money. Daddy would be walking Gordon, patting him to put him to sleep, and then I would take my turn, walking him, and patting him and putting him to sleep."

In 1956, Ann gave birth to her second child, the couple's first. They named him Gregory. From the day Greg entered the world, he was embraced by both sets of grandparents, but especially by Mister Johnny and Miss Martha. "Gregory was their first grandchild, and that was Mister Johnny's heart," states Ardis. They all loved him, in fact.

But being the sister of a woman married to a struggling musician was no easy chore. "Ann was like eight or nine years older than I was, but we were the same size when I got to be a teenager. My mom was a laundress. She did laundry for white

"He was very into his music. It was very clear that his whole life was music," says Ardis Hansberry, Grant Green's sister-in-law. Photo by Francis Wolff, courtesy of Mosaic Images.

Joe Charles, St. Louis drummer who played with Grant during the 1950s

Well, you know why Grant liked me? Because I played weird. I played different. I played off beat. See, Grant didn't like drummers to play just straight. When drummers play like I played, that suggested things for him, gave him ideas. I know a lot of drummers tried to get my gig because they [shot] dope with Grant, and they thought, "Oh, I shoot dope. I get the gig," but Grant said, "No. I want Joe Charles." He was a sweet cat.

folks all of her life and you know how white women are about trying to keep their size small, and so we would get their cast-off clothes," Ardis says. "After Ann got married, it was just me and my younger brother at home, so I was able to get the clothes, but she would borrow my clothes because she was basically this struggling musician's wife and they were steady having these kids. She would come over when I was in school, and the only way I would know she got my clothes was when I'd go to the closet to put on something and it wasn't there. At first I would go over to their house, ranting and raving. I'd get so mad because she and Grant both were very sloppy. For one thing, they'd be out every night wherever he played and they slept all day and they'd come home at two o'clock in the morning, and wherever they were when they got home is where they dropped everything. So I'd go over there looking for my clothes. Once I bought this dress. It was a blue and white check with these kind of puffed sleeves. I had never worn it. When I went to the closet to finally wear it, it was gone. I knew immediately that Ann had it. I went over to her house to get it. I looked all over the house. We were literally about to come to blows because she was saying that she didn't have it, and I was like, 'You have to have it. Who else would have it?' She and Grant were very terrible housekeepers. They would have weeks of newspaper around the house. So I looked through everything and finally, I just got down and looked under the bed, and there was my new dress under the bed. It was ruined. I didn't know how long it had been under there. I was so angry. We stopped speaking for three or four months."

But there were pluses to being the sister-in-law of a musician. Ardis and her sister, Jewel, often got special treatment at the various clubs where Grant played. They got in free and always sat up front. Drinks were often on the house. "We would go because Ann would have to sit at a table by herself, and even when he wasn't on the stand, the guys would get together and go outside. So we would go with her to keep her company. It was exciting because we were Grant's sisters-in-law."

Barbara Morris, St. Louis friend

Grant was down-to-earth and his wife, Ann, was a very sweet girl. The very first time she seen Grant, she told me, "I'm gon' get him." That's what she told me! "I'm gon' get him!" And she got him.

Ardis fell for a musician, too—a drummer named Ed Hansberry. It was Grant who played Cupid.

"Grant would try to match-make a lot," she recalls. "He was always trying to hook me up with somebody. I don't know if the guys were attracted to me or if he was just trying to hook me up 'cause I was Ann's sister, but he was always telling me about some guy or another who liked me. There was one drummer we used to call 'Hans.' It was short for Hansberry. So one day Grant asked, 'Did Hans call you?' And I'm like, 'Who is Hans?'" [Hans is the first cousin of Lorraine Hansberry, the author of *A Raisin in the Sun,* the first play by a black playwright to be produced on Broadway.]

As it turned out, it was Grant who gave Hansberry her phone number. Grant went on to give Ardis "this whole story about why I should be interested." In time, she was. They got married and Grant, Ann, Ardis, and Hans became a common sight on the St. Louis club scene. During that time, Ardis was able to observe Grant, whose disposition, according to her, was different from that depicted by some people years later. As the woes of the business and the accompanying ups and downs of his drug habit took their toll on him in the mid-1960s, band members would describe Grant as a bitter and even miserly man when payday came. But in the early days, he was an easygoing, peace-loving fella, she says. "I can't recall ever seeing Grant angry," says Ardis. "His thing would be a li'l smile and just going, 'Oooooh.' It was funny. A club owner or somebody might stiff the band for money. When they got through playing on a lot of the gigs, we'd be sitting around waiting for the owner to pay them, and then it would occur to us now, we been waiting for an hour and a half. And the other musicians would be like, 'Let's go find the mothafucka' and Grant was like, 'Well, let's just cool it.' He didn't like a lot of confrontation."

Albert St. James, the Quartet Trés Bien drummer, and his wife, Sarah, were another couple with whom Grant and Ann hung out, Ardis says. "Ann and Sarah were pregnant at the same time," says Ardis. "I can remember once babysitting Gordon and April, who was Sarah and Albert's daughter. In fact, the whole family remembers this, because both of them were crying all night long. It was one of those [times] when Grant and Ann and Sarah and Al were supposed to be 'right back.' There was like three or four couples that kind of hung out together. Chauncey Williams played drums. And he was married to this girl named Peaches. And so they had kinda like this li'l group, the musicians hung together and their wives. Some of the musicians smoked weed. Some used heroin. All of the wives smoked weed, and they were very happy."

Sarah St. James offers a view of what it was like to be married to a musician. She explains a musician's wife can have her up moments, particularly when she was at the table with the other wives. "We talked about everything that I guess most women would talk about, but then on the other hand, it was very, very fulfilling, especially when I was a young girl like eighteen or so, when Albert was playing with Jimmy Forrest. They would say, 'Oh, that's Sarah Marlo. Albert St. James, that's her boyfriend.' So it made you feel like you [were] walking on air. I lived on the South Side, and naturally my thing during that day was the Miracles and Stevie Wonder, and then Albert came along and says, 'Here's a different type of music, Sarah. Listen to this.' And when we had our children, they grew up listening to nothing but jazz. They could hum anything to you from Bird or Miles because that's what they heard all day."

But a musician's wife can also have her down moments, Sarah adds. "You can be very lonely on New Year's Eve's and holidays," she says. "You are sitting there in a chair while everybody else is having a good time because your husband is on the bandstand, but then after he gets through playing, that's when the excitement would come. I remember a lot of times Albert and Grant and Annie Maude would come to our house and I would make biscuits and fried chicken, and we would be up 'til five and six o'clock the next morning just laughing and talking and having a good time, and that seemed to be when the musicians would be relaxing. And that's when you enjoyed yourself. The only thing you could say is that they had a God-given talent and so they had to exercise it come what may, and you knew this when you decided to take one of them as your mate. But how you cope is a different story. Some did and some didn't."

Ardis says Grant and his musician friends had a certain code language she never could understand. And didn't care to. "At first, I really didn't listen to Grant because he talked in that musician's code a lot, and it was like I didn't have time to figure out what he's saying, but I did [eventually] start listening to him and having conversations with him. He would come up with li'l sayings that would keep people in stitches," she says.

Says Sarah, "You didn't have to be around them long before you could understand, though. Like Albert might tell Jimmy, 'Well, Jimmy, I'll see you later, man. I'm goin' home and I got to scarf and I'm a cop some z's. Well, pretty soon you learned that that meant, 'I'm going home to eat and I'm going on to take a nap.' Like they never say, 'money.' They said, 'my jingles.'"

This kind of talk made for a tight camaraderie between the guys, but everyone recalled Grant had a special friendship with one musician in particular, a local piano player named John "Albino Red" Chapman. Their relationship offers insight into the side of Grant that championed the outsider, and especially the underdog. Many say Grant probably learned lot from John, a quiet albino man who was a remarkable composer. "He could play 'Rhapsody in Blue,' all thirty-two pages, Concerto in F," says Barbara Morris, who was once married to Chapman. "[He] had a revolutionary attitude, and he did not play nothing but jazz. I don't care whether beans was in the pot or out of the pot, he didn't compromise. I've seen times when Chuck Berry come to the house to ask John to come play with him, and he'd...slam the door in his face."

Ed Hansberry adds, "He would tune his piano while he was playing and, as I recall, he and Grant were fairly close. By him being an albino, I think he was extremely shy. I remember him and Grant talking and it was the kind of thing where one would start something and the other would go, 'Yeah,' before they even completed the thought. It was kind of mystic stuff. There were a lot of implied things, but never actually spoken. John Chapman and I used to go out to the cemetery and sit on tombstones and talk about things. And we used to just walk from one end of St. Louis to the other, walk and just philosophize. It was always about music, about impressions we would make as musicians on people in the world or how you can influence younger guys coming up."

They also talked about money. Some musicians made just $15 a night, but they could find regular work in St. Louis, and of course, in East St. Louis. When clubs in St. Louis closed, it was here that musicians headed.

East St. Louis sits smack between Chicago and Memphis. Back in that day, blacks from the South, who might have been on their way to Chicago or Detroit, stopped in East St. Louis because of the jobs waiting at packing houses in the city. Swift was there. Hunter's was there. There were also steel mills, all with help wanted signs. And people worked hard. But when the time cards were punched on Friday, they got paid and headed for the clubs.

"East St. Louis is rather historic because there were a lot of things that went on here," says Leo Chears, a longtime St. Louis-area radio disc jockey and East St. Louis resident. "Duke Ellington wrote a song about it simply because when Duke and his band would come into town in the '30s, they enjoyed it. It was a very, very live town."

"A lot of these places were bars as opposed to actually a nightclub," says Ardis of the clubs in East St. Louis where Grant played. "They just had a little stage for the musicians and they would sell stuff like pickled eggs, pickled pig's feet. It was a lot of fun. They were crowded and people really, really appreciated jazz, so you really heard the musicians."

East St. Louis was actually known more for the blues and, later, rhythm and blues. Ike and Tina Turner became well-known entertainers in the city. Popular clubs at the time on both sides

During a 1995 visit to St. Louis, Grant Green Jr. especially connected with the late drummer Joe Charles, with whom his dad played during his early years in St. Louis. Photo by Sharony A. Green

of the Mississippi include the Judge's Chamber, Peacock Alley (formerly the Glass Bar), the Paddock Bar, the Club Riviera, the Barrel, El Patio, the Mellow Cellar, the Paris Lounge, Jorgie's, the Holy Barbarian, Gino's Jazz Central, the Blue Note, La Casa, the Blue Flame Club, and Club Manhattan. But it was in a tiny club in East St. Louis called the Sportsman that many believed Grant began to first make a name for himself.

The Sportsman "was really no bigger than, say, a truck in width because people...well, blacks had always liked to kind of rub up against each other when they passed by," says Leo. "But it was a very hip club. East St. Louis at 15th and Broadway. Everybody when they ever came to town wanted to come here."

In time, folks began to hear more and more about a guitarist named Grant Green who played there. Older musicians like Chuck Tillman were letting him share the stage more. "Young musicians always came around old musicians because we always had something to tell them in terms of bettering themselves, and Grant was one of the young musicians coming up behind me," says Chuck, who plays saxophone. "And when I say younger, I'm talking five to seven years, because in five years, a musician can be so much greater than someone just starting. They can almost look up to you because hey, man, you been around. You been playing and you've been there. And I don't exactly know when I met

Grant, but I've known him for it seems eons, and he could always play.

"I liked his concept. His concept was more of a horn player. Grant wasn't avant-garde. He was just a soulful musician that could express himself and he didn't mind being funky. He could play stank with the best. The patterns he could play were reminiscent of what I think horn players would play because of the single stroke and the way he moved it. He played things that were not basically guitar licks. I believe that if he had played another instrument, he would have still played like that. Grant would take his figures and play like a horn player. He could do that and play jobs. Like if your horn player didn't show up, we'd call Grant. He knew all of the heads that the horn players knew and played them like the horn players. And that's one of the things about him that I thought was rather unique."

Grant began to play alongside Chuck and others like Harry Edison, Sam Lazar, and Jimmy Forrest. When the big guys like Miles Davis came through town, Grant sought them out, too. Unfortunately, he was beginning to pick up more than music from them. He also picked up a drug habit.

Chuck Tillman, a St. Louis saxophonist pictured here in 1995, served as a mentor for Grant in the 1950s. Photo by Sharony A. Green.

"Charlie Parker did it in the early days," says Ollie Matheus, who readily admits to having used heroin in large quantities with Grant and Jimmy Forrest. But for years musicians really wanted to get with Charlie and Miles, two natives of the area who had already made a name for themselves. Whenever they returned home, their calling card was heroin.

"It's still the drug of choice for anyone who does drugs," Ollie says. "I was about seventeen when I met Bird and started using it. Bird says it's like a loan. You consolidate all of your loans into one payment; that's a junkie. All of life's problems are one problem. That's all he had. He doesn't have any other problem."

Ollie says the city's musicians might have been spared if Charlie and Miles had just stayed away. "When I would go over to Miles's house to pick him up, his mother would search me better than cops ever did before I could come in the house. I mean she'd go through the things in my pants and around my cuffs. They really tried to take care of him, but when Miles and Bird would come home, the junkies would come out of the woodwork. Their idols were here. Grant was with us."

No one is sure at what age Grant started using heroin. He was just twenty when Charlie Parker died, and there is no evidence to suggest any personal contact between the two men. Certainly by his teen years, he had begun to dabble a bit with the drug, and some say using it took Grant's playing to another level. "He was a chronic dope fiend!" says Joe Charles. "And it made him play better. Only thing is that we used to run around the city all of the time trying to find the man! We had a gig to play at nine o'clock and we'd be ten o'clock, trying to find the man. That's what made me mad! I had a family then. I was depending on that money to take care of my family, but musically he played better."

But Albert St. James shakes his head when he hears talk like this. Drugs don't make one play better, he says. "That's a misconception. That's not true. You can play, or you can't. Drugs have to do with the *fall* of the musician! Drugs gon' ruin your talent in the end. You can't perform if you're a drug addict."

But before the drugs took their toll, word was slowly getting out that St. Louis had a very special guitar player.

4 Shoot Me! Don't Shoot My Instrument!

The Mid- to Late 1950s

"I told Leo to send him, and when he got to New York, I met him and took him to Blue Note."

When Elvin Jones first met Grant, he was still working with Harry Edison and Jimmy Forrest. The year was 1956, and Elvin was himself playing with J.J. Johnson. He and J.J. had a gig in St. Louis, and while there, they met up with Jimmy Forrest, who said he had a guitar player they should meet.

"So we went over to this little place where [Grant] was playing—I forget the name of it—it was just a small bar. He had a drummer and a bass player, I believe. But anyway, we just sat down, had a few drinks, and listened, and then they came off the bandstand and Jimmy introduced me," Elvin recalls. "Grant asked me if I wanted to come up and play, and I [said], 'Well, sure.' So we played a couple of tunes together. I was just fascinated because I had never heard anybody play with that kind of purity before. I suppose if I had been a girl, it would have been love at first sight. It was just one of those things, an immediate rapport. To me, I always felt that this was a great artist, a great musician that I'd met."

"Cats coming through here heard Grant, they was running back saying, 'They got a man in St. Louis who can play,'" says Kenny Gooch, another St. Louis drummer. Like Grant, he would also marry into the Moody family. Years later, he married Annie's sister, Jewel.

In the mid-'50s, while Grant was slowly making a name for himself, he took up yet another interest—religion. In 1954 battles were brewing from Topeka to Birmingham. Black folks were fed up, and the black musician was especially sensitive. He needed to find some peace within himself and his place in the world. Grant Green was among a group of musicians who formed the first

Elvin Jones, drummer who played on several early 1960s dates with Grant including *Talkin' About, Street of Dreams, I Want to Hold Your Hand,* and *Matador*

Grant and I knew each other very well. When it was his recording session, he'd always call me. He'd ask for me. It worked out like that because we worked so well together. He didn't need to explain anything to me and I didn't need to explain anything to him. We'd just simply go in and it was a matter of him tuning up. And I'd say, "Well, what do you want to play?" So we'd start playing and that's how the recordings were made. There was not a lot of music, not a lot of manuscripts floating around. It was just from our souls.

chapter of the Nation of Islam in St. Louis. At the time, the Nation was a small but growing separatist movement. Too extreme for most black Americans, Grant found something within the organization that reinforced his identity as a black man.

Red Garner, a white St. Louis bartender, recalls the feelings of many black musicians at that time. "I would've called it kind of a black power thing, something like 'We're tired. We're mad. We've had enough. It's going to be a different thing comin' down,' and it seemed like Islam was what most of them were switching to," says Red, who also moonlighted as a musician. "I was on the inside of a lot of black lives at that time. I knew a lot of black musicians. I knew a lot of black musicians' families. I would say St. Louis, at that time, was probably primitive compared to a lot of places."

Barbara Morris recalls how the Nation's teachings captivated her and musicians like her husband, Albino Red, and Grant. "I was raised up in a home that was sort of progressive," says Barbara. "Like Easton Avenue used to be all Caucasian-owned stores, and black people used to spend all of their money there, but these stores didn't hire nobody black, so when I was a baby—this was during the Depression—my mother and father would form teams that would go out and walk up and down with signs that [said], 'Don't shop at this store. They don't hire nobody black.' It was in me from the get-go."

Injustices permeated every sector of society, especially the bandstand, which, ironically, was a place an artist would go to get away from it all, she says. But even there, there was no peace to be found. Many black musicians reached for drugs and alcohol as a way to cope with the times. Charlie Mingus's book *Beneath the Underdog* was named time and time again by the musicians I interviewed as a must-read if one wanted to know the extent of the racism within the music industry.

But drugs and other chemical abuse got Albino Red long before Grant. As the story goes, in a drunken state, he walked into an abandoned house in St. Louis one cold day and froze himself to death. But before his death, a local bass player named Herschel Harris introduced Albino Red, Grant, and other musicians to the Nation. Harris's own interest was sparked by a meeting with another musician while traveling on the road. He told them all about the Honorable Elijah Muhammad.

"Herschel came back and told us, 'The Honorable Elijah Muhammad is where it's at,'" Barbara says. "When we first started, we'd be meeting in different homes. We didn't have a mosque. And so you would be required to write your letter, and it [asked] are you married or if you have children and all of this, and if you were not married, they made you get married. They would say, 'If you want to be a member of the Nation of Islam, we are a righteous people. First you have to do this, you have to do that, and then you can become a member of the Nation of Islam. So the Nation made John and I get mar-

Barbara Morris, along with Grant Green, was a founding member of the St. Louis chapter of the Nation of Islam. Photo by Sharony A. Green.

ried because we was living together. There was John and I, Herschel, Albert St. James and Sarah, Charles Williams, the trombone player, Grant and Ann. We were the ones who started the Number 28 for St. Louis. We went to Chicago to see the Messenger. We wanted to see our leader and teacher. On Sunday he used to teach at the mosque, and afterwards he'd invited us all to his home for dinner and we all had dinner with him. Grant was with us."

Islam claims one fifth of the world's population. More than one billion people from a vast range of races, nationalities, and cultures, from the southern Philippines to Nigeria, are Muslims. While the religion enjoins many, fear of its teachings has created rifts between cultures and races in the United States and abroad for years. The Nation of Islam's self-reliance theories, in particular, frighten many whites in America. When asked what specifically about the Nation's teachings attracted the black musician, Barbara says the Nation's teachings offer the black musician what they offer anybody else. "It's a blessing for everybody, black, white, red, green, and yellow. It taught us to give an honest day's work for an honest day's pay. And it [teaches] you to [not] steal. Don't break the white man's laws as long as they don't conflict with your religion. And to be perfect and act right. All you had to do was stop doing wrong, stop doing things that violate your body, violate your sister, your brother. You don't covet your sister or your brother's home. And don't do nothing to nobody that you wouldn't have done to yourself. And they turn to the east and they pray to Allah five times a day. You don't drink, you don't smoke, you don't get high, and you don't eat hogs."

What was Grant like back in the days when he studied with the Nation?

She giggles. "I remember Grant was a very spoiled person, a big baby, and Ann catered to him, you know," she says. But Islam and its teachings "touched his heart like it touched everybody else's. Grant had a whole lot going for himself. I think that he was just kind of spoiled," she says. "And I think it might have been a little bit on the rigid side for him. But he was always a sympathizer!"

While he was exposed to the Nation, Grant still got an ample dose of the traditional teachings of Christianity, particularly when he played in sanctified churches.

"There was a time when Grant was playing with Sam Lazar, and they were right across the street from a spiritual church, and on intermissions, they would go across the street and listen to the gospel," says Chuck Tillman. "Humph, you think El Patio was jumping? You should've went in the church. Grant knew that."

However, it was the Muslim faith that touched Grant's intellect. It was the faith he clung to and lived by until his death in 1979. No matter what city he visited, Grant sought out kosher restaurants. His last manager, Jay Glover, described the times when Grant would rather go hungry on the road than eat pork barbecue ribs with his band members between gigs. According to Jay, Grant had been dead less than a month when some musicians came over to his house to reflect on his life. One of them joked to the other that it was not a heart attack that had killed Grant, but his eating habits. "This guy says, 'Grant didn't die of no heart attack. Grant died because he starved himself to death,'" Jay recalls. "I said, 'Explain that.' He says, 'Many times we'd be traveling on the road and Grant wouldn't eat with us. After we'd finish playing, we'd want some barbecue or some pork or something that Muslims don't eat. We'd be in a small town and Grant would drive all over town looking for a vegetarian restaurant, and if he didn't find one, he'd just go home and go to sleep without eating. That's what killed him.'" Jay pauses. "If they knew him, they'd know they were paying him a compliment. Grant was so particular about his diet. Me and him used to go to his favorite restaurant in New York, an Indian restaurant on 125th Street. The chef knew him so well that when we'd walk in the door, he would say, 'Ah, Monsieur Green,' and he'd just start shouting orders back in the kitchen: 'The famous Mr. Green is here again to have dinner, and you know what he likes.' That musician, out of ignorance, was saying that Grant starved himself to death, which was not true. He didn't understand that Grant was a Muslim, and if the food wasn't right, he wasn't going to eat it. I smiled when he explained himself. I says, 'Oh, well damn, that's a compliment.'"

Beyond dietary requirements, the Nation obviously offered more for black musicians. It taught them to be more in control of their music and their lives. And many black musicians listened.

"During that time it seemed like the only people who were really understanding what was going on with the teachings of the

Honorable Elijah Muhammad were the musicians," says Albert St. James. "Wherever we went it was musicians who were able to understand how the teachings of the Honorable Elijah Muhammad could turn you around and make you do better things."

"Elijah went to Chicago and started the movement, and it spread back this way in the early '50s," Chuck Tillman says. "And the movement reached all of the way to California. Some of them went in it. Some of us didn't," he says with a chuckle. "I was never in it because my wife is Catholic."

With the Nation's teachings under his belt, Grant braced again for the life of a black musician. It was something he confronted daily. As was true in many cities, in St. Louis there was a white musicians' union and a black musicians' union. Nightclubs paid the black musician a lesser wage for the same work. "Black musicians didn't even ask for raises in them days or they'd beat the shit out of 'em," says Ollie Matheus. He explains how some black musicians in St. Louis were forced to take work in strip joints. If they were lucky to get a club gig for a certain period, it was not uncommon for a club owner to suddenly tell them they were dismissed. Ollie recalls how he first came to hire Grant when he opened a club called the Holy Barbarian in December 1959. At the time, Grant was playing in Sam Lazar's band. "When I first hired Grant and them, they [had been] working at a strip joint down the street who fired them, and they didn't give them much notice," says Ollie. "When they got done playing one night, Sam told the owner, 'I'll come back and get the organ in the morning,' and the owner says, 'No, you take it out right now,' and they threw the organ out on the street, and then the guy takes his gun and starts shooting at Sam, and they tell a story of Sam running in front of the organ saying, 'Shoot me! Don't shoot my instrument!'"

Ollie was a different kind of club owner. He was best known for opening the short-lived club Holy Barbarian, located in a building at 572 De Baliviere. Ever the beatnik, he placed blacks and whites together on the stage—a radical concept for its time—much to the chagrin of city officials, who eventually chased him out of the city. Ollie went on to a life of saving the underdog, an endeavor that took him to Aristide in Haiti and the Chiapas in Mexico. But, in St. Louis, it was black musicians.

"We had Grant and Chauncey Williams on drums, Sam Lazar on organ, and Bobby Graff on tenor," Ollie says. "Bobby was the white boy. It was the first interracial club in the city. I put Bobby with them, and both of the unions gave me a lot of crap over that. But it was the happiest place. The wall opposite the bar was lined with booths. It was a long bar, and at the other end of the bar was a bathroom and I had a great big wooden round table where we all sat and carried on, and there was a wall with photographs. I still take a lot of photographs, but I don't have a picture of Jimmy or Grant. You didn't take pictures of [the] friends you ran around with."

Ollie wasn't the only one without pictures. Oddly, many people I interviewed, including family members, had no photos of Grant. Greg, my brother-in-law, says one of his uncles had photos of his father, even one of Grant as a child. But when that uncle died, the photos were misplaced and never found. (Hence, this book relies heavily on Francis Wolff's images from Blue Note.)

Ollie Matheus and Jorge Martinez, pictured here with Grant Jr. in 1995, both owned nightclubs in St. Louis and had fond memories of Grant's beginnings in the city. Photo by Sharony A. Green.

Grant's performances at the Holy Barbarian are significant because they were probably the last he did in St. Louis before he left for New York. Strangely, the club might have been there just for him, because it was open just eight weeks. Described in advertisements as a "beat" saloon, the Holy Barbarian (inspired by

Grant Green playing beside Bobby Graff in the Holy Barbarian nightclub in St. Louis. Photo courtesy Virgil Matheus.

Lawrence Lipton's book of the same name) was a place where bearded poets in turtlenecks took refuge, and where paintings of pubic hair by Ernest Torova were welcomed. As poets read at the mic, Grant would play behind them on his guitar. A local reporter used the word "unusual" to describe the combination of his guitar with drums and an organ. Grant would continue to be identified with the organ sound throughout his career. The Barbarian soon became a happening spot.

"I got Grant and Sam Lazar to crank up the volume. And I had to stay on them. The lady upstairs said the pictures would fall off the walls. She was always complaining. I told her to either move or take the pictures down," Ollie recalls. "I tried to hire all different colored waitresses. It was something no one had ever done before, and, I mean, there were places like in Kansas City where black people could come in and sit, but playing together—that was never done before and they didn't like it at all."

The city shut the place down. The police busted Ollie for employing a minor as a waitress. According to newspaper reports, Zerieta Coleman, then twenty, told authorities that she lied to Matheus about her age to get the job. The club lost its license, and the police set out to make Ollie's life miserable. "I got arrested 150 times in the city. I finally had to leave town. It was just totally unbelievable the things they did," he says, adding, "I am a very good sculptor. I started making statues. Once I made a statue of Dr. King, and they told me, 'You don't make statues of niggers.' I said, 'Well, I do.' They came in the middle of the night with the dump truck. The police who smashed all of my statues said, 'The next time we see you, you're dead.' I wasn't allowed in a white club. If I came in a white club, they'd come in and tell me to 'get over on the east end with the niggers where you belong.'"

Ollie, who passed away during the writing of this book, was pained by the memory. "After the Barbarian, I got into revolutions," he says. "Anybody who was fighting the government, I was helping them fight. I was just in Mexico. I still don't know a white man I trust."

Even with his anger, Ollie never lost his sense of humor. Before his death, my husband and I met him in O'Connell's pub in St. Louis, where his art work was displayed on the second floor.

"I have a funny story," Ollie says, unaware that most of his stories—even the tragic ones—were funny when he told them.

"Now Grant wasn't the prettiest man in the world," Ollie begins. "And neither am I. But I had a motorcycle with a sidecar. It looked like a German motorcycle, and I would put Grant in the side of the motorcycle in one of those little seats, and we'd drive along a row of big night clubs. This was back when the Barbarian was still opened. Our club wasn't fancy, but we had a line around the block every night, and these other places were starving and they all hated us. *Holiday* magazine sent a crew in to do a thing on Gaslight Square, and they came in our place and stayed for three days. Made everyone mad. So Grant and I are driving along in my motorcycle, and I pulled up in front of one club, grabbed Grant, and gave him a big kiss on the lips and stuck my tongue down his throat, and this guy who owned the club just went into a rage. He ripped the parking meter out of the concrete and came chasing us down the street with the parking meter. We used to do shit like that just to mess with 'em. It was hysterical."

The Holy Barbarian is where Jorge Martinez, another local jazz promoter, met Grant. "I was there every night," says Jorge. "In fact, I was kind of working there. I was checking IDs at the door, that type of thing. Grant was great. There was just something obvious that set him apart from the other guitar players in town. I mean, everybody was talking about him. Everybody knew that he was going to be leaving. He was obviously somebody too big for the town. Nobody expected that Grant was going to be here for very long."

Jorge was right. On December 10 and 19, 1959, Grant had already gone into the studio to record with Jimmy Forrest for a Delmark date that included Elvin Jones. The songs on the sessions were used on Forrest's *All the Gin Is Gone* and *Black Forrest* albums. Several months later he did an Argo recording with Sam Lazar. He was then invited to Chicago to do a recording with Miles Davis's rhythm section. "Lou Donaldson set it up," Ollie says. "Grant was going to use Miles's rhythm section. As soon as we got to town, Grant borrowed my car. I had an old Studebaker. I went back to the hotel to see what was taking him and his old lady so long, and they were laying in bed, nodded out, you know. They copped as soon as they got there, so that [session] didn't get recorded." There are some reports that the session did get recorded in November 1960, but the material was never issued.

When Grant made his first trip to New York is unclear. Many believe he left in the summer of 1960. Other say he left in late 1960 to play with Jack McDuff's band shortly after Lou Donaldson got him the deal with Blue Note. Red Garner, a St Louis bartender, recalls seeing the caliber of people with whom Grant was beginning to spend his time during this period.

Leo Chears, St. Louis disc jockey who interviewed Grant Green

Grant was never what you would call energetic. Matter of fact, during [an] interview [with me] he was very, very cool and quiet. You would almost have to drag out the conversation with him. But if he knew you, he was cool. I think I have learned to be an essential interviewer simply because I don't ask folks questions that everybody asks. When I jokingly say I had to kick Grant out of the studio, it's because he felt comfortable with me. I had to do the same thing with Stanley Turrentine. Wes Montgomery and Jimmy Smith. People that I have interviewed will come to town and say, "Where's Leo? Is he still on the air?"

"Grant and I had a mutual friend, a fella by the name of Clarence Hamilton. He was a drummer who went by the stage name of Sonny Hamp. At that time I was doing some playing myself and was bartending and working around Gaslight Square. I lived upstairs over the Dark Side. And Sonny knew that I would be up there, so one day they came over and asked if they could use the piano. It was Sonny, Grant, and John Coltrane. They just wanted to work out some riffs, so they came in and jammed. John played piano, and Grant was just playing along with him. He didn't even have his amplifier on or nothing. It might have even been an acoustical guitar," Red says. "And I just went downstairs and started cleaning up from the night before, and Grant and John just kind of fiddled around. I think about that time Grant was getting ready to leave, to go east somewhere to cut an album. As a matter of fact a couple of nights after they did that riffing on the piano, Sonny asked me if I could loan him a $20 bill because Grant was strapped for cash and was trying to get to the East Coast. I didn't know Grant well enough for Grant to say anything to me, so Sonny Hamp

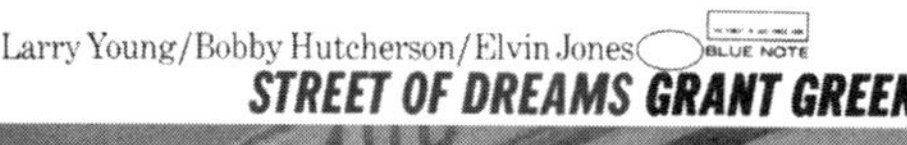

Grant Green's **Street of Dreams** *album features a guitar, bass, and organ trio. Courtesy of Blue Note Records, a division of Capitol Records.*

I WANT TO HOLD YOUR HAND/SPEAK LOW/STELLA BY STARLIGHT/CORCOVADO/THIS COULD BE THE START OF SOMETHING/AT LONG LAST LOVE
I WANT TO HOLD YOUR HAND/GRANT GREEN
STEREO
59962 BLUE NOTE

I Want to Hold Your Hand, *recorded in 1965, was one of Grant Green's many theme albums and showcased his long-standing desire to uniquely interpret popular songs of the day. Courtesy of Blue Note Records, a division of Capitol Records.*

asked me to make the loan, which I did. It just seemed like there was a lot of skidding wheels with jazz in those days back here in St. Louis, and I knew that Grant had the kind of talent that would put him over, but he was going to have to leave St. Louis to do it."

An interesting fellow would step up and offer his services. He was a stocky guy named Leo Gooden. He owned a club called the Blue Note in East St. Louis. He also managed a house band called Leo's Five. "Basically Leo Gooden was a 400-pound cat who struck you as being 'the Godfather,'" says Leo Chears, a St. Louis–area deejay who is no small package himself. A walking historian on East St. Louis, Chears can tell you a lot about Leo Gooden. Leo was just that unforgettable. And he became Grant's first manager.

"Leo was a very large man, and when he sang he sounded like Billie Holiday," says Kenny Rice, a drummer who played with Leo's Five. Kenny says Leo Gooden had a pervasive influence on his own music, and his life. "Leo's motto was: 'Don't be a follower. Be a creator.' Leo handpicked that band, Leo's Five. He picked me when I played a New Year's Eve in there with Albert King. I got off the bandstand and he says, 'Come here, boy. You look like a flower in a old band of weeds. I want you to be in my band. I'll give you $90 a week and all the food you can eat.' Leo opened the Blue Note Club and he made the Blue Note a mecca, a jazz mecca. People came from all over the world. They had written articles all over Europe about the Blue Note Club. We had some of the biggest names in the business come through the Blue Note," Kenny recalls.

One evening Redd Foxx, Lou Rawls, Bill Cosby, Miles Davis, Tony Williams, and John Coltrane were in the club all on the same night. "See, the Blue Note had a restaurant in there, and we didn't start playing until eleven o'clock at night because Illinois hours were later. We played from eleven to five or eleven to daylight, whichever came first. So after all of these places closed up, people would come to the Blue Note. The Gaslight Square was gone by then. So all of them came to the Blue Note. I used to go there back to his office and he'd have $20,000 or more, all kinds of money, sitting there.

"He wore diamond rings and he had brand-new Cadillacs. He said, 'Look, as long as you live, you're going to owe somebody.' He said, 'Get what you want and what you like to have and don't worry about paying the bills.' He says, 'Pay them if you can, but if you can't, don't worry about it 'cause you gon' owe as long as you are alive.' When he died, everybody came after him. They padlocked the Blue Note. The government came after him," Kenny continues. "He changed Cadillacs every year. He lived the way he wanted to live, but he was the kindest man you ever want to meet, especially to musicians. The waiters, the waitresses, all of them hated us. Most club owners treat musicians like they a dime a dozen. They'll tell you, 'You a dime a dozen!' Leo treated musicians like they were kings!"

Before he left for New York, Grant performed at Leo Gooden's club. By then, he was so self-assured, he insisted that everyone who joined him on the bandstand play as well as he did. "Grant was swingin'. And he would take you to church, too! He would take you to church on the gig," laughs Kenny.

Joe Charles remembers the night when he and Grant ended up in a fight over Grant's demands about how he should play. Says Joe: "We was playing at the Blue Note and [the] time kept picking up. And I couldn't keep the time down. And Grant got mad at me 'cause I couldn't hold the organ player down with my timing. So one night he came to pick me up and I was always high on my gin and he was always high on his dope, and he says, 'You can't hold the organ player.' I say, 'You right. I can't hold him, Grant.' I say, 'He too strong for me. I can't hold him.' He says, 'You ain't no good drummer, man. You can't hold the organ player,' and we got into it then! If you don't know Grant, he'll say anything on that dope. He sell a lot of wolf tickets. He say stuff like, 'Ah'll knock yo' butt down! I'll kick yo' butt!' So I say, 'Stop the car.' And I whupped him. Slapped him a li'l bit.

"Now when we got to the gig, Mr. Green was there. Talk about somebody who loved him? His daddy! Mr. Green was crazy about Grant! And I knew he was gon' tell his daddy, and Mr. Green had a big old .38. But I went on, and during intermission I went out and there he was. He says, 'Come here, Joe.' I was scared. My legs was shakin'. I says, 'Lord, take it easy.' I thought he was gon' shoot me. You know, Mr. Green was terrible. So he called me to the table and he says, 'I heard about you and Grant. Grant told me about it, and I said, 'That's good. He needed it.' He says, 'I'm glad you hit him.' Boy, talk about somebody was relieved! See, I thought Grant was gon' fire me. But he says, "I can't fire you.' You a good drummer.'"

Joe pauses and says something he has probably had on his mind for many years. "See, I was supposed to go to New York, too. Leo Gooden was supposed to send me *and* Grant. He was supposed to send me second. He sent Grant first."

Only Grant would make it to New York. Joe stayed behind, like many of the musicians in the area who had the talent, but lacked the connections or the nerve to leave. For every musician who left, there were those who couldn't. While many are proud of Grant, a few sound almost bitter when remembering how he left in the summer of 1960.

Looking back, Joe says, "I had seven kids. See, Grant *left* his kids! And he tried to get me to leave mine. I [said], 'No, man, I can't do that.' We made a whole lot of money with Grant, but we had our families. I wanted to go to New York a lot of times, but I [thought] about my kids and my wife scuffling with those babies and I [said], 'No, I can't.'"

While St. Louis was never a Detroit or a New Orleans, within the larger context of jazz history the city offered the world some great artists: reedman Gene Sedric; bassists Jimmy Blanton and Wendell Marshall; saxophonists Jimmy Forrest, Oliver Nelson, and Ernie Wilkens; trumpeters Louis Metcalf, Joe Thomas, Shorty Baker, Clark Terry, and Miles Davis—even though Miles was actually born in nearby Alton, Illinois.

And now making an exit was the town guitarist, Grant Green.

Al Harewood was traveling with Lou Donaldson's band when they made the infamous stop through East St. Louis. "I don't remember the name of the club," says Al. "But I'll tell you this much, before he got there, the club was packed. So [Grant] must have been doing something right. Oh boy, it was swinging, swinging, swinging. He was fresh. Lou told him, 'Why don't you come to New York?' and that's what he did."

Lou Donaldson confirms he was the impetus to get Grant out of St. Louis. "I told Leo to send him, and when he got to New York, I met him and took him to Blue Note," Lou says. "Leo Gooden got the ticket for him, and I took him to Blue Note and got him a deal."

Many say when Grant left for New York, his playing style was already intact. He had long plucked foxy lines in a way that turned heads, and he would continue to do so in the Big Apple, changing forever what people expected from a guitar. "To me Grant was one of the giants, and when he left St. Louis and went to New York, his style was already formed," says Virgil Matheus, Ollie's brother. "I really didn't notice that much change in his style on his recordings for Blue Note. Looking back, he was an original."

5 Arriving in New York The Early 1960s

"It was like he's listening to what that guitar is saying. The guitar seemed to have a voice that he wanted to hear."

Grant arrived in New York at a time when the city was busy and inventive when it came to jazz. Nightclubs were packed. There were jobs to be had. And artists with the skill and drive to make it could. Ruth Lion, who was a receptionist at the time for Blue Note Records, remembers the day Grant Green walked into their offices for the very first time. At his side was the round and yellow fellow named Leo Gooden. "I'll never forget the guy who brought him into our offices," Ruth says. "He was heavyset, a portly fellow who was lighter than Grant. Grant was kind of retiring. He could laugh and he could have fun, but he was thoughtful, musically thoughtful."

She continues, "They had taken a large elevator up to where I was. There was a waiting room, and I was behind this waiting room sitting at this little desk. When people would ring the bell, I would go and see who it was, and if Alfred and Frank were going to see them, I'd let them come in, and if they didn't have an appointment, it was kind of hard. But they mostly didn't bother with appointments. Alfred was doing everything. He was taking care of getting the records out. He was getting to the rehearsals. He was getting to auditions. He put in at least a seventy-hour week. Days off were very rare. Now when Grant and this gentleman came in...I immediately thought there was such a contrast with this older man and what I thought was a kid, because by that time I was certainly forty. So here's this very quiet kid. I didn't know what he played, but I can still see them sitting at Alfred's desk. Grant, like a kid, was not talking much. It was the other fellow who did the talking."

When Grant walked into the offices of Blue Note Records, Lion says, she and Alfred were not yet married, but the offices were in the third location for the label, signaling the company's success. She was there to see the company's climb. "They had been on Lexington," Ruth recalls. "There had been another office on the West Side, on 61st Street. When Grant came, we were in this loft building. This was a big step up for Blue Note because it had always been in some little, small place. But by then, they'd recorded Jimmy Smith, Art Blakey, Lou Donaldson, and Horace Silver. So when Grant came on the scene, the music was beginning to be received across the country. It was beginning to have what became known as the 'Blue Note sound.' A lot of people would say, 'We're waiting for the new Blue Note. We're not just waiting for the musician. We want to hear that Blue Note sound.'

Ruth Lion says when Grant Green arrived in New York in the summer of 1960, he quickly won the heart of her late husband, Alfred Lion, founder of Blue Note Records. Photo by Sharony A. Green.

It was something that Rudy [Van Gelder], Alfred, and Frank had discovered together."

How does one define the Blue Note sound? It is at once funky, jazzy, soulful, and other adjectives that mean little until one actually hears the music. It can make you dance. It can make you cry. It is cogent and hard to miss. It is what made Alfred's foot start tapping in Rudy's studio when the cats who gathered to play were on the right track.

Alfred Lion, long a lover of jazz, hightailed it out of Germany just before World War II and founded the record label in 1939. It would become an internationally known repertory of musicians. In the beginning, Alfred was "the one that recorded the guys when other people wouldn't even touch them," says Stanley Turrentine. "He came from Germany and started selling records out of the back of his car. And then he turned it into a big, thriving company."

With the assistance of Frank Wolff, Alfred began to pick musicians who had a certain feel. It was honest. It was raw. It was real. By the early 1960s, the company had established some stature, and when he and Frank heard what Grant had to offer, they quickly signed him on to fill in the gaps of their growing business. Between working as a staff guitarist for Blue Note, a wide-eyed Grant also stepped out with guitar in hand to make the rounds in local clubs.

"Grant came to Minton's Playhouse, and right away he was just in love," recalls Al Harewood. Minton's was just one club on the scene.

"During that period of time, they had a lot of places to work. You had about ten clubs in Harlem, man—Baby Grand, Small's, the Top Club, and so on," says Lou Donaldson.

Adds Ruth, "You could walk into one club and Miles Davis would be there, and you could walk into another club and Charlie Parker would be there."

Rama Lomax, a former deejay at the Palm Cafe and the disc jockey who first broke out Art Blakey's "'Moanin'," presented the most vivid picture of the New York that greeted Grant in 1960. After listening to her, it was clear that while many of the clubs were similar in size and setup to those back in his native St. Louis, there was something special emanating from the dark, smoky joints in New York City that helped Grant realize he had made it somewhere big.

"New York, in the 1960s, was the mecca, and this was before I knew anything about Islam," says Rama. "There were no security gates on stores like you see now. People would be walking up and down the street, and I mean it was just fabulous. This was our Cotton Club days, the '60s. It was wonderful. People had a sense of style. You'd find the people from downtown liked to come uptown. Nipsey Russell and I worked at the Palm Cafe. I remember...playing some records, and I'm up in this booth which is like see-through, looking down on these beautiful people. We broadcasted radio shows by remote. The booth was like an airship, and it was really personable then because you were with an engineer, as opposed to today. Then, you created a groove with an engineer. If you had a problem, he'd help you out and stuff. So we're looking down on the people. And in the middle there's a room divider with flowers and stuff. And then there are booths on this side and then there's a long bar. Seems like it was a quarter of a block long, like a long New York City block. And then on the other side, there [was] the dining room section. It was kind of fun because I'd look up and here come Big Maybelle. Oh, she was big. And that's where I met Grant Green. He was so sweet."

Historically, musicians have always migrated to New York, says Dave Bailey, a drummer and historian who has worked for years with Jazzmobile, a New York–based organization committed to preserving jazz. "I'd say from the '30s upward, they were coming, but by the 1960s the new migration of people had leadership. We had people who were at the top of their game: Charlie Parker, Dizzy Gillespie, Thelonious Monk, and Bud Powell. People that we all looked up to, and we were striving to get better. Everybody was into improving themselves. So the quality of the music was very, very hot."

Grant quickly settled into a musician's life. Blue Note often housed new musicians in a hotel at 59th and Broadway. It was outside this hotel that saxophonist Larry Smith met Grant. It was Larry Young, the organist, who made the introductions. "Grant Green was sitting right out front on a stoop, and Larry, a very fine innovator of the organ, introduced us," Larry recalls. "Grant got up and got a pencil real quick and wrote my telephone number down. He was absolutely beautiful."

Grant Green was in good spirits and obviously showing it. In 1961, he recorded an unheard of seventeen albums. I asked Ruth how it came to be that Grant was so busy at Blue Note. She replied, "I think [it was] because when Alfred liked somebody, he recorded them as much as he could because he didn't know how long they would be around. Guys had to travel to keep working."

Beyond his rigorous work schedule, something he seemed to enjoy, Grant also benefited from a special rapport with Alfred. "Alfred, as you probably knew and know, liked the real. He didn't like sophistication. And he did not like pop. And somehow when George Benson came along he had a lot going, but he was maybe...more sophisticated, more polished in a way, so he didn't get in Alfred's heart. He didn't get there the way Grant [did]," says Ruth. "Grant got nicely established, especially with Alfred, and that meant a lot in those days. If Al liked you, that meant that the other people were going to like you, too."

Ruth Lion, widow of Alfred Lion, cofounder of Blue Note Records

When Alfred was ill, I started playing Grant's **Am I Blue.** *I played it all day long, and my kids got tired of hearing it I'm sure, but it was just about three years before Alfred died. He was seriously ill for quite a while. I said to myself, "I better listen to this a lot because if I don't listen to it now and Alfred goes away, then I won't be able to bear it." So I did listen to it ...I got it out and I played it, and played it and played it and I'm sure it helped me to get through that real terrible time because, you know, you go into a denial when somebody is dying, and it made me—well, it was soothing and it was sad, but it was very real. I like that song so much.* **(Singing) Am I Blue. You'd be, too. Ain't these tears in these eyes tellin' you?** *There was so much pride Alfred had in the guys. He communicated that he expected the very best from them, and he just couldn't do any slouch jobs.*

Not only did Alfred and Grant get along well musically, they also got along well as people. "Grant and Alfred laughed a lot together," says Ruth. "They always had some kind of jokes going, and they did a lot of dates at night because Alfred had an idea that the guys played better at night. And they all enjoyed having whatever it is they were going to have, liquor or whatever."

Ruth recalls one night in particular when Grant and Alfred had her in stitches. They were on their way to Englewood Cliffs, New Jersey, where Rudy Van Gelder has a custom-built studio. It was in this studio that the majority of Blue Note's records from the late 1950s and on were recorded. Prefacing her story, Ruth explains how the musicians typically got out to Rudy's studio: "This is how it worked: Alfred would call for a cab company that had an account with us and order two cabs. The cabs came to the hotel to get the guys. But this must have been a large date. Alfred was also going to drive over to Rudy's. He had an old, large Buick that was gray with a red stripe around four doors. I was going to that date, too. So Alfred was in the front, another musician was sitting next to Alfred, and then there was Grant, Ike Quebec, and myself in the backseat, and oh, Alfred got lost on the way there, and everybody got a little panicked because it's awful to be in the woods like that at night. We knew Alfred was not a good driver as it was—he did not have a good sense of direction—and we were scared. Finally, Alfred says, 'I think I know how to get out of this,' and Grant hollered, 'Go the way you know, man! Go the way you know!' and it was so funny because Grant was usually pretty quiet and to hear him speak like that!" She laughs and then says, "So, yes, we did finally get there."

With Frank by his side, Alfred went to work overseeing the recording dates. Musicians say they made a good team and knew exactly how much involved to get with the work of the artists. They knew when to interfere and when not to. "See, man, Frank and Alfred were from Germany. They didn't know that much about our music. So they didn't bother you, you know what I mean?" Lou Donaldson says. "They wouldn't come out and say, 'Now you do this, you do that.' They didn't do that. They'd come to the dates you're playing and it would be like, 'Finish?' And you'd be like, 'No, I'm not finished yet.' And so they sat there reading the paper. Then, they'd pay you your money and go. They'd say, 'Well look. Black people play this kind of stuff. They know what they're doing, so we let them play it.' That's why they made so much money."

"There were other people who made fantastic contributions, you know, people like Bob Weinstock at Prestige," says Rudy Van Gelder. "He was responsible for all those great Miles Davis sessions. But it was a totally different atmosphere from what Alfred and Frank would create. Totally different, and also great in its own way. But when it comes to the Blue Note kind of approach to things, Alfred was the best."

Ruth Lion knew better than most the extent of her husband's commitment to the music and artists like Grant Green. Before they were married and long before she worked for Blue Note, she was a public relations woman who had a side gig as a disc jockey at the Palm Cafe. She recalls the first time she saw Alfred in the club. "He appeared to have nothing but music on his mind," she says. "I walked in one night and there's this little man sitting in a booth, and I said, 'This is the man I been looking for all of my life.' And he sure did look good," laughs Ruth. "And so I asked Jack Walker—Jack Walker was the guy I worked with—'Who's that guy down there?' He says, 'That's Al Lions.' They never did call him by his right name. He says, 'Al Lions, and he's got Blue Note Records.' So I said, 'Introduce me,' and so when Al came over to the booth, Jack introduced us, and I made a terrible faux pas because I was kind of like aggressive, and in those days I had a PR company and I was kind of brash. I wasn't a kid either. I should've known better, but anyway, I was so anxious to take over this guy. But he wasn't going to be taken over, and besides there was a very nice little girl named Georgia who also had a show and he was stuck on her. So he wasn't about to look at me, but anyway, I said something to him about records and how I was kind of business-minded. I said, 'How much is a record date? How much do the artists get?' He thought it was too personal. He really closed up because he didn't like me in the first place, and here I come asking him a business question. So a few nights he'd come and he just didn't pay me any attention, and I was so hurt about it. I found out he didn't like the way I dressed either. You know, he liked sleek, sophisticated women, and I was anything but that. I used to wear these full poodle skirts, and he thought that was the corniest thing. He was like, 'Where did this corny woman come from?' He'd sit there and look holes in Georgia. But I finally did get to Alfred. I had a wonderful thirty-

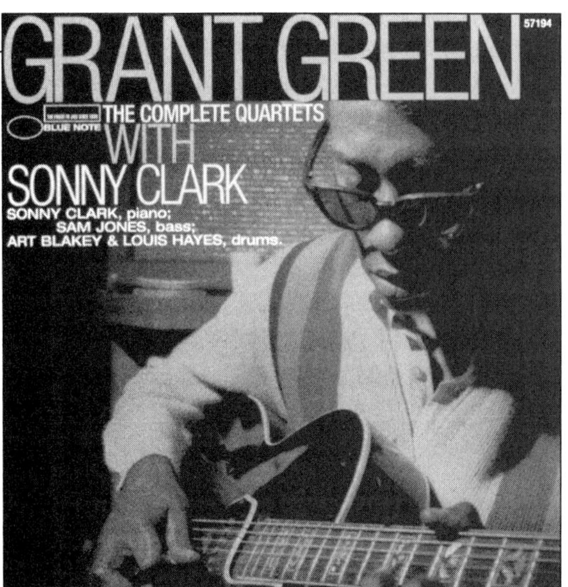

Released long after his death, **The Complete Quartets with Sonny Clark** *features sessions that bear witness to Grant's prolificacy at Blue Note: he made more music than they could put out. Courtesy of Blue Note Records, a division of Capitol Records.*

two years with Alfred, and it was filled with great music and wonderful people. Alfred was just a workaholic. The music was his love."

Beyond Alfred's undying love for music and his eye for new talent, Blue Note also benefitted from Frank Wolff's deft skill behind a camera. The company's album covers are legendary for their graphics and downhome feel. They depict a range of moods as varied as the music inside the jacket sleeves. "Those photos Frank took had a very personal view," Ruth says. "You could tell he tried to get the musicians in their most distinctive way, like cradling them."

Alfred and Frank began to put out Grant Green records like an assembly line. Because Blue Note always operated on the family principle, fermenting the sounds and skills of musicians with varying styles and backgrounds, the young guitarist recorded alongside nearly everyone who came through the doors between 1960 and 1965: Lou Donaldson, Baby Face Willette, Dave Bailey, Ben Dixon, Jack McDuff, Stanley Turrentine, Horace Parlan, George Tucker, Al Harewood, Hank Mobley, Winton Kelly, Paul Chamber, Philly Joe Jones, Kenny Drew, Booker Ervin, Harold Vick, Joe Dukes, Yusef Lateef, Wilbur Ware, Tommy Flanagan, Art Taylor, Ike Quebec, Sonny Clark, Sam Jones, Louis Hayes, Art Blakey, Willie Bobo, Carlos "Potato" Valdez, Sir Charles Thompson, Milt Hinton, Dodo Green, Johnny Acea, Garvin

Masseaux, Don Wilkerson, Tommy Turrentine, John Patton, Butch Warren, Billy Higgins, Barry Harris, Jimmy Cobb, Blue Mitchell, Sonny Red, Herbie Hancock, Joe Henderson, Duke Pearson, Bobby Hutcherson, Jimmy Smith, McCoy Tyner, and others.

From straightahead bebop to offerings with a more bluesy feel, Grant stood out. He often performed in simple trios where he was allowed to stretch. In his first year, he went into the studio more than two dozen times as a sideman and as a leader. The results: *Here 'Tis, Grant's First Stand, Face to Face, The Honey Dripper, Up at Minton's, Reaching Out, Work Out, Green Street, Stop and Listen, Sunday Mornin', Up and Down, Goodnight, It's Time to Go, Steppin' Out, Grantstand, Remembering, Z.T.'s Blues, Blue and Sentimental, Gooden's Corner, Nigeria, Oleo, Born to Be Blue, My Hour of Need, The Latin Bit, Elder Don, The Natural Sound,* and *Preach Brother.*

The tally of albums Grant recorded in the early 1960s is overwhelming, and the significance of each one is, of course, subjective, but it's important to mention the key sessions that signaled his apparent maturity even while new to the company. *Grant's First Stand,* the first date in which he recorded as a leader, is well regarded because it presents a young artist whose sound is exceptionally discernible. His playing is zealous and assured. Recorded on January 28, 1961, it features a strong catalog of songs, ranging from classics like "'Tain't Nobody's Business If I Do" to his own "Miss Ann's Tempo," named for his wife. Grant Green was a man who was decidedly on his way somewhere far beyond the beer and wine gardens of St. Louis.

Grantstand, recorded on Aug. 1, 1961, also garners mention. It features Grant beside Yusef Lateef, Al Harewood, and another organ player, Jack McDuff. From the homey "Blues In Maude's Flat" to the solemn "My Funny Valentine," the date is an admirable achievement. Grant's understanding of the guitar's possibilities is evident. He swings, and his guitar sings. "It was just incredibly brilliant playing," says producer Michael Cuscuna.

The album hailed most often in any serious critique on Grant is *Idle Moments.* It was truly revolutionary for Grant because prior to its taping, "Grant had recorded mostly in a kind of organ groove, whether it was backing up Lou Donaldson or

Grant Green, pictured here with Sonny Clark, made more albums as leader and sideman than any other artist at Blue Note between 1961 and 1965. Photo by Francis Wolff, courtesy of Mosaic Images.

doing his own records," says producer Michael Cuscuna. "*Idle Moments* was one of the ones with a piano, bass, and drums. Bobby Hutcherson was on vibes and Joe Henderson was on tenor, and all of the performances on it were very laid-back. It was pre–New Age New Age. But because it was harmonically brilliant. It was an album that was very hypnotic in the way later Miles Davis records like *In a Silent Way* would be. It was very riveting and very lyrical."

In the liner notes for the album, Duke Pearson reveals how it was a difficult date because the musicians kept going over the time Alfred had allotted for the lead tune, "Idle Moments." Al Harewood, who plays drums on the album, attempted to explain why the musicians couldn't keep the tune under the allotted seven minutes. "This was just a real happy date, really a happy date," Al says. " I think we recorded longer than we should have because of this. I think it was the first time Joe Henderson and Bobby Hutcherson played together. I believe it was the first time we all recorded together, and Grant—the minute he put his fingers on that guitar, that was it. That's how bad he was. He had so much soul. Like I said, when we went to the club where he was in East St. Louis, the place was packed. It was like a revival meeting. They well appreciated him, too. They well appreciated him. So did the fellas in New York, once they heard him."

There were other albums recorded in the early 1960s that were equally strong, but the label felt the people who purchased Grant's music were not ready for them. They collected dust for years in the company's archives. These unissued albums include *Gooden's Corner,* recorded on Dec. 23, 1961; *Oleo,* recorded on January 31, 1962; and *Nigeria,* recorded on January 13, 1962. All three were released after Grant's death.

"Most of his following was among organ fans," Michael says of Grant's appeal in the early days. "[Blue Note] figured they weren't ready to see him performing in this way."

The three albums, recorded with Sonny Clark on piano, Sam Jones on bass, and Louis Hayes on drums, were eventually released in a double-CD package. "This is just some of his best stuff," says Michael. "They got a lot of critical acclaim when they finally did see the light of day. I think at the time they were considered too modern, a little too pure jazz for the audience that was supporting Grant's career."

Ruth Lion says the company was simply responding to the musical tastes of people initially taken with Jimmy Smith and the organ as a jazz instrument. "When Jimmy Smith came out he was so striking," says Ruth. "I mean there had been organs out before, but with Jimmy it was so original and striking. When Alfred first got a chance to record with Jimmy, he [said], 'I'm going to sell Blue Note so I can travel with Jimmy so I can hear him all the time.' He went absolutely wild for Jimmy. Clubs would be packed for Jimmy, and I would go sometimes and the girls would be dancing like crazy."

Grant had no qualms about meeting the public's appetite for the organ. While some musicians have a certain prejudice against the organ, Grant loved it. This clearly was a result of his beginnings in the church. The influence of church music could be heard on many albums to follow. One in particular is his 1964 *Talkin' About* date. "*Talkin' About* is without question his all-time best," says producer Bob Belden. The album is once again a simple trio featuring Grant, organist Larry Young, and drummer Elvin Jones. Recorded on September 11, 1964, *Talkin' About* unveiled the growing savoir faire of Grant Green, who may have been bothered by the appearance of a younger guitarist named George Benson, who had arrived on the scene a year before. With *Talkin' About,* Blue Note stomped out any notions that Grant was old news. In printed advertisements they presented him as a wonder that people were, well, talkin' about, even though by then he had already recorded some fifty-three dates. Cuts on the albums like "I'm an Old Cow Hand" and "Luny Tune" showed his range and delivery and most refreshingly, his sense of humor.

Grant also did some of his most impressive work on dates with George Braith, most notably Braith's *Two Souls in One,* which offers the bewitching "Mary Had a Little Lamb" tune. Recorded on September 4, 1963, the session presents Braith backed by Billy Gardner, Donald Bailey, and Grant. But Bob Belden says with a chuckle that this session should have been "a Grant Green album with George Braith making a guest appearance. 'Mary Had a Little Lamb' was phenomenal."

Other jewels include some of Grant's theme albums like *The Latin Bit,* which featured a flock of Spanish tunes such as "Mambo" and "Besame Mucho"; and *Feelin' the Spirit,* a graceful and fluid batch of Negro spirituals and gospels like "Go Down Moses" and "Nobody Knows the Trouble I've Seen"; and *Goin' West,* a collection of western tunes. "I remember finding *Goin' West* at an auction," says Bob Belden, who speaks of Grant's music the way a kid speaks today of a new video game. "This is all really great stuff."

Not all of Grant's early sessions were with Blue Note. Some were done on Prestige and Black Lion, a Japanese label. No matter where he played though, his energy level and consistency was incredible, almost unreal, and left a lasting impression on every musician with whom he played. Grant was an artist who aimed not only to please himself, but others. He obviously knew that his position as Blue Note's staff guitarist moved him into a different arena. He encountered higher expectations from more seasoned musicians who had been around the block a few times. But they were all floored by what he had to offer. Dave Bailey, who appeared on Grant's very first Blue Note date, Lou Donaldson's *Here 'Tis,* says, "Grant was a new approach to the guitar. He was a very, very soulful player."

"I have an image of him holding his guitar like it's a very live object...very lovingly," says Ruth about seeing Grant in the

Dave Bailey, drummer who performed on several early-1960s dates with Grant including *Green Street* and *Reaching Out*

Grant was different, and that's what makes, in my view, an artist—someone who develops a style, a sound, that kind of thing of their own. I don't like to compare people, but he just came here with a different sound, a different way of playing. When you hear him play, you could tell, "Oh, that's Grant Green." So the quality of his playing, made him, to me, a standout on his instrument. I miss him. I just wished that he, along with everyone else whose lives were shortened by this sickness, were still with us. I think we'd have a much better world to live in if more of those fellows had been able to overcome their situations and be productive.

studio. "It was like [he was] listening to what that guitar [was] saying. The guitar seemed to have a voice that he wanted to hear."

Says Bob Cranshaw, a bass player who joined Grant on several dates including *Idle Moments, Solid,* and *Matador,* "Grant was a very easy person to play with. He had a great feel."

"Grant had the natural ability to know when not to play," adds pianist Horace Parlan, who played with Grant on several dates, including Parlan's own 1963 session, *Happy Frame of Mind.* "In other words, there's also an art to knowing when not to do something. And he had that. He would never play on top of me. He gave me a lot of room. We gave each other a lot of room. It worked out very nicely because there can be big problems when piano and guitar play together because they're both chord instruments."

Barry Harris, a pianist who played with Grant on two Sonny Red dates, was especially impressed with Grant's melodies. "He was very melodic," says Barry. "There are a lot of people who are more technical and all that kind of stuff. But Grant wasn't like that. Grant was sort of on the order of...one person who comes to mind is Blue Mitchell. Grant and those kind of people, they were just naturals. Grant was a good guitarist, one of

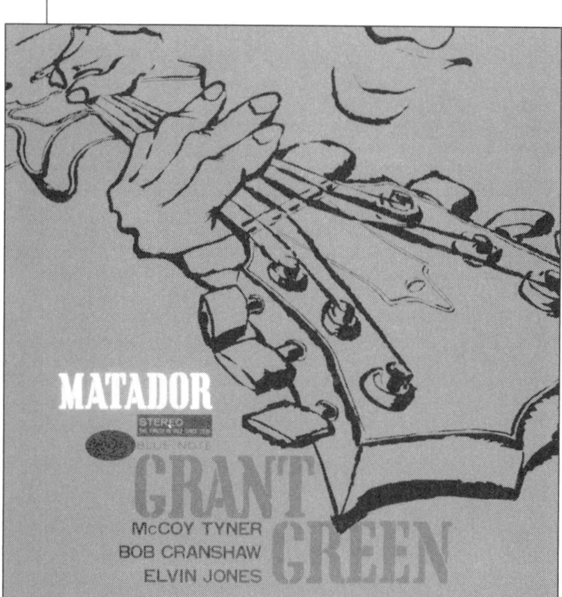

Assured of Grant's mastery as an album leader, Blue Note showed no hesitation in placing him in the studio with two members from John Coltrane's legendary band—McCoy Tyner and Elvin Jones—assisted by bassist Bob Cranshaw. Courtesy of Blue Note Records, a division of Capitol Records.

the best, one of the greatest—if not *the* greatest. And I have played with Kenny and I played and recorded with Wes."

Elvin Jones, who sat in with Grant on the *Matador, Idle Moments, Talkin' About,* and *I Want to Hold Your Hand* sessions, says, "I always thought Grant Green was one of the greatest guitarists that ever existed since Charlie Christian. I haven't seen anybody before or since that could compare to his artistry and conceptions of music."

"Grant sort of fell right into getting a beautiful, groovy, mellow sound," says Rudy Van Gelder, who is known industrywide for being very strict and precise in his craft as an engineer. "I had no problems with him. I knew what to expect when he came in. We were no strangers."

Stanley Turrentine has special memories of his 1961 *Up at Minton's* session and how it came to be that Grant was invited to play on the date. "At the time, I was working with a quartet, Horace Parlan, George Tucker, and Al Harewood. And Alfred Lion said, 'Hey man, I'm really interested in doing a live date, a record date at Minton's.' He said, 'Have you heard about Grant Green?' I had already met Grant Green and jammed with him a lot of times at Wells, and he came into Minton's and sat in a lot of times. I was really familiar with him. So I said, 'Solid.' And it turned out real nice. It was a lot of fun. It was packed. It was always packed. At Minton's, you'd never know who would stop by. Miles would drop in. Everybody, Dizzy, Monk, all of them, would be dropping by. Eddie 'Lockjaw' Davis, everybody was there. That was the place where all the jazz musicians hung out and they jammed."

Shortly after his arrival in New York, Grant received an invitation to join a band headed up by Jack McDuff, one of the leading organists of the day. Again, it was Lou Donaldson who set the deal up. Jack recalls: "He'd just come to New York, and Lou Donaldson said, 'Hey man, got a good guitar player in town.' And Lou Donaldson gave me his number and name and we hooked up. I checked him out and I hired him. I'm from Champaign, Illinois, and he was from St. Louis, which was close to me. He was a great player, but he was also a helluva cat."

Jack hinted at other sides of Grant that began to concern some of the musicians even while they remained impressed by his

Grant, pictured here with organist Larry Young during his 1964 Street of Dreams *session, always believed the guitar went well with the organ. Photo by Francis Wolff, courtesy of Mosaic Images.*

talent—his lack of maturity outside the studio. Even as he approached his thirtieth year, he was still playful and irresponsible. "Girl, I could tell you some stories about Grant Green!" Jack says. "We were playing in Asbury Park, New Jersey, and I was a cosigner for him so he could get a Cadillac. It was a used car! We were all driving used cars then. And Grant Green never made one payment on that car. Never made one payment!"

It was not long before he left Jack's band. "I hated to see him leave because I missed that guitar playing, but I could understand him wanting to go on his own," Jack acknowledges. "It was Joe Dukes, Harold Vick, Grant, and myself. And boy, that was a band."

As for the car, Jack recounts, "The man at the dealership never asked me anything. I didn't know where Grant was, either, and if I did know, I wasn't going to tell the man, you understand? By that time, he got his own band. And they'd go and play Pittsburgh, Buffalo, all those places. And he drove his car until it was time to get the license renewed. It was then he had to give it up. He couldn't get the license renewed because if he did, they'd find out where the car was. It was a green Cadillac. And he had a green suit. It was Grant Green on green on green!"

"He was very country," says George Benson of Grant. "He liked what real simple people liked. He still acted like he was in the streets in St. Louis. His speech was slow and slurred-like, but he did this on purpose. He had this kind of hip cat-cool talk. He wore green suits. He had a green Cadillac. Had a green guitar. Does that tell you how Grant felt about Grant Green? But, see, people forced him to think like that because they worshiped him. Everybody loved him."

6 Ha' Mercy!

"He just sat up on the bandstand by himself, and every record that came on that jukebox, he played with it. He sat there and played with the record like he was on it."

In 1962, when *Down Beat* magazine was still giving out its New Star awards, Grant took the honors in the guitar category. That he got it proved he was a man who was very much in command of his instrument, his destiny, and his place in New York. "I dig New York," he said at the time. "I wouldn't want to be anywhere else, that's for sure."

So comfortable was he in his role as an artist, he began to have a more elaborate dream. A lush ambition. A covert longing. "I don't know if I'll ever get around to it, but I would love to get with some violins," he said.

But he also began to look back at the things he had left behind. His family. His friends. These were situations that were a little less visionary, less formal. He missed the down-home feeling of St. Louis and her people. He especially missed the jam sessions where the brothers used to just let it all hang out.

"Musicians don't get together like they used to," Grant said. "That good feeling seems to be gone. We had it back home, and I understand it used to be that way in New York, too...guys would get together and jam, have fun. Look, a friend of mine has this great big loft, with a good piano and everything, and nobody wants to come by. If there are guys who'd want to, I don't know where they are. The other day, I asked some cats to come by, and they acted real suspicious, asking all kinds of questions. So I just froze and told them, 'Later.' What it is, I don't know. Maybe there are too many musicians and not enough work, and people get jealous of each other. That might be it."

Matthew Nelson, guitarist who met Grant during the 1960s in New York

Grant will always be—along with Wes and Kenny and all the cats that can play—here. You see, when a musician leaves the world, unless somebody destroys everything there is, if he had something to say, it's profound—it never leaves. To me, he didn't die because his music is still here. And I don't have to hear his music to know it's still here. I can hear all the young cats coming up.

He was right. New York was a place where everyone wanted a piece of the action. Matthew Nelson, a guitarist, confirms what Grant felt at the time. He recalls walking down the street one day and noticing an unusual number of guitarists in one club. "I was on the way home and stopped by this bar to get myself a beer," Matthew says. "I noticed that it was kind of early, but it's packed. And I'm saying, 'What's going on? I live around the corner. I should know about this.' So I notice that there's a lot of guitar players in the place. And we didn't care for each other that much. A couple of them came up to me and said, 'I know you're not going to play because Grant Green's here tonight.' And oh, I was crazy about Grant, but I had never seen him in person. I had a lot of his records, though. So I said, 'Where is he?' and they pointed him out. He was sitting at a table talking to a young lady. They kept egging me on, and one guy said, 'Well, I played.' So I said, 'Well, I guess I'll have to play.' So I walked over to the table and I said, 'Mr. Green, my name is Matthew Nelson, and I play guitar and I'd like to use your amplifier.' Well, I guess he was annoyed, but he said, 'Go ahead. Everybody else is.' Fortunately, I had played with the organ player who was there. The organ player was very good. His name was C.C. Williams. So I went up on the stage and I said, 'Hey C.C.,' and he says, 'Hey, man, come on up and play something.' So I went up and I started to play. And I was scared to death because Grant Green was in there. So Grant gets up from the table. And I think, 'I guess he's going to come and yank the plug out.' But he didn't. He came up on the bandstand, he leaned over, and he whispered in my ear, 'I hear you playing that Kenny Burrell shit.' And he walked back and sat down at the table. I felt very good then, and I kind of opened up a bit. And anyway, to make a long story a little shorter, Grant came up on the bandstand

and sat down. And he started to play, too. He hooked up to the amplifier, and we sort of played together for a minute. He kind of washed me away. But I still felt good, and when I went down, one of the people sitting at the bar said, 'He had to do that, man. You were putting a lot of pressure on him. He had to just come up and show you.'

"So after that set was over, Grant came down and we got to talking. I said to him, 'You know, I'd like to take some lessons or something from you.' And he kind of looked at me and smiled, and he said, 'No, you've got to get it the same way I got it. But you're really on the right track.' He was going to be there about two more nights, and he said to me, 'Anytime you want to play while I'm here, come on in and play.' Well I had my chest out a million feet, because I told the other cats, 'Hey, did he ask y'all to come in and play?' I went back the next night, but I didn't play. I wanted to sit back and listen. The band was getting ready to go on, but somebody had a lot of money in the jukebox. Most musicians would just turn the jukebox off so they could go ahead and play, but Grant didn't do that. He did something that, to me, was very phenomenal. He just sat up on the bandstand by himself and every record that came on that jukebox, he played with it. He sat there and played with the record like he was on it. The last night he was there, I came in and we talked for a moment and he said, 'Hey man, just keep on doing it because you sound good. I think you'll make it.'"

Matthew, who was giving private guitar lessons at the time of our interview, says he never made it big like Grant, but he has certainly proved himself on the instrument over the years. "See, I've been around a long time. If you play a phrase, I don't care who you are, I'll tell you where you got it from. I can hear all the young cats coming up. My wife looks at me, and she's gets amazed because I'll sit there listening to a young guitarist and she'll say, 'That guitar player can play.' And I'll say, 'Yeah, he stole all that from Grant Green.' Or Wes, or whoever it was. I purposely for a long time wouldn't even play octaves because I didn't want people to say, 'Oh, you're just imitating Wes.' I don't care what you play, try to play yourself. People might not like what you play, but if it's good, they'll come around to it. People didn't like Thelonious Monk. They used to say, 'What is he playing?' Well, today they're not saying that. And those are some of the things that Grant had. He played how he felt. He really played how he felt, and that's why he was as great as he was because you couldn't pin him to somebody else."

Matthew went on to describe how he saw Grant Green years later with Kenny Burrell and two other guitarists in a concert at Carnegie Hall. "Everybody that I spoke to who saw that concert said the same thing. They say that Grant Green kicked everybody's butt," says Matthew. "But people have to know that music isn't even about who plays the best. I remember Les Van telling me a story about he and Dizzy Gillespie working at the Newport Jazz Festival one year, and he said he was standing at the bar and some people came in and said, 'When are you going on?' And he said, 'Well we don't go on until tomorrow.' I think Duke Ellington and somebody else was going to be on that day. And they said to Les, 'Well, we hope you win.' And that seems to be the American thing—competition. But it really isn't competition. There are artists that I love very much, but if I go to see someone else, I completely take those artists out of my mind because I just want to focus on who I came to listen to. I don't want to be looking at Grant Green and thinking about Wes Montgomery. I think I've heard some of the greatest jazz musicians that one could hear who never will be known and who, in some cases, could outplay all those people on those records you buy."

However, Carlos Santana said, "Once you get into Grant Green and Wes Montgomery, you're on your way to picking up your own individuality as to where you fit into all this."

But Matthew offers this with a chuckle: "We used to say, 'Now when you go to one of them little hick towns, it's that guy in them big overalls that's gonna take your instrument from you and run you right out the door.'"

Despite his growing rank as a musician in New York, Grant continued to respect his peers. While still acknowledging his own contributions to the instrument, he once told Leonard Feather that Kenny Burrell was one of his favorite guitarists. "I met him right after I came to New York. We used to give concerts right off 142nd and Broadway in a little club there...Battle of the Guitars. Me and Kenny, and, of course, Wes Montgomery used to stop in for a minute. Three of the world's top guitar players...just a little bitty place, and it would be packed."

But no matter how much praise he gave to others, Grant was still prone to cockiness and had some thoughts on Wes's potential. There were the obvious differences between the two: Wes played octaves and Grant was a single-note line player, which made his sound crisper and clearer. Wes used his thumb, Grant used a pick. "Grant always thought Wes should get him a guitar pick," George Benson says, laughing. "So I asked him, 'You mean Wes can't play?' And he said, 'Oh, he can play, but he gotta get a pick!'"

As Grant made a name for himself in New York, his family remained in St. Louis. On March 23, 1962, his wife gave birth to Grant Jr., their fourth child. Ardis Hansberry, his sister-in-law, recalls his wife, Ann, going to see Leo Gooden in East St. Louis to see about Grant sending some money home to his kids. Leo always had an excuse about why Grant had no money to send home. The family knew the obvious: his drug habit was getting worse. But they still expected something.

Reno and Mack, Grant's brothers-in-law, had reputations as ornery as Leo's own. Ann and her sisters once sent Reno and Mack over to Leo to shake down some of Grant's money. Sometimes there simply wasn't anything to shake.

Drummer Kenny Rice recalls how often Blue Note Records called Leo to tell how much Grant had already borrowed against what he was supposed to be paid. He was so in the hole that many times, Grant owed Blue Note more often than not. Shaking his head in disbelief, Leo would show Rice the paperwork. "He would laugh about it," says Kenny. "He'd show us some statement[s] from Blue Note Records and they'd say, 'Grant owed so and so something.' After Grant would do a session, they sent Leo a statement saying that's what *he* owed them!"

Lou Donaldson felt some measure of responsibility for the young guitarist he'd brought to New York and tried to help by taking Grant's paychecks and putting them to the side. "Yes, I kept the money and put it in my pocket because of his problem," Lou admits. "But Grant would come by my house every day until finally I said, 'Look Grant, fuck this. You take it.' He came everyday, sometimes twice a day. I took his money and put it in a bag

WOMEN'S RESOURCES

Grant Green Jr. shares a laugh in 1995 in Plantation, Florida, with Lou Donaldson, who brought Grant Green to the attention of Blue Note Records. Photo by Sharony A. Green.

and [said], 'You've got it.' I couldn't take it. Then he started bugging Blue Note. A guy told me he was down there everyday to get some money. When we made a date, he never got paid because he owed the company. He'd go down there every day trying to get some money. And every time he got paid he'd owe money."

Ruth Lion confirms that Grant did in fact go down to Blue Note and demand cash advances. "Grant always needed money. They would argue about the money and they got okay with the money, and then he would laugh."

Bob Cranshaw witnessed firsthand Grant's temper outside Blue Note's offices. "I just remember going there one day and Grant was there waving, ranting, really, really angry, wanting to rip the place apart, hoping they would give him some money," says Bob. "He didn't seem like he was a really educated guy, but he worked hard for his money and he wanted it. I guess he was trying to get an advance. See, quite a few of the guys at that time were really strung out. It's not that they didn't pay them, but it was always he needed the money before we did the record date."

Bob explained that the drug scene was so bad, musicians got advances just to show up for rehearsals. That was the way Blue Note worked. "Each guy would get like $10 or $15 for making the rehearsal," says Cranshaw. "This was a nice situation 'cause that meant the guys had some money in their pockets. In [that] day, $15 really meant something. It was an incentive to make the rehearsal."

How much Blue Note enabled their musicians is a dubious question. "Getting high was part of the environment...Alfred Lion and Frank Wolff knew that a lot of the guys were strung out," says Bob Cranshaw. "They had alcohol, so the guys could drink, assuming they would just take a little bit at a time. They wanted you to be comfortable. A lot of the guys who recorded for Blue Note Records—not all of them, but there were a lot of them who were very, very talented—they were messed up. It didn't make that much difference as long as they made it to the record dates and as long as they took care of business."

Grant clearly took care of business. He made the record dates. Besides the fact he played so well and with such versatility, his output was so enormous because he often volunteered to play. And Blue Note brought him on. It also helped that he was good friends with Ike Quebec, who was doing much of the A&R work for the company in the late '50s and early '60s.

Some musicians were openly bothered when asked about Grant's drug use. Stanley Turrentine, in particular, was the most protective. "Grant was a lot of fun and he was a good musician, regardless of his physical challenges. Charlie Parker had them, too. I can name them off. So did Elvis Presley. What about Elvis Presley? Why does mention have to be made for only the jazz musicians?...I can't mention those things. We're not suppose' to be talking about one another."

Bob Cranshaw, bassist who played with Grant on several early 1960s dates, including *Idle Moments* and *Solid.*

I don't think that Grant lived long enough to really be known. His thing was short-lived. All of a sudden I look up and he's gone. By his being strung out, there were a lot of people who wouldn't call him. There were a lot of things he wasn't allowed to do. But Grant was a big influence in my musical biography of people.

In those years, musicians received scale wages, maybe $100 for their gigs, says Bob Cranshaw. "That was some money. We would come right back after the recording, and there was a drug store on 50th and Broadway that would cash our check for those who wanted to take it home. For the others, I guess they went out. I know this happened not only with Grant, but with Lee Morgan and all of 'em. They would get high and whatever with the money they had and use it however they chose to use it. Sometimes the guys were messed up before we could even finish the dates. They would start to drink and by the time we finished the last tune, the guys would be on the floor."

Other musicians, however, wouldn't even touch the stuff. "I'm from the country. I'm from the sticks," chuckles Lou Donaldson. "Ain't no way in the world I'd ever do nothing like that. I'm asthmatic. I can't even smoke. I never really thought I'd live as long as I have. But you know, that's just one of those things. But I never smoke or drank; never did nothing like that."

Bob Cranshaw says there was another reason, though, why Grant relied so much on his paychecks from Blue Note. Unlike many jazz musicians, he didn't do much studio work on the side. Bob suspects this was because he could not read music very well,

and many studio jobs called for that skill. For years, Bob worked as a staff musician for the PBS children's show *Sesame Street,* and went on to work for *Saturday Night Live.* "I was doing a little bit of everything," he says. "I was working with different singers—Barbra Streisand, Frank Sinatra, Lena Horne, and all of these people, and Grant and some of the jazz players were just involved in the jazz thing. They were having a much harder time...See, Grant was not the kind of reader where he could ever be called into that kind of situation. He wasn't known in those circles. He was only known in the jazz circuit."

How well he read music is debatable; some said he could read music, but chose not to. He once told an interviewer, "I know a lot of good jazz guys who have gone into studio work and played what they've been told to play. But I feel they lose something. Something seems to happen to them."

Clearly, no matter how much drugs were affecting his life, Grant Green had some understanding of his unique place in the jazz field. He had taken the baton from Charlie Christian and took a detour around the icons of the day like Tal Farlow, Kenny Burrell, and Wes Montgomery to make his own mark, cross-fertilizing with some of the best players on other instruments. He had become a masterful soloist with a clear, singing sound. For these reasons and more, he had a few concerns when a young George Benson showed up in New York in 1963.

Grant Green performing at **The Latin Bit** *session in April 1962, one month after his wife, Ann, gave birth to his fourth child, Grant Green Jr. Photo by Francis Wolff, courtesy of Mosaic Images.*

7 Pitting Players, Dogging Demons

The Mid-1960s

"He surpassed himself."

George Benson struck me as someone who never forgot his roots despite obvious compromises. For months, his wife, Johnnie, endured my measured, but steadfast phone calls. George was not there. George was overseas. George was on the West Coast. George was in the studio. Finally my phone rang and on the line was the voice I'd long been waiting for: "Hello, may I speak to Mrs. Grant Green."

"This is she," I said.

"Well, this is Mr. Benson. Ann?"

Since he mentioned my mother-in-law's name, I knew that he and Grant went way back. Any musician who mentioned her name was immediately placed in a certain era of Grant's life. When George and I spoke that first time, he held firmly to the steering wheel. Perhaps, all that talk about him usurping Grant had bothered him, too. Still, he gave credit where credit was due. He quickly acknowledged that when you hear George Benson, you hear Grant Green.

His love affair with Grant's playing began shortly before he left Pittsburgh in the early 1960s. At the time, George was gaining notoriety not as a guitar player, but as a singer. A buddy turned him on to Grant's records, which were burning up the jazz airwaves at the time.

"We would get together and play records at one of my friends' houses. He was the only one who had the money to buy these records. He would introduce us to what was going on in the music industry, because we didn't know anything about that," George recounts. "We were rock 'n' roll people. He was introducing us to great jazz guitar players. One day he said, 'Here's a new cat, man. You're gonna like him. He's got a nice

Recorded in December 1962, **Feelin' the Spirit** *showcases Grant's penchant for church music, which was the origin of many of his compositions. Courtesy of Blue Note Records, a division of Capitol Records.*

groove.' His name was Grant Green, and he put him on and, sure enough, he was cooking."

The friend who had this smashing record collection also owned a guitar and happened to be the best guitar player in the neighborhood. George said he had been playing guitar since he was nine years old, but until then considered himself more a vocalist. "I was known around Pittsburgh as a singer," he says. "I sang pop tunes and R&B. I used my guitar as a backup instrument."

Then George started listening to Charlie Parker records. He became more interested in jazz and how the music allowed its instrument to sing. He began strumming on his guitar. Though he had little experience, he had some obvious skill with the instrument, certainly enough to convince Jack McDuff to hire him. In 1963, he left Pittsburgh to play in Jack's band. "I had nothing. I had no money, no nothing. And he took me on the road. That was my first real chance at playing the guitar. We traveled to a lot of little cities out in the Midwest."

Jack actually fired him the first night. George had been telling Jack that he didn't have any jazz experience, but Jack didn't listen to him. Once they got on the road and the band started playing songs, George was in trouble. "We started playing songs and chord changes, and he was trying to name the chords, and I didn't know what he was talking about," George said. "I could only play the blues. Anybody could play the blues. He told me when we got to New York he was going to find me another gig. He said he thought he knew a band that would really like what I did because they were more blues-based. But by the time we got to New York several weeks later, I had learned so much of his book that when his manager heard his band, he liked it the way it was. He said, 'No, you can't fire this kid, man. The band sounds better than it did when you left.'"

And so George stayed with Jack in New York. George was in awe of what he saw in the city. "I was starstruck, you know," he says. "I wanted to meet all of the stars."

He'd already heard about Grant Green and quickly set out to study his style. After a few months, he was bold enough to ask Grant if he could sit in with him. He will never forget Grant's reaction. "He laughed," George recalls. "Lou Donaldson was there and I did sit in. Lou Donaldson called me a rock 'n' roll guitar player, which I was, really."

But George wasn't bothered by the older cats. He had a plan: He would get Grant to become his friend.

"He was not an easy man to approach," says George. "He always felt like people were trying to steal his stuff. And indeed everybody was. But that's the way all players learn. They all take from each other. He could tell from the time I first came to New York that I could play. From the time that Grant heard me until two and a half years later, I was battling with him."

Many say 1965 was the year Grant reached a recording plateau. By the middle of the year, he had recorded *Joe's Blues* with Johnny Hodges and Wild Bill Davis, and *Matador,* on which his performance of "My Favorite Things" is among my favorites.

"For me, I thought it was his peak. He surpassed himself," says Elvin Jones, the drummer on *Matador.* "He did everything absolutely flawlessly. Everything he did was just so creative and so beautiful. He had such a delicate touch. I've never seen anyone who could get that kind of tone quality from an electric guitar. He just had that ability more than anyone else. He was a great artist, a great musician. I don't think he had any peers. He might have had some enemies and people who were envious. But I don't think he had a peer in the whole world."

Two other albums that year, *I Want to Hold Your Hand,* a bundle of Beatles' tunes, and *His Majesty King Funk,* were early signals of Grant's dissatisfaction and desire to reach a wider audience. *His Majesty King Funk* in particular was the buzzer announcing baby steps in a new direction. He did dates with the Cadet, Verve, and Limelight labels before sitting down as a sideman on Stanley Turrentine's *Rough 'n' Tumble,* recorded July 1, 1966. The session, which also featured Bob Cranshaw, Mickey Roker, Pepper Adams, Blue Mitchell, and James Spaulding, would hail the end of his first spree with Blue Note. Grant was anxious for acceptance on a wider scale, and despite his obvious achievements, few people outside the jazz circuit knew of him. By then he had recorded sixty-eight albums.

Elvin says having the ability to put out a lot of records—as Blue Note did—was easy. But having the budget to promote them, especially to a mainstream audience, was a different story. "It was relatively simple to make a recording. The economics were very low on the jazz artist side, so it was easy for the record companies to make a lot of recordings because there wasn't a big outlay as far as money was concerned from their point of view. So they made a lot of recordings with a lot of jazz artists. But I don't think very many of the jazz artists received any of the benefits of the marketing process," Elvin says. "So some got notoriety and some got known in the industry. But on the economic side, it was sort of a life-and-death struggle all the time. It was very difficult economically for the musician."

That Grant's career seemed to come to a halt in the mid-1960s should not be a surprise. There were many changes in the air. Because of Alfred Lion's failing health, Blue Note was sold to Liberty, a recording giant at the time. The industry was going through a transition. The country was going through a transition. There was a political war in Vietnam and a civil war on the streets of America. Jazz players got lost in the shuffle. The smartest ones quickly learned how to reinvent themselves. Wes Montgomery continued to benefit from a smooth marketing machine. His contributions to jazz guitar were documented in *Time* and *Newsweek.* Meanwhile, George Benson had formed his own band that year and was gaining ground.

George recalls, "People started saying, 'You heard this new kid?' and Grant would say, 'Who are you talking about? George Benson? You mean, George Benson!?' Remember, I couldn't

Grant Green, pictured here in his 1964 **Talkin' About** *session, was often called a simple, elegant stylist on the guitar. Photo by Francis Wolff, courtesy of Mosaic Images.*

Herbie Holland, former A&R promoter for Prestige

The guy who started this guitar solo thing was Charlie Christian. Grant was closer to Charlie Christian. Anytime Grant played—I don't care if Grant played gospel—he was swinging. A lot of these guitar players got into this real cool thing where they would put you to sleep. But Grant was swinging on the guitar. He kept that thing going. Grant had the ability, but he didn't have the outlet. I don't think he accomplished what he wanted before he died. Could he? I don't think that Count Basie and them accomplished what they wanted to before they died. I think that they were put into a situation to survive, you know? Like I always said, Ella [Fitzgerald] was a slave. They ran Ella all over the world and made millions and millions for somebody. I don't know how much Ella's got out of it. I don't think that any black artist got that much because, see, we don't control the top.

play nothing when I came to New York. But two and a half years later, Grant sat in with me at Count Basie's. He had sent the message: 'Tell him I'm coming down there to get him.' Once my reputation started growing, Grant said he was coming to get me. So he came over, and I knew how to escape him. I knew I couldn't play one-on-one with him in his own bag. You couldn't play a medium duo or anything because Grant would chop you to pieces. So I've always been smart enough to know to never try to beat a man at his own game. I made him play my game. I played so fast he couldn't keep up with me. I was eleven years younger than he was. So I played all night. My band played up-tempo things all night. We were crazy. That's why everybody loved us because we would play ridiculous tempos. But we didn't know any better. We were just playing fast just for the sake of playing fast. Grant had outgrown all the craziness years ago. He was a settled, smooth, soulful guitar player. Not a speed demon. I knew that. I never let him get comfortable.

Grant and George, besides being phenomenal guitarists, had something else in common: a man named Jimmy Boyd. George recalls distinctly what Jimmy, who was their manager, told Grant when he and Grant left the bandstand. "Jimmy told him, 'I told you not to go down there and mess with that young boy,'"

George says, laughing. "So I won that date in the minds of people. But Grant and I both knew there was no way I could be on the bandstand with Grant Green. Nobody could."

A year after this phone interview with George, my husband and I made a personal visit to George's home in New Jersey. When we arrived it was evident George was still a student of Grant's work. He counts *The Latin Bit* as one of his favorite Grant Green albums, but on the turntable in his music room was Grant's last recording, *Easy*. It's an album critics don't give the time of day, but one that has given me immense pleasure. Though Grant is clearly on his last leg—and the Commodore tunes like "Easy" and "Three Times a Lady" make you want to bow your head—the energy on cuts like "Empanada" and "Wave" is bizarre. George admits that he has played this album so often he's misplaced the album jacket. In fact, he says he and a buddy were just listening to it a week before our visit. He says he continues to be amazed at what Grant could do on the guitar several months before his death. Walking over to the turntable, he put the needle on "Empanada." We listened quietly for a minute. We heard a Grant who, though seriously ill, was still trying to throw some punches.

After listening to "Empanada," my husband casually asked George if he knew where his father's guitar was. My husband was under the impression that his brother Gregory had sold it to George some time in the early 1980s. (Greg viciously refutes the rumor. "What, you think I'm an idiot?" he once told me. He says that after their father died in 1979, a relative sent his father's guitar to be repaired. It was never picked up and was later sold at auction. When asked how they could ever let it get away, Greg couldn't answer. There is much about the circumstances surrounding his father's life and death that no one seems to remember or want to talk about. Years later the family also let his house in Detroit sit unwatched and uninhabited. Back property taxes piled up and the family lost the house.)

But in recent years as Blue Note began to release his old albums again, people started asking about the guitar. Everybody seemed to want the guitar. When my husband told George that he was looking for the guitar and wanted it back, George laughed and said, "I betcha I find it before you do!"

He did. For years, George reportedly looked for the guitar, which was believed to be in the hands of a Japanese collector. Not long ago, George purchased Grant's guitar for a reported $47,000. Owning Grant's last guitar was a dream come true, he says. Today, any talk of rivalry between him and Grant seems to bug him. "The world is always trying to pit one against the other, just like Muhammad Ali and George Foreman. They have to find a place to put you in their memory. I learned from those cats, so I don't consider myself in their category. That's how I learned to play, listening to all those cats. I had the privilege of hanging out with the greatest musicians in the world at the time. I hung out with Grant Green, Wes Montgomery, Kenny Burrell, Jim Hall, Barney Kessel, Tal Farlow, so I was the beneficiary of a great school. Can you imagine going through school and having those guys as teachers? That's why there's a George Benson today. When I left, I was a singer. I sang whatever was on the jukebox. Pittsburghers didn't know me as a guitar player. They knew me as a singer. So when I came back with a reputation as a guitar player, my hometown people didn't like it because they wanted me to sing. They thought I was going to come back a singing star. As a matter of fact, that's what they were telling me. 'Get out of here. Go to New York and cut you some records.' But they didn't mean as a guitar player. Now that I went out and won all the Grammy awards and top guitar honors and all that stuff, now they want me to play now. But when I first came back a couple of years later, I was like in the Top 10 guitar players and had accomplished that in two years' time."

Lou Donaldson has another view. He says there really was no premier jazz guitarist in the 1960s—not Wes, not Grant, and not George. "Wasn't no premier guitarist then! If you're talking about who got the publicity, well white cats got the publicity. Tal Farlow, Barney Kessel, all of them. They got the publicity. I played with Grant and Wes and George occasionally. George had a group at one time. It was Lonnie Smith and Ronnie Cuber. That was a great group, man. They had a great group. They were with Columbia Records. Columbia dropped them. George was kind of scuffling until he made that record with me, *Alligator Boogaloo*. That made him famous again. Then Creed Taylor got him and then they had a big star. Started singing. He always could sing."

George knew it, too. He also knew that his presence was obviously beginning to needle Grant, whose life was taking a major turn by the mid-'60s. With his career on hold, Grant turned to drugs even more. George says he wasn't aware of the extent of Grant's drug use, but he says Grant certainly had a reputation that suggested one should be careful around him. "One time he needed to borrow my guitar, and my manager said, 'George, he's gonna pawn it.' And I said, 'Well, I'll just sit here and wait until he finishes and I'll take it with me.' And I did. I went to the club and he thanked me very much. And then one day they stole my guitar off the Apollo stage, and Grant loaned me his guitar. Paid me back. See, if I had not done that for him, he wouldn't have been as willing. Because you talking about messing with his guitar? Boy, Grant didn't play that! At that time, he had a beautiful black instrument—[a] black Gibson L-7. He loved that instrument, boy. He would never cut the strings. If you see his pictures, you'll notice that those strings are wild and uncut. One day, I volunteered to cut them for him, and he said, 'No, man, don't do that.' I said, 'What are you talking about?' He said, 'You're gonna mess the tone up.' He was like a big brother. But he was a god, and a lot of that is still in my mind about him."

St. Louis jazz historian Richard Henderson (left), pictured here with Grant Jr., loved the elder Grant's interpretation of "Stella by Starlight." Photo by Sharony A. Green.

While he wasn't signed to any major

Grant Green, shown here with John Patton at Patton's 1965 Oh Baby *session, parted ways with Blue Note a year later to lead his own band. Photo by Francis Wolff, courtesy of Mosaic Images.*

label, Grant continued gigging in the New York area. Richard Henderson, the St. Louis jazz historian, remembered being in New York around this time. "I went to a place called Slug's, and he was playing with John Patton, and there was about six of us that had traveled up from St. Louis. We were all there, and he looked up during intermission and said, 'Oh, homies!' And he says, 'I know I'm gon' have to play some "Stella by Starlight"' 'cause when I used to see him, I use to always ask for that tune."

In 1967, Grant's only recording appears to be a Cobblestone album he did titled *Iron City*. On it, he reached for some old formulas with John Patton and Ben Dixon. The dark album featured tunes like "Old Man Moses," "Work Song," and "Sometimes I Feel like a Motherless Child." In 1968, he worked as a sideman on Rusty Bryant's *Rusty Bryant Returns* for the Prestige label, and then fell on some unusually hard times.

Herbie Holland, who worked as an A&R promoter for Prestige, saw Grant playing in the city around that time and recalled that he wanted to talk. He had a lot on his mind. "I used to hear him at different clubs, and then I got to meet him," says Herbie. "And we kinda struck up a pretty good relationship because he was interested in the business aspect of the industry by then. We used to talk about how the artists were being ripped off. They would make an album. They would be paid a few dollars up front, but they never got any of their royalties. If they wrote a song, the publishing was taken over by the record company. So the guys really didn't get any of the money from their compositions either. See, when an artist is young, the first thing he wants to do is just make a record, you know. Well, Grant had made records by the time I met him. Now he was a businessman. He was interested in the business aspect of the music business, as was I, because I used to see how the artists were getting ripped off because I was right there in the company. You can't believe some of the discussions that I had with some of the people in the business. Some of these artists should have been millionaires!! The companies were making money off these albums. Half of them weren't reporting their income to the artists. And Grant knew this. So Grant said, 'I'm not going to record.' So he didn't record for a while."

More than music was on Grant's mind. He was still trying to beat his drug habit, and though he tried to keep it hidden, he couldn't. He was becoming a man of pure contradiction. On one hand, he would hail the wonders of Islam and eat healthy meals while simultaneously destroying his body and mind with a needle and a sinister liquid. He would tell interviewers how much he missed his family, but stay on the road for months. Maybe it was to provide for them. Maybe it was to save himself from them. An artist's biggest burden has always been on the home front.

Rama Lomax, the Palm Cafe deejay, shedded light on the conflicting signals Grant gave. As she tells it, sometime in the mid-1960s, she walked up to the second floor of the club and found a group of musicians sitting around, alternately shooting up heroin and nodding off. "I can't recall why I went up there, but I went upstairs where the band was," she says. "It's a great big old room. Did I have to use the ladies' room? Maybe. I don't know. But I remember feeling uncomfortable because the bathroom was like a closet right in the middle of the floor almost. And all these brothers—musicians—were all over the place. Some of them were doing the bad thing. And I was really scared. I was really young. I was like, 'Where am I?' Grant rescued me. I remember that he actually rescued me. He came over and said, 'How are you doing?' and took me by the arm. He was looking around like, 'You don't want to be here' and he took me downstairs and we talked. He was really nice to me. I knew a lot of guys. But every time I saw him, he was always so gentlemanly. That's what I liked. He was always a gentleman. I don't care when I saw him, where I saw him. I'd never seen this situation before. Some of our people—black people—had a problem, especially at that time, with drugs. Many of them died. It was the first time I saw anybody with a needle or anything. I had never seen anything like that in my life before. I don't know if Grant did it, too. He certainly wasn't doing it when I opened that door. And if he did, hey, that's the way of the world sometimes."

Lottie "De Body" Graves, an exotic dancer who opened shows around the country for many jazz musicians and the Harlem Globetrotters, also recalled seeing this gentleman quality in Grant. "Grant was a quiet person. I don't know if anyone has ever told you that," she said one evening on the phone from her Detroit home. Like many women in the entertainment business or on its perimeters, her past is ever present despite the passage of time. Lottie, still kicks up her fat, pretty legs at Bomac's in downtown Detroit nightly. Now a woman nearing her winter years, she will readily tell anyone her name is Lottie "De Body" because "she had a body like a Lottie." In a low, cool voice, the kind that could easily place her in a Hollywood movie, Lottie continues, "Grant would stand off to the side unless he knew you. If he knew you, he'd hug and kiss you and 'Hi, Baby' you and buy you a drink, but he was not going to stand there and tell you his personal business. He was busy with his work. He was constantly thinking about the next act, the next gig, the next time they go back up. All musicians are like that. All great musicians anyway."

While he was forever a gentleman in the company of women, for whom he had an eternal weakness, Grant began to show a harder, more stubborn, even nasty side to his male band members. Those close to him blamed drugs.

Lottie "De Body" Graves, dancer who opened shows for jazz musicians during the 1950s and 1960s

I loved him. Grant just had a style of playing that everybody wanted to copy. The way he played, he made everybody applaud him. We used to go over to Little David, and Little David loved him. Little David was right here on Tireman [in Detroit]. He'd be in that corner and he'd play. I mean, it was just beautiful. He had a trio, and I mean, they would throw down. He was just like a big brother. I mean, you had to love him to know him, and you had to know him to love him. He was a musician that helped a lot of other musicians. He cared about people. I cried so hard when I found out that he was ill. But he's not gone. He's just resting. Making a little place for the rest of us.

"Grant was a funny guy," says Lou Donaldson. "He could tell you a lie and look you right in your face. He looked pitiful until you'd believe him. He'd say things like, 'Ah, baby, give me this money. I've got a gig.' He knew he ain't had no gig; he just wanted to get that money. Grant was a mess, man."

Grant's drug habit was spiraling out of control, and the waves sent some in his circle running for cover. Wendell Harrison, a clarinet player, remembered working in one of Grant's bands in the 1960s. "Although he was very good in terms of getting me on the scene and actually teaching me the ropes of performing and stuff like that, I had problems getting my money," says Wendell. "Grant was strung out on drugs. So I couldn't stay with him that long because I was up in New York trying to pay that rent. I ended up going with Hank Crawford because he would pay. Hank would pay. See, you'd go on the road with Grant, and you might not get but half of your money. He was sick. All the money he would get would go for drugs."

Wendell says he wasn't the least surprised to hear of Grant's death a decade later. "He should have been gone long before that with all the drugs. You should have seen this guy. He wasn't healthy at all."

Wendell holds Grant responsible. Not the music industry. Not society. "Every time we fail it's ultimately our fault as an individual. We have to take the credit. Grant would have been very, very successful, but the record companies took advantage of him. His managers, everybody just took advantage of him because he was strung out, he would go for anything. One reason why he worked a lot and made a name for himself was because he took any kind of gig. He was just one of those guys that would do anything to be high. The contracts and the things he did just to get high! After awhile, it wasn't about getting high, it was about feeling normal. Because he was using so much dope, he would be sick if he didn't have it. So drugs was like mainly medicine for him, and he didn't care who he would mess over to get the drugs. And a lot of people just took advantage of the fact that that was his weakness. Once you start, you meet all kinds of people that's doing the same thing. It's really hard to break away from it because your whole day revolves around getting high. You get high to reward yourself. It's just like factory workers; they'd go to work and come home and drink a beer. Druggies, the least little thing they accomplish, they've got to get high to reward themselves. They say, 'I just played a gig. I think I'll get me a hit of coke or something.' It's associated with good times and relief. They try to rationalize everything for getting high. Justifying it, giving many different excuses.

"He was a genius in his own way. Grant was like a pioneer. He was out there before George Benson on the guitar. Old George was playing, but Grant is the one that had the name and was getting recorded a lot. He could have had a lot of money. He could have left a lot of money for his kids if he hadn't been on the drugs."

Emmanuel Riggins, who joined one of Grant's bands in the late 1960s, expressed similar feelings about how Grant managed money. "He'd hold my money up and I'd be mad. I'd be like, 'Man, later! You keep that shit and shove it up your ass,' and I'd jump on a plane and come on home. I'd fall out with him and get me a ticket home and say, 'Fuck you, Grant,'" Emmanuel recalls, laughing. He doesn't hesitate to add that he did this even though Grant was his best friend.

"I always seemed to get my money because he wanted me back!" says Emmanuel, who has had his own challenges. "He always wanted me back! All of them damn musicians were on heroin! Miles was on. John Coltrane was on. Everybody was on. Bird died young. Lee Morgan was on."

Something finally got Grant to get his drug habit under control—a brief prison sentence in 1968 for drug possession.

Initially, Grant received almost a slap on the wrist. Grant ended up with a longer sentence after he failed to report to the penitentiary at the agreed-upon time. He left New York for a gig in California. Federal cops came to one of Grant's gigs to pick him up. And they even waited until he finished his set. They waited because they liked the music he played.

Emmanuel laughs as he recounts the story Grant relayed about what it was like to see the officers show up at his gig. "He says, 'Emmanuel. I wasn't gon' report to no penitentiary.' He says, 'But I had to tell 'em, "Yes, sir!" But they was nice guys by not embarrassing me and telling the whole audience who they were.' They waited 'til he finished his job and got his money. They even bought him drinks and stuff, brought drinks up to him! And put his ass on a plane! And flew his ass all the way back to New York City and then put his ass in jail and threw away the key. But he said, 'Emmanuel, they were so nice. They were *so* nice. They were *so* respectful, and I'll tell you one thing, I ain't gon' do that shit no more!'"

OPENING ACT — Grant Green is the first artist to perform in Detroit's newest after-hours club, Jazz West, through Jan. 6.

JAZZY GUITAR—Recording artist Grant Green, quintet in tow, heads for Watts Club Mozambique, checking in Friday for a ten-day engagement.

RAPEVINE LOUNGE

9 Joy Rd. at Schaefer

834-6606

COMING DEC. 11th thru 17th

"FINAL COMEDOWN"

INCOMPARABLE

GRANT GREEN

QUARTET

8 Shifting Gears The Late 1960s

"Grant used to pull me up early in the morning and tell me to listen to James Brown."

Besides his prison sentence, something else happened in 1968. Wes Montgomery died.

And so the year emerges as a pivotal one for Grant. He was free to start again in many ways. Released from jail, he returned to New York. With his most well-known rival off the scene, he began 1969 working as sideman on a Charles Kynard date for Prestige. The album was called *The Soul Brotherhood,* and it featured Grant and Charles alongside Blue Mitchell, David Newman, Jimmy Lewis, and Mickey Roker.

Some time in the late 1960s, Ann and the four kids joined Grant in New York. Reports of when and how they all got there are vague and inconsistent. According to Gregory, he did not spend much time with his birth mother and instead lived for years in St. Louis with Grant's parents. There seemed to be a lot of going back and forth to St. Louis for all of the family members. The kids were often shuffled between Grant's parents and Ann's parents, relatives say. They never had a stable home life.

But before the end of the decade, they finally all made it to the Big Apple. While Grant was an accomplished musician who had by then had considerable success, he was still unable to fully provide for his family. They made their home in an apartment building in Brooklyn, and Ann took a job with a government agency to help with the household expenses. "She worked because she had to work," says Ardis Hansberry, Ann's sister. "She worked for the New York Model Cities agency. In the '70s, after the civil rights movement, they had all of these different programs, and Model Cities was one in which the government put up funding to try and rehabilitate [the] neighborhoods. Ann could always get

good jobs because she had excellent secretarial skills."

Though he was an accomplished musician with considerable success by the mid-1960s, Grant Green still struggled to provide for his family. Photo by Francis Wolff, courtesy of Mosaic Images.

While Ann was supportive of Grant's career, and even his antics, his life was putting obvious strains on their marriage. She wanted out. "I [think] the fascination just wore off," Ardis says. "Grant was very into his music, so it was pretty much left to Ann to raise the kids, so I think to a certain extent she outgrew Grant, [but] of course, that's just me speculating. Being a musician and even being somewhat famous and all that, just wasn't enough. Plus he still had the drug problem, so I don't think they ever benefited completely from what he was able to do with his music because of the money that he spent on drugs."

Ann did show her support in her own way. Thomas Basir, a drummer who worked with Grant in the late 1960s and even lived with him at one point, remembered how Ann came through for him the day someone stole his drums. "She was a very strong woman. To live with Grant, she was extremely strong," Thomas says. "I was always thankful for her. At the time I was working with Grant, some junkie stole my drums. And I was pissed, to say the least. Ann said, 'Don't worry about it.' She happened to be there at the time and she had the money. Saved my butt. I bet she don't even remember it. The main reason I got another pair of drums was because of her. She cooled it right out. I will always be thankful to her for that. It came at the right time. It was the late '60s, and there was a lot of turmoil in the streets."

Rama Lomax recalls: "You know the thing that used to frustrate me with some of the musicians here in New York is that they didn't know what time it was. All they knew how to do was play this stuff. They didn't even know we were into a cultural revolution. It was like they never read the paper. Of course, they must have known. But they didn't seem to take an interest."

But Grant was different.

Rama remembers him as a contemplative man who would join her at a table in the Palm Cafe for a cup of coffee and conversation between his sets. "Grant would talk about whatever was current. Sometimes it would be about basketball games and stuff like that. And I was always flattered because guys were so sexist and macho in those days. But then he would talk about racism and he would say, 'This makes me sad.' I could sense [his] frustration, as I had with so many so-called jazz musicians. It was difficult being totally disrespected for this brilliant thing they pulled together for the world to enjoy, and you couldn't even make a living. And then you turn on the TV, go to the movies, and you'd see your music being played by European Americans or whomever and they're making the money! And this is your stuff! So why not get high! Why not! The pain. The pain. That has to be dealt with. You can't pretend it didn't exist because it does. It still does."

Thomas remembers how Grant continued to cling to the

Muslim faith. It showed in his diet. It showed in his music. "When I began to live with him, he noticed that there were certain things I didn't eat," says Thomas. "He finally said, 'Oh, you don't eat meat? You mean, you're Muslim?' I said, 'Yeah.' Then we said, *'Asalaam alaken,'* to each other. He had no idea. We were always into eating correctly. I could cook. Grant *wished* he could cook. We'd go to the store and just buy tons and tons of food. And we'd get in the kitchen with all that food. Everything was kosher. Grant was one of the first so-called big names that was Muslim, and people knew it."

The energy that ignited his spiritual thinking mirrored the music being heard on the radio across the country, namely funk. Grant, who had been in a slump like many jazz players, was excited again.

Thomas recalls, "Grant used to pull me up early in the morning and tell me to listen to James Brown. He used to wake me up and tell me, 'I want you to hear something. Listen to this.' And it would be somebody else's record, especially James Brown. It didn't make no difference, though. It was the rhythm he liked. He liked James Brown and the P-Funk, too. Any funky tune, any so-called R&B stuff that had the real slick rhythms, he would be in it. This was because the jazz thing was kind of second nature for us, but the funk thing was different. We listened to all the funk groups, every last one of them because he was into it."

Grant got his second break when he was asked to perform on Reuben Wilson's *Love Bug* album, which was recorded for Blue Note on March 21, 1969. By then Reuben, who came to New York in 1967, had already recorded his first album, *On Broadway.* Reuben remembered well how happy Grant was to come on board (he was actually more honored that Grant wanted to participate. After all, Grant was already a man with some fame.) "After the *On Broadway* album, I wanted to do something with some really established people, and among those established people was Grant Green," says Reuben. "So I went to visit Grant. He was living in Brooklyn then, near New York Avenue. I had this idea about doing pop music with jazz players. That's where Grant and Lee Morgan and Idris Muhammad and George Coleman came in. I was a little concerned about approaching them because they were really at the top of the shelf when it came to jazz players. And I was thinking,

'Maybe these guys wouldn't be interested in this thing.'"

But they were, especially Grant.

"See, I came up with this idea of playing pop music with jazz," says Reuben. "I didn't think they should be limited. In a lot of ways it had already been done, but not necessarily given the appreciation. They used a lot of jazz musicians in Motown. They were background players. So instead of having them in the background, it was just a matter of bringing [them] to the forefront. When I went to Grant with these things I wanted to do, he was just ecstatic. He was like, 'Yeah, man. Let's go. This is hip. Come on Ru, let's do this thing.' He was just really excited about it. I found out soon enough they really liked the idea of what I wanted to do. And so we all sat down eventually and we started rehearsing. And the amazing thing about Grant, I found, was that when I played something that he'd never heard, he could pick up his guitar and play it like he wrote it. He was a genius, this guy. And he was eager to do the pop music. I think he was at a low ebb when I came along. This was really good for him. I think this

Thomas Basir, drummer who was Grant's roommate in the late 1960s in New York

Grant was very, very outgoing, and he had his faults. But who didn't? You'll have somebody who will say, "He was like this and that!" And I say, "So what?" I'm telling you about what's really happening because we broke bread together. We were very close. I'll say there's always a dark side to everybody. But when I'm talking about the history of my people, especially those that I had the opportunity to know, the negative part does not necessarily need to be known because that's something between him and God. You understand? Like I tell my children, "Anything good that comes from me, please take it. Anything bad is between me and God. Anything good that comes from me comes from God. Anything bad comes from me." In other words, some things are left between me and the Creator. Grant and I never recorded together. We did all live stuff. One day we were talking and he got a call from Prestige Records. I said, "Yeah, we really should do this." But we never got around to it. We would have made great albums. We'd have made great albums.

brought him back, to tell you the truth. Well, for one thing, he did not have a deal. I had a deal. And it was just perfect for him."

The *Love Bug* date got Grant back into the Blue Note family. By this time, Alfred Lion was no longer with the company. The business was killing him, and Ruth insisted that he retire. She took him to Mexico. "We actually left in '67," Ruth says. "I wanted to be in Mexico because I was afraid. I thought he was going to come back and record again. He was a person who was stuck, absolutely stuck on his music, but then I became his music. I think we lived for twenty years when music was not the number one thing in our lives. He became a photographer. I became a journalist. We did a column for the *Mexico City News*."

But Frank Wolff was still at the helm of the company, and he was anxious to get Grant back in the studio. According to Emmanuel Riggins, who joined Grant's band in the late 1960s, Frank wanted Grant to go more commercial, something Grant was not sure about doing, even though he did enjoy the energy of funk and soul music. "Grant couldn't do the commercial stuff. He couldn't think that way," says Emmanuel. "*I* got him to think that way! As soon as I got with the group, they started to sell records! Frank Wolff started smiling, you know? And he said, 'You keep Emmanuel Riggins!'"

Recorded in 1970, Grant Green's* Alive! *album marked a newer and funkier direction for the St. Louis–born guitarist. Courtesy of Blue Note Records, a division of Capitol Records.

Grant Green albums began to come off the Blue Note assembly line like hot cakes again: *Green Is Beautiful, Carryin' On, Grant Green Alive!, Shades of Green, The Final Comedown,* and *Live at the Lighthouse.* On these albums, he did everything from Mozart to covers of Karen Carpenter, Kool & the Gang, and even Jackson 5 tunes. But while doing them he always performed with straightahead musicians who had the talent to keep it real—among them, drummers Idris Muhammad, Greg Williams, Claude Bartee, and Neal Creque.

The music was danceable, and much of it was played on the radio. His 1971 *Visions* album almost took him over, even as many industry observers slammed it. "It simply was not his best playing," says the London jazz guitar professor Adrian Ingram.

Carryin' On was recorded in 1969 and demonstrated Grant's continued desire to interpret popular music of the day. On this album, he tackles a tune by a man he greatly admired, James Brown. Courtesy of Blue Note Records, a division of Capitol Records.

Still, Grant clearly was making a slow climb back to the top. What was in store for him on the climb up was unclear. He was determined to give it one last try. So he did the unthinkable. Realizing he needed an international reputation, he overcame his fear of flying and got on a plane to attend the London Jazz Expo. He shared the stage with Kenny Burrell and Barney Kessel. It was actually a fluke that he even participated. Tal Farlow had been promised as the third man, but Tal canceled and Grant stepped in. The fact that his name wasn't advertised on the marquee outside made him play "that much harder," Grant would tell an interviewer.

By the time Grant returned to the States, his marriage to Ann was over. Ardis Hansberry recalled walking into their home only to discover that the kids were essentially living alone. She decided to take Grant Jr., the youngest, to her new home in California for the summer. "The summer that I brought Grant Jr. out here with me, there were no adults anywhere in the household. His brothers and sister were all teenagers, so it was a lot for them to have this house by themselves. Junior was only like nine or ten years old, and basically there was nobody taking care of him, so I took him for the summer," Ardis says.

After his summer in California—he especially loved the train ride to and from the West Coast—Grant Jr. reunited with his brother, John, his sister, Kim, and his mother, who soon remarried. "She met this Jamaican guy and they started dating, and he wanted to move back to Jamaica and start his own business and just raise a family in Jamaica," my husband once told me. "I remember meeting him a few times, and he was like pretty sharp, man. He was real neat. So one thing led to another, and I remember my mom told us we were moving to Jamaica, and she gave us a choice like, 'You guys can either come or you can stay with your dad,' and Greg stayed with my dad. Me, Kim, and John, we all went to Jamaica. We drove down from New York to Miami and then from Miami we caught a plane there, and the car got shipped over on the boat. My stepdad rented a house in Kingston for us until he got situated. Then we moved to a part of Jamaica called Mandeville, and we all pretty much got oriented with Jamaica and that way of life. It was like a serious culture change for us because we were kids living in New York, so what the hell [did] we know about Jamaica, West Indies? But everything fell in place eventually. I started going to school. I was doing good in school. Kim was going to a private school. John was like the deviant. He was always in trouble in school. And he was always against my stepdad."

My husband has often said that he doesn't remember much about his life in St. Louis, and very little of his years in New York—except for sitting on the floor of his grandparents' house as a toddler, cuddling an album depicting his dad wearing a big sombrero, and getting a butt-whupping years later in a New York apartment for bringing home a bad report card. (His dad reluctantly delivered the blows.) However, he has very vivid memories of his time in Jamaica.

"I had never seen my dad too much, so when I moved to Jamaica and started living this family life and having a mom and a dad, or a stepdad, I finally started to realize what it's like to live as a family, to have two parents, and it was easy for me to deal with that because I had never seen my father anyway. He was always on the road. But if I had spent most of my life with my dad, I probably would have some trouble with it. See, that's probably what happened to my brother, John, because he probably remembered more times with my dad than I did," my husband told me.

Greg, who by then had started to play guitar, lived full-time with relatives in St. Louis. But his father did come to visit from time to time. One visit in particular stands out in his mind. "I was living with my grandfather and my grandmother, and he came to town," says Gregory. "By then, he and my mom had split up. I remember he came to town and he took me shopping. He bought me this red knit suit. I thought that was cool because he bought it. I really didn't know him because I never spent that much time with him. I never spent much time with either one of my parents. I was shuffled around a lot. I was like at either my father's parents' house or I would stay with my mother's parents."

James Edmonds, South Carolina jazz guitar record collector

I love Grant's music. I was listening to classical guitar players, and one day I stumbled across an album of Lou Donaldson playing some funky music, and this guitar player was wailing away on guitar, but instead of playing that twangy Duane Eddy sound, he was playing these clear lines. And I could understand what he was doing. And that was my first introduction to Grant Green. Grant Green takes a simple melody and he builds on it, and he's got something to say and he takes his time. Grant Green is a storyteller. And anybody can understand what he's saying.

Gregory is now forty-three, the age his father was when he died of a heart attack. Shortly before this book was finished, I pointed this out to him, and he chuckled and said, "Don't jinx me." And then his face grew distant. Reality set in. It was true. All of the older men in his family are gone. Both grandfathers. His dad and all of his mother's brothers. Most had battled chemical abuse, mainly alcohol. Greg prides himself on clearing his own chemical hurdles and being clean for several years. But he is especially proud of following in his father's footsteps.

Thirty years ago, Grant bragged to a reporter in London about the son who was still learning how to play guitar. In the following years, Greg would have a great teacher in his father and his family's friends, like Earl Klugh. Today, Greg's promotional literature boasts that his conservatory was simply "the environment in which he lived." He has memories of playing football with Marvin Gaye and hanging around other Motown stars when he and his siblings

Greg Green performing in New York in 1996 at a session in tribute to his father, Grant Green. Photo by Sharony A. Green.

finally joined their father in Detroit.

Though he is still making headway in national and international circuits, Greg is without question known in New York, particularly in the Village, where his band, Ge Ge Be, plays at various clubs like Terra Blues on Bleecker Street. (The name of his band looks like a fascinating play on the initials of him, his father, and George Benson.) Greg is close to George and will readily call him up to chat. He says George is mesmerized by how much he plays like his dad, and once asked him exactly how his father tuned his amp to get "that sound." George gave Greg his best guess. Greg says he just laughed. "I wouldn't tell him how he got it," says Greg, smiling. "I won't tell *anybody.*"

Like his father, Greg plays it all—jazz, funk, rhythm and blues, and rock 'n' roll. Does he have a preference? "Yeah, jazz," he says. But he's gotta eat, and he says he'll play anything. Last time we chatted, he was doing a Whitney Houston session. He had also done an album issued in Japan with Reuben Wilson as one of his sidemen.

Unlike his brothers who are on the slim side, Greg is more stocky, but equally tall. He's known to have a temper and is unequivocally dedicated to the music business. However, he is steadily making a name as Grant Green Jr., not as Greg Green. It's a name he hasn't been able to shake, despite some effort to do otherwise. In New York City, he's Grant Green Jr. Period. Greg says it was his father who told him to use the name, even though it was the legal name of his youngest brother. He grows visibly irritated by any suggestion that he did it on his own accord. "My *father* told me to do it," he said. "He said no one would know who Greg Green was."

I once asked Greg whether the shuffling between homes had any long-term effects on him and his brothers and sister. He grew quiet, and then answered, "I can't say whether I regret it or not because, I mean, I love my grandparents like they were parents, because they were the ones who were providing for me and stuff like that. But I guess logically I don't think it's healthy to shuffle kids around. I think they should either be with one parent or both parents. Maybe it did affect me in a way because I am older now and the majority of my friends that I grew up with are married with families and kids, and I'm not."

In time, his father decided once and for all to do right by his kids. After reuniting with Blue Note, he had enough disposable income to purchase his first home. In 1970, Grant Green moved to Detroit. Unable to resist another opportunity to play on his name, he selected a two-story brick house on a street called Greenlawn, on the city's West Side.

Around this time Blue Note, which was later purchased by Capitol Records, had moved to the West Coast as had other record companies, including Motown. Gigs were no longer as plentiful in New York for jazz players. Grant's move to Detroit was partly due to the fact that he had a strong base in the city. His music was played regularly on the airwaves. There was money to be made there; the automobile plants were still hiring. And what was especially attractive was that black people seemed to be more in control of their destiny even after the riots. They still had homes. They still had jobs. "Brothers had money in Detroit!" says Emmanuel Riggins, who made the move to Detroit with Grant and bought his own home, too. "They ain't had no money in New York! No businesses either! People had businesses here, man! Brothers had restaurants! They owned homes! These brothers had money, baby! Real money!"

Detroit had something else—a strong musical tradition. Grant wanted to be a part of it.

9 Looking for the Perfect Beat The Early 1970s

"From time to time he would call to tell me about what he was doing. He'd be playing in the Mozambique and he'd say, 'I killed them in there! Boy, it's hot in there. I'm telling you it's hot in there.'"

Grant Green went to Detroit for one reason.

"He moved here to save himself," says Wendell Harrison, the clarinetist who still lives in the Detroit area where musicians and deejays from all backgrounds—techno, pop, rock, soul, blues, and jazz—are nurtured by a musically sophisticated audience. When my husband and I first moved to Detroit, we were moved by the city's appreciation for music, especially black music. We could go into the whitest establishment and still hear the latest R&B tune from the radio piped in. Little wonder Motown got its start here. Detroit was also a city that welcomed Grant Green in the 1970s and honors him even today. He was a constant presence in the area, especially at the popular Watt's Club Mozambique. Located on the city's West Side night spot, Watt's Club, like many jazz clubs around the nation, lost a lot of business due to crime, arena concerts, and cable TV. Today, Watt's is a second-rate strip joint. But enlarged cardboard photos of the greats who came through its doors like Art Blakey and Lonnie Liston Smith still hang underneath dusty frames behind speakers booming, "Get it, get it! Rock wit' it!"

Cornelius Watts, the club's owner, spoke proudly of the club's more dignified beginnings. "I had a club on Linwood and Davison called the Parisian Club. It was in an old bank building," says Cornelius. "My attorney called me and told me about a building out on Fenkell. My opening date at that spot was Palm Sunday, April, 1968. When I got there, I didn't start with jazz right away. I opened up with a band called the Metropolitans. They were the house band. I did that for about a year before one of the disc jockeys at WJZZ at the time talked me into bringing in jazz. And that's what made Mozambique. We opened up with Spanky Wilson and behind that, Charles Earland. Then, someone told me about Roy Ayers. Then, Grant Green, who had been in a little trouble, was back on the scene. The deejays had told me that he'd just gotten out of prison and that Blue Note had dropped a new album and it was going to be hot because he had been off the scene for a while. I guess people were just waiting on him to come back and put out something new.

"Blue Note hurried up and put a record out on him. To tell you the truth, he was my biggest draw. He was my biggest draw until Lonnie Smith came out with *Move Your Hand.* Lonnie Smith came in and broke all records. But as a consistent drawer, Grant Green was it. I would book him three times a year, and I'd always make money with him. Grant was a very good artist to work with.

Grant Green bought this house on Detroit's West Side where he lived from the early 1970s until his death in 1979. Forever infatuated with wordplay he was first drawn to the street's name—Greenlawn. Photo by Sharony A. Green.

He was cooking. Jimmy Boyd was his booking agent at the time, and Jimmy would always call me and say, 'Watts, let me know when you want Grant back because he's booked up pretty solid. I've got a few dates open,' and I would always grab one of those dates."

"Grant Green's records got really popular in the '70s here, and the guy who really brought Green to focus in Detroit was Cornelius Watts," says saxophonist Eli Fountaine, a former Motown musician, best known for his stirring solo at the beginning of Marvin Gaye's "What's Goin' On."

Cornelius says Detroit appealed to Grant because it is and has always been a city of homeowners, both black and white. Once folks got a job at one of the motor companies, the first thing on their mind was the proverbial house with the picket fence. Historically, Detroit has never been a city with a lot of rental property. Says Cornelius: "Grant always liked Detroit because he [said] it was more of a residential city. He was used to living in an apartment all of his life. He wanted to buy a home here. He made a lot of friends here. Detroit is a warm city. The people are more congenial. You're quick to get hooked up with the neighbors next door. It's more like family to you than a city like New York or Chicago. Those are cold cities. I've been to both of those cities. I find that they're very cold."

Herbie Holland, the former A&R man for Prestige, says Detroit had another appeal—it was a record-buying community. "At that time he moved there, we had no black record companies," says Herbie. "Motown was a different story, but even Motown is not black anymore. Gordy sold out and everything. But it started out as a little company in Detroit. Other than Motown, all the black record companies had been put out of business. All of them, like Stax, were put out of business. I'm talking about payola and what have you. The white companies were the ones who had the payola. They used to send guys around the country with bags of dope and money to give to the deejays. And some of the deejays were dogs. They would play anything as long as they got some money for it. But I never paid any money because I felt that jazz was our music and we should hear it. Detroit was probably our best market. Detroit was the market where we knew that things would hit right away. You had guys

Calvin Brooks, Detroit guitarist and member of Grant Green Legacy Band

I worked with Martha and the Vandellas for about twelve years. And we're doing stuff like "Dancing in the Streets" and "Heatwave," and this is not jazz guitar. We were just playing what we call triads—chank, chank, chank. But working with Martha, we would get a chance to do a couple opening numbers. So this particular night she said, "Do whatever you want to do." I said, "Okay. Fine." So I think we did some instrumental tune. And this brother ran out of the audience after we finished the tune. He said, "Grant Green! Grant Green!" He said, "Man, you took me back to Detroit. Watt's Club." He said, "Where are you from, brother?" I said, "I'm from Detroit." He said, "I knew it. Grant Green!" And that's happened on numerous occasions. If you go back and listen to some of his early music, you would see that that music can't be copied today. We're talking very intricate melodies. As far as his style of playing—it was phenomenal.

out there like Ed Love. He was doing a heck of a job. There was Martin Douglas. There was a girl there named Cookie Cox. Detroit has a lot of talent."

The city also had money. Calvin Brooks, a Detroit-area guitarist who, along with Emmanuel Riggins and Greg Williams, formed the Grant Green Legacy Band in 1993, says the dollar signs in Detroit proved to be an obvious lure for Grant. Brooks has heard many stories from Riggins and Williams, who have both played in Grant's band.

Says Calvin, "I once said, 'Emmanuel, why of all places did you and Grant come from New York to Detroit?" He says, 'Calvin, during the late '60s and '70s, there was so much money here in Detroit.' He says people were riding around in El Dorados and fur coats. Everybody had houses. I said, 'You're right!' Because I can remember in college—I went to college in '72. I was at the University of Michigan—you could go to Ford, General Motors, Chrysler, any plant, fill out an application and you'd get hired the next day. People were doing so well here during those times. There was no worry."

But Detroit's rich musical resume was the city's most obvious draw. As far back as the 1920s, the city was booming when Henry Ford offered the then-unheard-of wage of $5 a day. Ballrooms like the Graystone, the Arcadia, and the Palais de Danse began to spring up around town for those looking for places to enjoy music when the workday was over. In the 1930s, Paradise Valley, located in the heart of the black community on the city's near East Side, became a major entertainment center. Among the well-known clubs during that time were the Chocolate Bar, the Cozy Corner, the Club Plantation, and the Melody Club. In the 1940s, the Paradise Theater, now called the Detroit Symphony Orchestra Hall, featured some of the best in black entertainment, including the biggest names in big band, rhythm and blues, and bebop. By the 1950s, urban renewal and its by-product, urban decline, swept away Paradise Valley. Clubs on the West Side like the Crystal Lounge, the Parrot Bar, Klein's Show Bar, and the Blue Bird opened and gained a national reputation as the places to hear good modern jazz. "The Blue Bird was really a neighborhood bar on the West Side," says drummer Elvin Jones, a Detroit native. "There were other places on the West Side and all kinds of places around

Over a diverse collection of songs, Grant Green reveals his beginnings in the blues tradition on his 1961 album **Sunday Mornin'**. *Courtesy of Blue Note Records, a division of Capitol Records.*

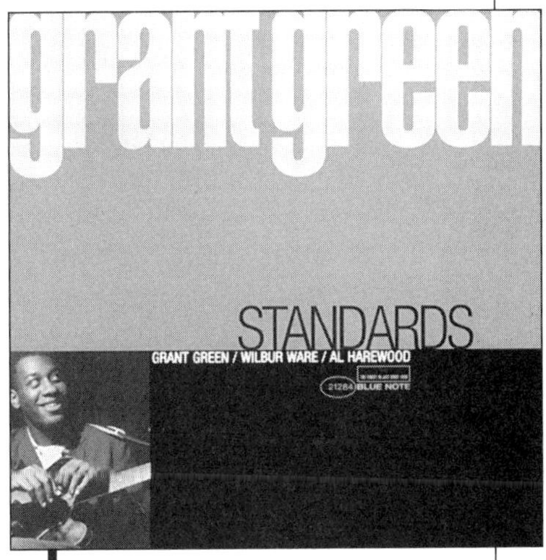

The recently released **Standards** *CD showcases Grant's smooth handling of mainstream modern jazz compositions. Courtesy of Blue Note Records, a division of Capitol Records.*

Detroit. There was also the World Stage. It was really a theater playhouse for young actors developing plays, developing their craft, and so on. And we used that room for jam sessions once a week. It was a wonderful thing. There was all kinds of activity like that that motivated young musicians to go out and study and learn, and it also gave them an opportunity to perform. There was a place out in River Rouge called Blair's Hotel, and we would go out there after hours. Sometimes on weekends, we'd stay up all night. We'd just go from one place to another. It was just a beehive of activity and development. You could listen to young musicians and older musicians. Everybody would come together and hear their knowledge. And the music was not just for black people or white people. It was for everybody. Everybody there got the benefit of all that."

In the 1960s, Motown began offering even more enticing opportunities for the city's jazz musicians. Many of them were session players for groups like the Temptations and the Supremes.

When I think of the names that came out of Detroit, I am reminded of the photograph of jazz musicians lined up on a sidewalk that was made famous by the movie *A Great Day in Harlem*. But if one could line up the cats who came out of the Detroit area—Pepper Adams, Geri Allen, Dorothy Ashby, Marcus Belgrave, Norma Jean Bell, Bess Bonnier, Lester Bowie, Roy Brooks, Kenny Burrell, Donald Byrd, Betty Carter, Ron Carter, Paul Chambers, Tommy Flanagan, Curtis Fuller, Wardell Gray, Roland Hanna, Barry Harris, Teddy Harris, Louis Hayes, Milt Jackson, Ron Jackson, Elvin Jones, Hank Jones, Thad Jones, Hugh Lawson, Terri Pollard, Dianne Reeves, Sonny Stitt, Lucky Thompson, Donald Walden, Doug Watkins, Holly West, and Lyman Woodward, among others—that would be something to see. Watt's Club was no stranger to any of them, just as it was no stranger to Grant Green. Eli Fountaine remembered the impact Grant had in the club. "As one of the world's premier guitarists, he had a li'l bit of everything, a little jazz, a little blues. It was a round situation. I'm not too locked into the word *jazz*. If a cat can play, he can play," Fountaine says.

During that time, children were allowed to attend Sunday matinees at Watt's Club. Rod Sibley, another Detroit guitarist, recalls his first trip to see Grant perform there. "I can't remember the exact date, but I'm going to place it around 1970," says Rod. "Grant Green was coming to perform at Watt's Club Mozambique. I had never seen him live before. Matter of fact, I had never been to a concert before. So my stepfather and my mother decided that they would take me to see Grant Green. And I was like, 'Oh boy, this is going to be totally, totally great.' It was a Sunday matinee performance. So we got there and I had with me two albums. I brought his *Alive!* album and I had his new album, *Visions*. It had just come out and I wanted to get him to sign them. So we got to the club, and the show was supposed to start at around four o'clock. Well, the lights dimmed and this announcer came on stage and says, 'Now ladies and gentlemen, we are glad to welcome you to Watt's Club and blah, blah, blah. But we are going to have a fashion show now.' And we were like, 'Wait a minute. This is supposed to be Grant Green.' So we waited, and they [did] this fashion show for like around two and a half hours! They had this cheesy comedian up there with this processed hair. It was just really a low-budget type of thing, and you know black folks were getting mad. They were saying, 'Bring on Grant Green!' The band was getting ready to come on, but they found out they had problems with the Hammond organ. So they get the organ fixed and Grant finally comes on. I think he had a quintet. He had a xylophone player with him as well as an organ, bass, and drum[s]. He played for something like one and a half hours. I can't remember the exact time. But he sat up front on stage and he was just burning. At the time, I didn't know anything about the technical aspects of guitar playing. But I knew that I liked what he was doing, and even at that young age I was like, 'Man!' He really swung. It was almost over as quickly as it began as far as I was concerned."

Rod quickly hurried onstage to get his albums autographed. "They were packing up the gear and everything, and he didn't even notice me. But the organ player pointed me out to him. So he signed them and he seemed to be pleased that I had had that *Visions* album because it had just came out. As a matter of fact, when Grant first came out on stage, that cheesy comedian said to him, 'You got a new album out—*Contusions, Allusions*?' And Grant says, '*Visions*. It's *Visions*.' And then the guy told Grant, 'Well, you know when I drink, I have visions, too. Ha, ha, ha!' The guy was totally awful. In fact, in the process of being bored

Though increasingly bitter through the years, acquaintances say Grant, pictured here with George Braith, remained a dedicated musician until the end. Photo by Francis Wolff, courtesy of Mosaic Images.

with that fashion show I wound up scribbling the ink pen so much that I almost ran the ink out of the pen. But Grant had enough to get clear signatures on the album covers. He put his name on one side of each lens of the sunglasses he was wearing on the *Visions* album. So I've got those big G's on both of the sunglass [lenses]."

While getting his albums autographed, Rod noticed something about Grant Green he will never forget. It is something others have mentioned, too. "He had big hands," Rod says. "When I gave him the albums to sign, he gave them back to me, and all I could see were those hands. To a ten year old, everything is big, but his hands felt heavy and they were big!"

Calvin Brooks, another Detroit guitarist, recalls seeing Grant at Watt's Club. He attended an evening show. He and his buddies were just teenagers at the time and lied about their age to get in. After the show, Brooks had to go up and meet Grant. "I introduced myself, and Grant was very much a gentleman," says Calvin, who always includes a Grant Green cover during his gigs. "He invited me into the dressing room, and he had his guitar back there, and he showed me some basic fingering and things like that. I was really thrilled just to be in his company. I was very nervous at that time and really didn't know much. But I just had a real keen interest for the instrument and his sound. I never heard anyone with that tone and quality. I think the reason I never really tried to play another instrument is because I think it takes a lifetime to master this instrument. Grant was a master of the guitar."

The 1970s was without question Grant Green's second chance. Industry types were glad to see him back at work, and the public was waiting for him. On the notes for his 1971 *Visions* album, recording engineer Rudy Van Gelder sings Grant's comeback praises, saying he had never heard Green play as well in any previous session.

Grant's mental disposition seemed to be more solid in the studio and on the bandstand, not just at Watt's Club, but at Baker's Keyboard Lounge on Eight Mile Road and other night spots from Flint to Ann Arbor. Jack McDuff recalls Grant calling him to tell him about a night at the Watt's Club that went particularly well. "From time to time he would call to tell me about what he was doing. He'd be playing in the Mozambique, and he'd say, 'I killed them in there! Boy, it's hot in there. I'm telling you it's hot in there,'" laughed Jack.

Grant's humor and obvious celebrity status soon got him invitations to perform throughout the city. He was a regular at benefits for the local black organizations and became friends with city commissioners and Coleman Young, the city's first black mayor. His recent slump was something he was determined to get beyond.

Larry Smith, the saxophone player who saw a young Grant on a hotel stoop a decade before, recalls an afternoon when he and Grant were scheduled to do a gig at a local television station for Mother Waddles, a community activist in Detroit. "I had just come into the building and was standing there looking around to see where I was going [to] set up to play," says Larry. "So I'm setting up, and I felt someone tapping me on the shoulder. I looked behind me, but I couldn't tell who it was. I couldn't see anything because the person tapping me kept ducking. It was Grant. He did little playful things like that. He was always laughing, and he had this thing he'd do with his hands all the time. He would try to spank the plank when he gave you five. You know like how you give a person five? Well, when you'd go to do that, he'd move his hand back. Grant had a great personality."

"He was exciting," agrees Emmanuel Riggins. "That cat would have you laughing. He was the life of the party. When he come in the house, he was the life of the whole party."

Adds Wendell Harrison: "He was always kidding around, a real Uncle Remus. He had conversation. His personality was out of sight...Charming personality. He could charm the socks off of folks!"

Grant's personality went over especially well in Detroit restaurants, where he got special treatment, just as he had in New York. Still following certain Muslim teachings, Grant continued to eat mostly kosher and East Indian cuisine. "There was an East Indian man named Oscar who had a place out by Tiger Stadium," says Shelton Laster, who was a member of Grant's band in the 1970s. "We used to go out there and order food. And we always ate kosher."

There was one place where Grant wasn't always welcomed—the black Muslim mosque. Grant's other weakness, besides drugs, had long been women, including the Muslim sisters. "I used to say, 'Hey, Grant, want to go down to the mosque with me?' And he'd say, 'Oh, uhn uhn! I ain't goin' down there, man!'" says Emmanuel with a chuckle. "He had a phobia about going down there 'cause he knew those brothers were probably gon' whup his head!"

Riggins says many of the city's black Muslims loved him regardless. "The brothers still loved him and loved his music, so he would get hired for jobs. He played a lot of Muslim gigs. See, Muslims were businessmen. They would have a bazaar and the brothers who worked in the restaurant, or the wig shop, and the women who were doing jewelry, fingernails, and selling Korans, hats, and shoes, would get a big hall some place, and they would advertise that this was taking place and Grant was gon' be there playing. And you know they gon' come to hear Grant. They called him Brother Grant!"

Emmanuel Riggins, keyboardist who recorded with Grant on several albums, including *Visions* and *Shades of Green*

I went two years to Youngstown State. I met Grant; I dropped out. My old man said, "Boy, why you dropping out of school for?" I said, "Daddy, I got a chance to play with Grant Green." He said, "Who is Grant Green? I want to meet this Grant Green." So I brought him home. Later, I asked Grant what did Dad say to him. He said, "You make sure that boy pay that car note." I had just bought my first car off the showroom floor. It was an honor to play with Grant.

Grant was also well received in black Islamic communities across the country, especially in his hometown, St. Louis. One year the city had a Muhammad Ali Day, and the great boxer and Grant were invited. "We were giving Muhammad Ali the key to the city. All of the politicians and even the mayor came. It was nice. And so we had Grant Green come down," says Barbara Morris, who helped found the city's first chapter of the Nation of Islam with Grant and other black musicians.

Greg "Vibrations" Williams, who was in Grant's band during that time, recalls, "We were at the temple playing and Muhummad Ali walked in," Greg says. "He looked at us. We stood up and gave him a salute. He gave it back. He understood that we understood what he was about. He was honest in what he did. He respected us and we got to talking for a minute. Him and Grant talked for quite a while."

Grant played the old standards at the Muslim gigs, but he also played his newer and funkier material. He knew how to appeal to an audience. He once told an interviewer, "You have to be a businessman first and an artist along with it. You can't play something people dislike and stay in the business."

Whether he preferred the commercial music over straight-ahead jazz is unclear, but a more seasoned Grant seemed to know how to play the game now. He would tell the same interviewer that the recording industry was only interested in what sold, not how good you were. And he eagerly tried to get with the times, even if it meant branching out into other areas. He finally got his break. In 1971, he was asked to do the soundtrack for the film *The Final Comedown.*

Leo Chears, the disc jockey best known as the "Man in the Red Vest" when he did local promotions for Budweiser in St. Louis, shared a radio interview he conducted with Grant during this time. In it, Grant talked freely about where he was in his career and how he was making inroads in the business, commercial and otherwise. The interview on radio station KSD, presented in part below, unveils the voice of a modern jazzman who realized his own worth by the 1970s and was now furiously going after everything he felt was owed him.

LC: *Well, that's Herbie Hancock with a thing called "Maiden Voyage," and we were telling you earlier that we were expecting Grant Green to come down tonight. As you know Grant's at the La Casa over on Jefferson and Olive, and he'll be there through the rest of the week. Boy, this cat is so nice and so red hot, so check him out. After this word we'll come back with more sounds.*

[Commercial]

LC: *Twenty minutes now past the hour of two and we've sorta passed the Bud around to some good folks in the studio this morning and toasted one of the better people that I know, and I'm very happy to say, 'Hello, Grant Green.'*

GG: *Hello, Leo.*

LC: *How's everything goin', man?*

GG: *Oh, it's goin' good, Leo. You know, you're my favorite disc jockey. You've been doin' this thing a* looo-ng *time.*

LC: *We've had a good time with it. When I came out of the Army back* *in the '50s, you were over in East St. Louis at the Sportsman, remember that? Listening to you play was a beautiful, beautiful thang and we had such a great time.*

GG: *I went on to be sort of a household word in Blue Note.*

LC: *The way we were keeping informed as to what you were doing was the fact that Blue Note had one of their strong offices here in town at that time, and we'd go down and pull things off the shelf, and invariably we'd always pull Grant Green down 'cause it was good to see you—a hometown cat taking care of a lot of business. I had the pleasure of seeing the movie* The Final Comedown, *and that filled me with a lot of happiness 'cause here you were doing that soundtrack.*

GG: *Yeah, it was a challenge because it was something different, man. I always wanted to do a score for a movie, and so the president of the company said, "Well, Grant, look at the movie and see what you think. If you can do anything musical with it, just please go ahead and do it." So I was in Hollywood, so we went out to the studio and I checked it out and said, "Well, I'll take a shot at it." It was my first and I did it, man. It came out beautiful.*

LC: *The entire soundtrack is great, but everybody, including myself, jumped on "The Battle." Here you are with this very swinging group. Everything is there. It rolls. I can sense the feeling, the height of the battle. Imagination is a great thing, and the music that you have composed for the motion picture* The Final Comedown *is something to be talked about.*

GG: *Well, we have a nice staff of musicians, a young group of men I've been playing with. Of course, I couldn't do it by myself. We have Mubutu, the conga player, who's playing all of these different African things, y'know. I don't know what they are myself.* [Laughs] *It sounds like "Jingle Bells" and 'course, Greg Williams, the drummer with the whistles.* [Laughs] *I gathered up this group from all parts of the country. The drummer is from my part of the country, Flint, Michigan, and his name is Greg Williams, and Mubutu, the conga player, is from Pittsburgh, Pennsylvania. The organ player is from Springfield, Massachusetts, Shelton Laster. And we have Desmond Norman on vibes; he's from Asbury Park. And I'm from St. Louis, so we're rounding 'em up from all regions. We got a good blend there.*

LC: *You've done what I've noticed seems to be a trend with some of the good groups today—you pick some of the younger musicians.*

GG: *Right, man. I got a lot of fire there.*

LC: *And I like your ideas there.*

GG: *Excellent.*

LC: *Look like y'all have a lot of fun.*

GG: *Man, we be wild.*

LC: *Well, we can talk about a lot of other things, Grant, but I have to talk about that particular number because as I said before, I never seen anything quite like it. Grant, we go back a long time. We paid a lot of dues.*

GG: [Laughs] *I'm telling you!*

LC: *A lotta dues, man. But Blue Note was mellow for you.*

GG: *Yeah, Blue Note was the company for me, man. And we're doing some great things now that I'm proud of, y'know. We also did* Shades of Green *with the big band. It's on the jazz charts and it's doing well.*

LC: *'Course now we must [say that]* The Final Comedown *is on United Artists and then there's another album released [on] Cobblestone, and this makes me feel good to see a lot of good jazz labels coming out now, man. People—I won't say everyone—have a tendency to get away from the word "jazz."*

GG: *Well—*

LC: *But we got to know that this word is there.*

GG: *But I don't like it. I don't like to use it, Leo. I like to use "music" because—*

LC: *—because you do a lot of other things.*

GG: *Right and to put a title on it—a lot of times we've lost a lot of people by connecting up with jazz because they think it's in the same old form that it was in and we're just trying to get people to sit down and listen to music.*

LC: *Well, a lot of things are going on in one bag.*

GG: *Right. I just use "black music" in general.*

LC: *...It's got to be something that makes people want to stay up and listen.*

GG: *Riiiight! That's riiiiight!*

[Commercial]

["The Battle" from *The Final Comedown* begins. It is very upbeat with the "wack" twang reminiscent of the theme song for the 1970s film *Shaft.*]

LC: *That's called "The Battle." That's a gas, man.*

GG: *Yeah, we did a thing there. I really enjoyed that.*

LC: *There's gotta be something else in the wind, man. Sticking around Hollywood, you gotta be coming up with some grooves.*

GG: *I got something. Yeah, I got something in the wind, man.*
LC: *Alright, if you're just joining us and I surely hope that you aren't because if you [are], you've missed our interview with Grant Green, who is at the La Casa on Jefferson and Olive. It has been held over 'til the 26th of August and boy, I tell you, that's ample time to catch him, and I surely hope you do 'cause boy, this is a St. Louis cat that's really taken care of a lot of business.*

The Final Comedown, which starred Billy Dee Williams, was a film about an angry black man. Written, produced, and directed by Oscar Williams, it mirrored the emotions of black men in the United States at that time. In one scene, Johnny Johnson, the lead character, declares, "Bitter, baby. I'm not bitter. I was bitter 350 years ago. I'm violent! Hear me, violent." Angry. Violent. By the time America rolled into the 1970s, Johnny Johnson and Grant Green may have had every reason to be both.

My husband has strong views about the soundtrack. "That shit's crazy," he says. "I am certain that Wade Marcus, the guy who composed that shit, must have been standing in the studio wearing a clown suit conducting everyone! It's garbage. It sounds like confusion. It sounds like they were all confused. My daddy was just crazy back then. The one time I put that album on, I kept picking up the needle to move on to the next song. Finally, I just took it off. It was too painful. You'd think they could've put [out] something better than that. They should've been listening to James Brown."

As I continued my research on his father's life, he grew increasingly vocal about the direction his father's career had taken. He was frustrated with the people who benefited then, and who continue to benefit now. His tongue-in-cheek takes on current royalty statements, record companies, and certain musicians were not the kindest. They keep grabbing for his daddy's stuff because they can't create their own, my husband said more than once.

While the reissued CDs and glossy calendars that arrive in the mail are welcomed, they are reminders of the many who are still crawling on the graves of the greats. It is too bad his father is not here to see the comeback, rather than the comedown, he began to say more and more.

10 Six Eggs for Breakfast

"He used to drink this syrup, which was like some kind of depressant, and [with] him doing cocaine and depressing [his system], that probably [led] to his heart trouble."

I once asked my husband what he thinks about when he's listening to one of his father's records, and he told me, "When I hear his music, I don't listen to it to say, 'That's my dad.' I listen to it now to understand what was jazz like back in those days. Where was his state of mind in those days. I try to listen to something he did way back in the early days, and then something he did more recently, like in the '70s, and just to compare the styles. I listen just to understand it, to understand how he played, to understand all his riffs, to understand his style, to understand him. I know that he made some mistakes that damaged his music career... If he could've realized what those mistakes were, he'd probably be living now, and he would've been a lot more successful now.

"I remember so many nights I cried when I heard he died. And then again, that's just the saga of a black musician, man. It's like when they die, people always say that they were taken too soon. There are so many you can list like that. They were just taken too soon. "

Grant Green might have been taken too soon, but before he left here, he had a bigger vision for himself. There were still some things he really wanted to do. This seemed to be especially true after *The Final Comedown* project. On the heels of that production he publicly expressed a wish to arrange and produce. "There's more feeling in it when you put the package together for yourself, without interference from anybody," said Grant, who seemed determined to explore all avenues available to him, including doing live sessions, which would allow him the chance to stretch out. First there was the *Alive!* album taped at the Cliche Lounge in

Shelton Laster, organist who performed on *Live at the Lighthouse*

I miss him. Matter of fact, the other day on that BET thing,* Jazz Central, *I thought I saw him. Did he ever do a gig in St. Lucia? I woke up and I swear at the end of the thing as it was going off, they showed this guy sitting there with these white shoes and white socks. Then they went all the way up, and I saw this guitar—this hollow-bodied guitar—and I looked up and I swear it was Grant. He had sunglasses on. He was wiping his brow, and he wiped the guitar and put the rag over the guitar, so I guess the sun wouldn't hit it. But I'd swear it was him.

Newark, New Jersey, in 1970. Then there was a much-hailed live date he recorded at the Watt's Club in Detroit with Houston Person. And then there was the *Live at the Lighthouse* date recorded in 1972 in Hermosa Beach, California.

Greg "Vibrations" Williams, the drummer on the *Lighthouse* session, was in Grant's band at the time. A spiritual guy, Greg finds great meaning in dreams and says he knew about the date long before Grant announced it to the band.

"I use to dream a lot," he said, sitting cross-legged on the floor of a house in Royal Oak, a Detroit suburb. Holding his drumsticks in his hands, he began to tell about one particular dream in which he saw himself and Grant Green doing a live gig. One day he told Grant about the dream. "Grant didn't say nothing for a while," says Greg. "Finally he said, 'I know. We will be making a live record. We're going to California.' I didn't go to the rehearsal. I stayed in my room. I practiced all day. Grant didn't bother me because he knew what I was getting ready for. Wilton Felder was on the record date. He played saxophone with the Jazz Crusaders. He was playing bass. He could really play. Bobbye Hall was playing congas. She could really play. And then we had the regular band: Shelton Laster, Claude Bartee, myself, and Grant." (Also on the date was vibraharpist George Coleman.)

Shelton Laster says he was called in at the last minute to participate on the date. "Grant said, 'Look, you've got to do the best you can,' and I guess God smiled on me," says Shelton. "I can retain pretty quick. I don't have a photographic memory, but I can retain things. There wasn't a lot of charts there that I could go by, so a lot of things I just had to do by ear. I think I had maybe a week and a half, maybe two weeks to get four albums together, to know every tune on those four albums. He was living on Greenlawn in Detroit. We had a lot of rehearsals at the house. We had the organ up in the living room. We all stayed there and got up at different times of night. If we felt like rehearsing your part, there was never no problem. On our breaks, we'd just eat and relax and then go back to work."

Shelton says while living in Grant's home, he got a chance to really see the musician up close. He saw how Grant would only eat kosher food, and how he loved Neutrogena soap. "He was a character," says Shelton, who also goes by the name of Big Man. "He would say, 'Big Man, you be out on the road, you can brush your teeth with that Neutro! You can do everything with that Neutro, Big Man!' He always told me I was a little militant. He had this walk

The 1998 release of Grant Green's Breakbeats *reflects the record industry's effort to satisfy a younger generation's hunger for old school, funky jazz beats. Courtesy of Blue Note Records, a division of Capitol Records.*

In 1972, Grant Green had all the makings of success—a strong band, several well-received commercial albums, a soundtrack album, and this live album, Live at the Lighthouse. *Courtesy of Blue Note Records, a division of Capitol Records.*

about him, almost like a pigeon-toed walk, and he'd rub his hands together and he'd say, 'This Big Man, he's kind of a militant brother. He's kind of questionable, ain't he Claude?' Him and Claude go way back."

Shelton is grateful to Grant for allowing him to be on the date and for letting the band do "Flood in Franklin's Park," one of his own compositions. With some reluctance, Shelton told the story of how he came up with the tune. "All of us used to smoke that reefer, and by me being on the road, I used to bring home that good smoke. Well, there was a club we played at—the only black jazz club in Springfield at the time—called Jinxy's. The club's parking lot used to flood all the time. One Tuesday, this big electrical storm flooded the parking lot. Jinxy had a son everybody called Frankie, but I used to make him mad. I'd call him Franklin all the time because I'm a teaser. I pulled my van up into the lot next door because the parking lot was so flooded. So here you have all the little—I call them Pepsi Cola pimps—tiptoeing through that water to get to the van to see what I had, and the tune just floated in my head. The construction of the tune—how the notes and things go—are like people [tiptoeing] thru the water trying not to get their feet wet because they're too cute. I just wrote it in the course of like—I don't think it even took five or ten minutes. It just popped into my head just like that."

Shelton went on to describe the atmosphere at the legendary club in Hermosa Beach, California: "The Lighthouse was a very intimate setting. One thing I remember, they had a super large aquarium with big goldfish. I had never seen goldfish that big. A lot of my friends that I grew up with had moved to L.A. So they came down for the recording. We had a lot of support. There were a lot of people hollering and cheering."

"The record was a success for Grant," adds Greg. "It was a big hit. It got three and a half or four stars in *Down Beat*, and Grant was climbing up the ladder like he was supposed to be doing. Me and that brother used to have a lot of fun together playing. He used to tell me, 'I'm going to get you tonight, Vibrations! You ain't got no chance! I'm gonna play and you're gonna fall out! You're gonna faint! He was one of the most feelable guitar players in the world. You could *feel* him a lot. That's what people dug. He played music that you could really feel. He used to put his amp at the back of the stage and turn it all the way up. And then, there was no talking to your woman. If you came there to pick up a woman, you was in the wrong place, because she wasn't gonna hear you and you wasn't gonna hear her. Grant made sure of that. He used to play very hard.

"I remember one time we were in Indianapolis and there were a bunch of white people in the club. They got there before everybody else. Black people had to wait until the second set to get in. So we was playing real hard and people were looking. They had their eyes open in amazement. And one cat just jumped up from the back and screamed real loud, 'Owwww!' Then this cat ran up to the stage, picked up a tambourine from the stage, and shook it at us. He shook it at us and put it back down and ran back to his seat. Grant turned around and looked at me. I said, 'He had the vibrations that time, didn't he?' That was some funny stuff. That let me know that people was into what we were doing though. They could very well get into what we were doing."

Grant also made periodic treks back home to St. Louis. Deanetta James, who use to waitress at La Casa, remembered when he came through her club. James is married to conga player Percy James of the St. Louis band Quartet Trés Bien and took pride in seeing the return of her homeboy. "Grant was clean," Deanetta says. "You never saw Grant looking shabby. He was always clean. And he would just sit on his stool, you know. He had a stool, and he'd just sit on his stool and put you into a different groove."

During that performance at La Casa there was someone special sitting in the audience—Grant's father, Mister Johnny, who was now older and moving slower. Ollie Matheus, the former owner of the Holy Barbarian, sat next to Mister Johnny and recalls watching an especially proud father, who was finally realizing all that his son had accomplished. "I was with his father and, boy, his father was so proud of him," says Ollie. "Me and him sat at the table through the whole show."

After these shows on the road, Grant always hurried back to Detroit. Once he was surprised to find his homeboys waiting for him in the city. "We were just beginning to do things out of town," says Albert St. James, a drummer for the Quarter Trés Bien, a group known for its intricate rhythms and Afro-Latin beats. "We did one engagement in Detroit. We didn't know that the man who owned the club was going to bring us in with Grant Green. And when we got there and saw this sign, 'Grant Green' we were like, 'What!' And Grant run out the door and grabbed us! He hugged us. I never will forget that."

Along with grabbing the reins of his career, Grant tried to make improvements on the home front. By 1973, the three children who had gone with his first wife to Jamaica—Kim, John, and Grant Jr.—came to the States to live with him. "When I finally moved to Detroit to live with him, it was like a dream come true," my husband said. "Detroit [was] the best years of my life. I missed him, y'know? We had so much to catch up on. I loved him more than anybody could love a person. During all of the years that we spent apart from each other, there was something I always longed for, to be around my dad, a father figure. I never had that most of my life. He was always on the road, or he was in California or somewhere."

At the age of eleven, my husband says he was finally able to live with his dad in a normal way, or as normal as living could be with a jazz musician for a father. Band members were frequently in and out of the house. Money wasn't steady. But it was a time when his old man tried to make good. One of the best peacemakers proved to be a minibike for his baby boy. He also bought instruments and placed them in the basement for his children and his band members. "In the basement, we had a lot of instruments. We had like two guitars, and we also had a drum set. I don't know where this stuff came from. But I started playing drums and my brother, Greg, he played the guitar and John was like playing drums, too," my husband says.

During these years, his dad would sometimes sneak him into the local bars where he had gigs. "We always had a table that was like for immediate family. It was up close. I drank soda and I used to watch my dad play. And the way he used to play—the sound had so much feeling. He used to sit there and play and hold his fucking big guitar in his hand, and play this shit, and it was like he never smiled. He used to look at me every now and then and smile, but that's it. He was expressionless, but the sound that came from the guitar had so much expression, so much feeling it was unbelievable. I was overwhelmed. That's when I really started to understand, damn, what this man did for a living. It was awesome.

I wish I had listened more. I wish I had known more. I probably would've been a guitar player myself, but I was never exposed to watching him play, and when I finally started going to his gigs, I was like, 'Man, this is my dad. I love it, man. He's awesome.' This was when he had all of his hair shaved. He was bald!"

Drummer Al St. James and his wife, Sarah, were among the many musician couples with whom Grant Green and his first wife, Ann, spent time in St. Louis. Photo by Sharony A. Green.

On the rare occasions when Grant was not performing, he tried to spend quality time with his children. They recall the night he took them to the drive-in to see *The Exorcist* only to be most freaked out himself. They also remember the time he was driving along an icy highway in Detroit and howled like a ghost after losing control of the car. His screams sent his three boys into a fit of giggles. "I think my father was like a scary chicken kind of person," my husband chuckles.

Today, Grant's kids live in different cities. Greg is in New York. Kim is in Port St. Lucie, Florida, with her mom, stepfather, and other relatives. John is in St. Louis, and Grant Jr. is in Detroit. They don't see much of each other. There are some obvious strains in the family, but much of the pain is unspoken. There were times I believed it was because of this book. I wondered whether I had forced the family to remember things they'd rather forget. "No," my husband once said. "We were already like this."

His father's lifestyle affected them all in different ways. My husband's joy about finally being able to live with his dad was tempered by the reality that he could possibly lose him again. To what, was the question? Drugs. Another gig. These fears weighed heavily on his adolescent mind. "I remember one day me and my dad were

Part of the Green family, from left to right: April Moody, Grant's grandniece; Sharony Andrews Green, author; Ann Moody, Grant's niece; and John Green, Grant's son; 1995, St. Louis.

home and we were playing in the bed," my husband said. "We were wrestling and stuff, and I got up and started running, and he ran after me, and we had these pretty steep steps, and he fell down the steps. I mean he tumbled down the steps. And he fell to the bottom of the steps, and I thought he was having a heart attack. I was really scared 'cause I knew he was always on the road. I was kind of worried about him. To Greg, it was the funniest thing in the world when he fell, but to me, it was funny just a little bit, but then I realized he could've really broke something. I think it was just human nature because I never had spent any kind of substantial time with my father and I wanted to keep him as long as I could."

Greg's stories tend to focus on the lighter side of having a musician for a father. One in particular is quite riveting. As Greg recalls, he was a teenager trying to be a lover-boy. His dad proved that even in old age, he was the real Romeo. "We were in St. Louis and he was playing at La Casa...and there was this waitress there. And here I am, fifteen or sixteen years old. I was a kid, but I meet this waitress and she's nice, and she's an older woman, and she's grown and I want her. So I start talking to this waitress, and I invite her to this party one of my dad's friends had. She comes to the party and for some reason—I should've known something was fishy—my dad was really nice to me. I was in the basement smokin' pot and he didn't say anything. I was like, 'Oh, he's treating me like one of the fellas. I'm grown.' So we're all downstairs smokin' pot and she decided to go upstairs. She had been gone a good fifteen to twenty minutes. She said she was going to the bathroom. After another twenty to twenty-five minutes, a guy said, 'Well, your girlfriend has been upstairs a good while, hasn't she?'" Greg realized that not only had his female friend slipped away, but so had his father. Strangely, earlier in the evening his dad's own girlfriend had gone home. Greg decided to go check on things.

"So I go upstairs, look in the bathroom; she's not in the bathroom. I'm lookin' around the house for her, can't find her, and I walked past this one door that was closed, and in the bedroom I hear all of this [*he mimics heavy sighing*] in the bedroom and I'm like, 'This is not happenin'! This is just not happenin'!' So I go knock on the door and say, 'Man, let me in!' Let me tell you something, it was terrible for a kid. I knew she was in the room with my dad; my heart just broke in two. My little heart was just crushed. So I'm kickin' on the door, and finally he opens the door and he tells me, 'Man, take your clothes off.'" His dad insisted that he now have a turn with the woman. While recounting the story, Greg laughs hysterically. He says in many ways he and his dad were more like two friends than a father and a son.

Greg also shared how when he first got interested in the guitar, and how in the beginning his father was simply not impressed. "I would go to my dad and say, 'Hey man, listen to what I just played,' and 'Check this out,' and I would play it for him and my dad would look at me and say, 'That ain't shit.' Or he would say, 'Man, that ain't nothin' but chicken scratch.' And it would make me upset," says Greg. "I would get mad, and I would go upstairs and I would practice and practice and practice and practice, and you know it took years for me to realize what he was doin', because he came up in a different era than I did and what he was actually doing, I guess, was using psychology on me. If he told me that wasn't shit, either two things were gonna happen: either I was gonna give it up—and if I gave it up then it wasn't for me in the first place—or I was going to practice. So I would go upstairs and practice, and that's the way my dad taught me to play."

By the age of seventeen, Greg's father was letting him play with his band members. "I used to rehearse some of his band members. Like if they got a new keyboard player, or somebody would come in the band—because I knew all of his tunes—I would rehearse the guy. My dad would be upstairs asleep," says Greg, laughing again. "I remember one day I wrote this song, and I started playing it, and my old man comes downstairs and was like, 'Whose song is it? That's a great song.' He thought somebody else had wrote it. So the keyboard player says, 'That's your son's song.' And he was like, 'Really?' So he goes and gets his guitar, and he was like, 'Show me that melody.' So I showed him the melody and stuff, and it was then that I think he started taking me kinda seriously as a player. I remember one time they were playing at the Mozambique and they were playing the song I wrote, and he forgot the melody. I was sitting in the audience just watching. He was like, 'C'mere. C'mere! C'mere!' So I come to the stage and he says, 'Hum that melody in my ears.' So I hummed the melody in his ears so he could remember. He just bent down and I whispered the melody in his ears. It was pretty funny."

But Greg is most proud of the time he and his father performed together on *The Scene*, a Detroit-produced teen dance show. The show, hosted by WGPR-FM deejays Nat Morris and Ray Henderson, was so popular that Jefferson Avenue was bumper to bumper with traffic from the kids determined to meet the celebrities who performed.

Ann Moody, his cousin, also has memories of the good times in Detroit. In fact, going to visit Grant's kids and her other relatives in the city was the first solo trip she and her sister, Jene, would take. "We were visiting my great-grandmother, Mama Maude, who lived in Detroit, and Grant and his kids were also living there, so we went by," says Ann. "And when we got to the house, there were like a lot of musician types there, just hanging out. We sat in the living room, and I remember when Grant came in. He had on this green robe, a green silk-like dressing gown! And he had on house shoes. I don't know what was under the dressing gown because his legs and stuff was showing. He was just this big hunk of a man. I was kind of intimidated because I didn't really know him, but he made me feel right at home when I walked in. He said, 'Hey, girl, you done got big!

The last time I saw you, you was a li'l bitty thing.' He gave me a big hug. He smelled real nice, too, and made me feel very much at ease. We stayed up 'til early the morning, which is really strange because I'm coming from a strict background where kids go to bed at certain times."

The house on Greenlawn was a popular spot not only for musicians, but for the neighborhood kids. The 1970s were still a time when children could stay outside late in the summer and rarely fear a bullet. Friends came over to the Green's house to play basketball and football. It was a musical street. The Hardaways—Stevie Wonder's family—lived next door to the Greens. Life was good. The sounds of the BarKays, the Whispers, and the Emotions floated over the air with the smell of barbecue from backyards. The music in Grant's own home was more versatile. His sons' record collections had everything from Led Zeppelin and Rush to Gino Vannelli and Earth, Wind, and Fire, my husband says. And of course, there was the jazz.

Percy James, St. Louis conga and bongo player, member of Quartet Trés Bien

I am a Muslim. I was turned on by the Honorable Elijah Muhammad. And I'm still turned on by the Honorable Louis Farrakhan. I'm not a vocal cat. I don't get up and make speeches and down people for what their habits are. I am not into that. None of us are into that. You don't hear that from the Muslims of the Nation of Islam. What we're doing is the olive branch, because we got to relate, and that's what Grant did. The last time I seen my brother, he was at Baker's Keyboard in Detroit. I could've cried. Some famous artist didn't show up, so they called Trés Bien, and they called the Grant Green Trio in there, and they had the family in there. It was one of the most beautiful weekends that we ever had. He's sorely missed. You can't replace him. You can't replace a musician. He'll live through guys like myself who can think of yesterday.

But he cannot recall his father ever fully relaxing at home. "He wasn't into sitting outside, looking at the trees and all of that kind of shit. He was a musician. He was playing, trying to make money just to survive. Jazz got lost in the '70s. A lot of jazz people didn't know what to do. The disco was out. Funk was out. These guys were lost."

In 1974, Grant married Karen Duson Wallace, a fair-skinned nurse from Batavia, New York. My husband said he and his brother and sister had no special regard for her, or the women who came before and after her. "She was just another fixture who tried to play the mother role. And we had a mom," my husband says.

Around this time their father began to form bad eating habits and seriously neglect his health. While he still patronized kosher delis and East Indian cafes, he ate unhealthy amounts of food in his own kitchen. "I used to watch him eat like six eggs for breakfast, and then he would have half a slab of beef bacon," says Greg. "When you get to a certain age you really have to take care. The body can only take so much."

In addition to the huge helpings of food he ate, Grant began to snort cocaine, the drug of the '70s. It wasn't hard to come by. As a former cocaine user himself, Greg knows well. "When you play music in this business, there's always drugs around you," Greg says. "You really don't even have to pay for it because when you're playing music, everybody wants to get close to you and be your friend and be cool. They think you're cool because you're a musician, so they want to hang around you, so they give you that shit."

Cocaine wasn't the only thing his father was using, Greg says. He also began taking a certain syrup. "It had codeine in it. Now if you were a junkie and heroin is a downer, you could drink that codeine and it would probably give you that same effect, but I think what he was probably doing [was] what they would call speedballing because it's hard to drink codeine," says Greg, who made special runs to local pharmacists for his father. "We used to get stuff from pharmacists when I was a kid. I remember we used to get like these jugs of pharmaceutical cocaine. We didn't even know the value of the shit. We were young. We used to give the shit away to our friends!" He laughs and then says quietly, "It's a weird thing. You get caught up in that lifestyle and it's hard to break."

My husband says he never knew of his father's drug problems. It was only when he became an adult that he learned about them from Greg. "Greg told me that he had a drug habit, which I never knew of growing up in Detroit because I was at that age where I

never knew much about that kind of stuff, you know," he told me. "And he used to drink this syrup which was like some kind of depressant, and [with] him doing cocaine and depressing [his system], that probably [led] to his heart trouble—that and his bad eating habits."

Grant Green, pictured here in his 1961 **Remembering** *session, was a man of many contradictions. While he adhered to certain teachings of his Muslim faith, he rebuked others, including the one explicitly forbidding the use of drugs. Photo by Francis Wolff, courtesy of Mosaic Images.*

11 Ahead of (His) Time

Of Skinny Ties on London Dance Floors

"He opens up a groove and then opens up a groove and then opens a groove, and so on."

In the beginning, Grant seemed to be managing his family life and the transitions in the industry fairly well. But he was still searching for the right formulas, the right band members, the right home. Filled with conflict, he signed contracts and made deals with other labels like Prestige, Atlantic, Creed Taylor's CTI, KUDU, and Versatile.

While the bulk of his work from the 1970s is generally dismissed, some recordings bear mentioning. *Live at the Lighthouse,* the last he would ever do for Blue Note Records, is vital to any discussion of Grant's second decade as a jazz player. "Jan Jan," in particular, is notable. On it, his dexterity soundly refutes those who say technique was not his bag. How can fingers move like that?

Of the date, Stevie Ray Vaughan once said, "*Live at the Lighthouse* is knocked out. It moves. A lot of people can't keep up to it. It...doesn't rely on effects to get cookin'. This guy plays on a D'Angelico and it's movin'."

But it was *Visions, Green Is Beautiful,* and *Shades of Green* that got radio airplay. On them were popular tunes readily identifiable to the everyday person. Many are funky and telling of his ability to groove. Certainly the one album from this decade that has had the biggest belated impact is *Alive!* The date was recorded on August 15, 1970, at the Cliche Lounge in Newark. Featuring Claude Bartee, William Bivens, Ronnie Foster, Idris Muhammad, and Joseph Armstrong, Grant turns out four tunes that reflect, again, his versatility as a performer, his roots in the blues, and his growing business instincts. Included are the rhythmic Kool & the Gang tune "Let the Music Take Your Mind," the sweet "Time to Remember," and the hopping "Sookie, Sookie." "Sookie, Sookie" could be the song that will place Grant forever in the annals of jazz history. The irony is that it isn't a classical jazz tune, but is the one that finally got his name out there.

When the London-based hip-hop group Us3 lifted riffs of "Sookie, Sookie" from a bootlegged tape, they never knew they would end up with a contract with Blue Note Records and ignite the acid-jazz movement. Their 1993 debut album, *Hands on the Torch*, sold millions of copies worldwide.

Of its success, Idris Muhammad, the percussionist on the "Sookie, Sookie" tune, says, "I hope somebody in the family is getting this money because I ain't gettin' it. They took the rhythm and they took all of Grant's stuff, and they sampled it. Nobody's paying nobody. They's quiet about this shit. But I'm happy that something is happening for him. See, it always happen to us, that we got to get out of here before somebody does something to respect what we've done and why we're here. It's a sad thing, but I hope somebody in the family is reaping the benefit."

I first met Idris in 1996 at the Paddlewheel tribute date for Grant. When I walked into the studio, I saw him from afar, sitting before his drums wearing a colorful knit tam, a black T-shirt, and baggy pants. Proudly, he announced that he was using Art Blakey's cymbals and has done so for twenty-eight years. Between tapings, he would tell the recording engineer "not to lose the bass drum. That's what Grant liked."

When I ask him about Grant, he says, "Ahhh, maannn. You know what a big teddy bear is? That's what he was. He was like a big sweetheart. He'd hug me and squeeze me and we'd talk, and then we'd play somethin' and go run and hug each other. He wasn't only like that with me...he was like that with everybody."

Of the *Alive!* date on which "Sookie, Sookie" appeared, Idris Muhammad has this to say: "It was easy to do. We had this audience that was fantastic. Newark at that time was a fantastic place to record. Everything was live there. All of the guys, they always ask me about [Grant]. All of these cats that I played with—Melvin Sparks, John Schofield—all of these cats ask me about Grant. As a matter of fact, John Schofield wrote another head to 'Sookie, Sookie' and asked me to play the rhythm on the record, but I played a different rhythm. It's on John Schofield's record.

The author pictured at the 1996 tribute session in New York with percussionist Idris Muhammad and her brother-in-law, Greg Green. Photo by Jim Eigo.

It's called 'Cool.' Check it out."

Though Grant could not have possibly known it at the time, his version of "Sookie, Sookie" would eventually bring him some measure of the fame he desperately sought. In the 1980s, one of the best jobs available in the music industry was as a copyright lawyer. This is because many young artists and rappers began to reach back into the archives of record companies to "sample," or digitally fuse, the works of old-school musicians with their own. *Hands on the Torch* was by far one of the most successful of these undertakings. The album featured samples from Blue Note artists like Reuben Wilson, Horace Silver, John Patton, Art Blakey, Lou Donaldson, Herbie Hancock, and Grant, and became the best-selling album in the history of Blue Note Records. I asked Geoff Wilkinson, one of the group's producers, what it was exactly about Grant Green's version of "Sookie, Sookie," which appears on the album, that turned on young English people.

"There was a big kind of jazz dance scene in London in the early to mid-'80s, specifically around '86–'87," he answers.

Idris Muhammad, drummer who played on several dates, including *Green Is Beautiful* and *Alive!*

Whenever I've recorded with Grant, I never needed any music. He never gave me music. He would just say, "Hey, Li'l Bruh. Listen to this." He'd say, "Hey, Li'l Bruh. This is how this song go. Play me a rhythm." And he played the song and I played the rhythm. One time we were doin' a record date and he really wanted to do a certain tune, and Frank and Alfred didn't want to do it, and I knew what it meant to him to do it, but he didn't get frustrated where he threw something down. He just came over to me and said, "Ah, Li'l Bruh, we'll do it on the next date." I don't remember what the tune was, but it was something he really wanted to do. And you know what, he did do it on the next date. And then he did this album with some of the Beatles' tunes. Ahh, he played that music!

"There was a massive kind of revival of interest in the classic Blue Note sound. People were actually dressing up in suits and skinny ties, and clubs were just playing Grant Green, Art Blakey, Horace Silver the whole night. I was lucky to be deejaying at that time, and I got to play a lot of the things. 'Sookie, Sookie' was just a classic dancefloor track. I always described it as one of those kind of James Brown tracks of the jazz dance scene. When we first sampled it, we released it on a track called 'The Band That Played the Boogie.' Back then the album on which 'Sookie, Sookie' appeared was so rare in London. It was just impossible to get hold of, and it had actually been bootlegged. It was such a rare, such a classic thing."

Geoff says, "Ain't It Funky Now," which appeared on Grant's 1970 *Green Is Beautiful* album, was also well received on the dance floors in London. Of Grant's overall playing, Geoff says, "I like the aggressiveness, the way that he can go from playing something really peaceful to playing with aggression. I always describe the first time I ever saw Art Blakey and the Jazz Messengers as kind of witnessing...an iron fist in a velvet glove. It was so powerful and so smooth at the same time. That's what appeals to me in Grant, too."

It was Grant's funky playing on "The Band That Played the Boogie," originally released in September 1991 on Enja Tune

Grant Green and Art Blakey take a breather at a 1962 Blue Note session. Photo by Francis Wolff, courtesy of Mosaic Images.

Records, that took Us3 over the top. "Some of the guys who owned the label were deejays at the local station here," Geoff says. "So we got a lot of airplay, and it kind of became a cult record in London. That was what really got us the deal with Blue Note. An A&R guy in London heard the tune on the radio and he recognized what we used—because we used quite a lot of it—and he called us."

When Blue Note first contacted them, Geoff and his partner, Mel Simpson, feared that they were about to get sued. Instead, the company invited them to rummage even more through Blue Note's dusty archives. Little did they know, this Grant Green tune would make the company a ton of money more than twenty years after it was recorded.

With the release of *Hands on the Torch,* Us3 brought jazz, which went from birth to decline in sixty years flat, to a new generation. "The whole point," says Geoff, "was to fuse jazz and hip-hop together, and show that jazz had relevance to young people in the '90s."

Acid jazz didn't do it on its own, however. The emergence of younger jazz performers like trumpeter Wynton Marsalis and Roy Hargrove helped make jazz in general more relevant for everyone. Suddenly, it wasn't just the old cats from yesteryear cookin', but younger performers who were on the scene. So pervasive was this youth movement that Marsalis, the most visible and influential of these under-thirty musicians, and his peers were featured on the cover of *Time* in 1991. The announcement by Lincoln Center in 1991 that it would make jazz a major component in a mix that included the New York Philharmonic, the Metropolitan Opera, and the New York Chamber of Commerce, as well as the Smithsonian Institution's establishment of a jazz repertory orchestra, was an acknowledgment that jazz as an art form was here to stay.

But some of the young artists and deejays benefited from the revival of interest in the music in a different way than older players like Lou Donaldson and Horace Parlan, who made their mark performing the straightahead stuff. The hip hoppers, in particular, just put new twists on old tunes. Sometimes the originals, like "Sookie, Sookie" were played as is; other times the older tunes were remixed with words or new beats over or underneath the original beats.

Publishers, lawyers, and record companies were quick to capitalize on the public's interest. They saw how jazz music, particularly the music from the 1950s and '60s, could revive a tired industry. The first ones to catch on were veteran jazz producers Michael Cuscuna and Charlie Lourie, cofounders of Mosaic Records. As early as 1983, the two took a chance and purchased the licenses to jazz classics that the bigger record companies had no interest in reissuing. Mosaic reissued more than fifty boxed sets of music by various artists including Nat King Cole and Thelonious Monk. They also issued sets by lesser-known artists

Ike Quebec's 1961 **Blue and Sentimental** *session, on which Grant performs, is among the many albums reissued by Blue Note. Photo by Francis Wolff, courtesy of Mosaic Images.*

like saxophonists Ike Quebec and John Hardee, and guitarist Grant Green. Their company grew from a word-of-mouth setup in a Los Angeles apartment to a full-fledged operation in Stamford, Connecticut. Since it was founded, Mosaic has won a Grammy award, garnered praise from critics as the best label in jazz, and gained almost fanatic devotion from jazz consumers.

GREEN IS BEAUTIFUL
GRANT GREEN

1. **AIN'T IT FUNKY NOW** .... (9:57)
(J. Brown)

2. **A DAY IN THE LIFE** .... (8:55)
(J. Lennon-P. McCartney)

3. **THE WINDJAMMER** .... (5:40)
(E. N. Creque)

4. **I'LL NEVER FALL IN LOVE AGAIN** .... (6:40)
(From the musical production "Promises, Promises")
(B. Bacharach-H. David)

5. **DRACULA** .... (6:03)
(E. N. Creque)

PERSONNEL:
Blue Mitchell – trumpet
Claude Bartee – tenor sax
Emanuel Riggins – organ
Earl Neal Creque – organ (on "The Windjammer" only)
Grant Green – guitar
Jimmy Lewis – Fender bass
Idris Muhammad – drums
Candido Camero – conga
Richard Lendrum – bongo

PRODUCED BY FRANCIS WOLFF
Recorded by Rudy Van Gelder
Cover Illustration and Design by Bob Venosa
Reissue Design by Patrick Roques
Recorded in Englewood Cliffs, New Jersey on January 30, 1970.
Originally issued as Blue Note BST 84342

Recorded in 1970, **Green is Beautiful** *was one of Grant's many attempts to play on his name in his song and album titles. Courtesy of Blue Note Records, a division of Capitol Records.*

"You can see the dry tears on the stationery thanking us for continuing to put out vinyl," Lourie once said.

Jazz isn't the only music being recycled; so is funk. Thousands of James Brown and George Clinton samples have been featured on albums by rappers and young R&B artists, effectively reviving the careers of these two funk masters. Ironically, Grant saw the magic in that music at the time. He liked a good groove. He knew how to get inside of it and tear it up, even though then critics dismissed his efforts as lame excursions. It may be that he was simply ahead of his time. In the *All Music Guide to the Blues,* Michael Erlewine chastises critics for suggesting that Grant's work from this period was typically commercial, and thus of little value. The fact is, he was also a pioneer of funk. It was just that he was a jazzman doing it. The groove was there. Critics just couldn't see it. Or feel it.

Writes Erlewine, "Critics only seem to know how to rate what stands out. This won't work for groove music. In groove, the idea is to lay down a groove, get in it, and deepen it. Groove masters always take us deeper into the groove. These artists are our windows into the groove, and their hearts become the highway over which the groove can run. They reinvest. And we ride the groove. This is why jazz critics have either passed...over groove masters like Grant Green and Stanley Turrentine or heard something, but did not know what to make of what they heard (and felt). If music is not viewed as such an intellectual thing (something to see) but more of a feeling kind of thing, then groove masters can be appreciated. You may not see the groove masters, but you sure can feel them. In groove, the solo (and all else) only exists if it adds to the groove. Witness Grant Green's incredible single-note repetitions. Who would ever think to do that? You wouldn't dare think of that. It is done by pure feeling."

Erlewine expresses surprise about how many encyclopedias fail to mention musicians like Stanley Turrentine or Grant Green. He hails producer Bob Porter and Bob Rausch of *Cadence* magazine as being exceptions. He credits recording engineer Rudy Van Gelder as being another preeminent groove expert, saying that more than half of all great soul jazz sessions were recorded by Van Gelder. "The next time you hear some real groove music, in particular if there is a Hammond organ on it, just check the album for this engineer's name," Erlewine writes.

But Grant Green is the ultimate groove giant, says Erlewine. "He is so far in the groove that it will take decades for us to bring him out in full. He is just starting to be discovered. To get your attention and make clear that I am saying something here, consider the singing voice of Bob Dylan. A lot of people say the guy can't sing. But it's not that simple. He is singing. The problem is that he is singing so far in the future that we can't yet hear the music. Given enough time, enough years, that gravel-like voice will sound as sweet to our ears as any velvet-toned singer. Dylan's voice is all about microtones and inflection. For now that voice is hidden from our ears in time so tight that there is no room (no time) yet to hear it... Someday everyone will be able to hear it, because the mind will unfold itself until even Dylan's voice is exposed for just what it is—a pure music.

"Billie Holiday is another voice that is filled with microtones that emerge through time like an ever-blooming flower. You (or I) can't hear the end or root of her singing, not yet anyway. As we try to listen to Holiday (as we try to grasp that voice), we are knocked out by the deep information there. We try to absorb it and before we can get a handle on her voice (if we dare listen!)

she entrances us in a delightful dream-like groove and we are lost to criticism. Instead we groove on and reflect about this other dream that we have called life. All great musicians do this to us. Grant Green's playing at its best is like this too. It is so recursive that instead of taking the obvious outs we are used to hearing, Green instead chooses to reinvest—to go in farther and deepen the groove. He opens up a groove and then opens up a groove and then opens a groove, and so on. He never stops. He opens a groove and then works to widen that groove until we can see into the music, see through the music into ourselves. He puts everything back into the groove that he might otherwise get out of it. He knows that the groove is the thing and that time will see him out and his music will live long."

With this essay, Erlewine seems to be ushering people who struggle with jazz music towards a player like Grant Green. While Grant's music has been called "deceptively simple," it is in fact not. It is complex, but even its complexity is accessible to almost anyone, especially someone who digs the blues. Writes Erlewine, "You can always head back to the solid ground of blues if you can't get into the jazz. Blues and jazz are not mutually exclusive. Blues in jazz has been a thrilling ride (groove) for me and I have found a whole new music that satisfies much like the blues satisfy."

Rap has played a pivotal role in changing how we hear music, period. Generation X-ers have been exposed to significant recording directly as a result of acid jazz, hip-hop, trip-hop, and other electronic and techno recordings. It is the beat young people are obsessed with. Jazz is no longer a music to sit down to in a smoky club with a Hennessey in hand. It is something to groove to again. When Blue Note Records reissued five vinyl LPs from its funk era in limited editions of 3,000 each, the albums, including *Alive!*, sold out immediately. Two tunes from that album—"Sookie, Sookie" and "Down Here on the Ground," reworked by A Tribe Called Quest—were easily big grooves on the dance floors of clubs worldwide.

Those in the business of promoting and selling old-school music saw the money that could be made from this younger audience, and no one was surprised when Blue Note released a

Bill Heid, organist who sat in with Grant during the 1970s

When Grant Green died, I used to go over to his house on Greenlawn, park my car, smoke a joint and just sit there and reflect. The last time I saw Grant would have been at Baker's Keyboard Lounge in 1977. I remember he was still smoking squares. He had a lot of kids playing in that band. These guys were too young to even be in the joint. He was playing a little funk. I don't know if he got these guys because he was paying small money. Maybe that was the deal. I remember once I sat in with Grant at this joint down on Joy and Livernois. It's what we called "bash out clubs." These chitlin' joints where the club owner has the grand illusion of bashing out a wall and having a funk band on one side and a jazz band on the other. Orange chairs everywhere and those crazy mirrors. Those joints are like Coney Island, they're so bizarre. It's funny, I always tell white people, "If you go to Paris and you want to stand under the Eiffel Tower and eat a Big Mac, that's like the highlight of your silly, meaningless lives as far as experiencing culture, 'cause if you could go up into one of the chitlin' joints and just see these bizarre orange chairs everywhere, and gaudy chandeliers, and just watch the way these people carry on and behave, it's just nutty." You can watch the travel guide on the Travel cable network to stand under the Eiffel Tower and look for a Big Mac. You go in those chitlin' joints, you'll see shit that no white man has ever seen before.

CD of Grant Green playing jazz standards and then turned around and released a CD of his "breakbeats."

Thankfully, today's musicians themselves, at least the ones who are still living, have been able to also capitalize on the public's appreciation. Early on in my research, Reuben Wilson told me how he was headed to Ireland, where his 1969 *Love Bug* album was a dance floor hit. The fact that Europeans and other foreigners appreciate jazz more than Americans is old news. It is widely known that many black artists sought refuge in German and French nightclubs, seeking the appreciation their comrades back home did not offer. It is not accidental that those on foreign soil would be responsible in part for the rebirth of jazz. Blue Note gave Us3 free reign to sample the company's extensive library of landmark jazz albums not only because the music sounded good, but because its two English producers had a thorough knowledge of Blue Note's history and jazz in general.

In 1994, producer Nellie Hooper included Grant Green's "Down Here on the Ground"— also from *Alive!*—on Madonna's *Bedtime Stories* album. Purists may be moaning, but jazz has made exceptional headway into the pop culture. And Grant Green is slowly getting the commercial success he longed for.

But by the mid-1970s, it was evident that he would never have another hit like *Visions*. But he kept working even as disco reared its glitzy head, tripping up many in the industry, not just jazz musicians. Grant could still play, but everyone could see he was moving slower and growing increasingly bitter. Bill Heid, an organist I met in 1994 at the Montreux Jazz Festival in Detroit, confirms this. He ran into Grant in Newark.

"I was playing at the Key Club, and Grant was playing across the street at this place called the Cadillac," says Bill speaking from his home in Allen Park, just outside Detroit. "It was the first time I'd met him. Naturally, I was awed just because I'd heard his records for years with Larry Young and John Patton and Herbie Hancock. There was [a] song off this album *Got a Good Thing Going* called "The Yodel." It's like a 24-bar blues that had this little melody and it sounded like a yodel. Grant and John Patton would play this melody in unison with this crazy-like tempo, almost like a New Orleans funeral march tempo. The whole album was really great. So I approached Grant, introduced myself, and said, 'I'm playing at the Key Club right across the street here, and on one of my breaks, it would be a tremendous honor just to sit in and play one song with you.' Grant was being friendly, but at the same time he figured, 'Well, this young white boy probably ain't happening.' He said, 'Well, I don't know if you know any of my material.' I said, 'Well, Grant, I know all the stuff that you did with John Patton, some of the stuff with Larry—because Larry Young's stuff was so deep—but there's one tune that's just so hip that you did with John Patton called “The Yodel,” and I would just love to play that bad boy with you.’

“So he just kind of mumbled, but he came over on one of his breaks and heard our little group. We had an organ trio—a guitar player out of Pittsburgh, my brother George playing drums, and myself playing organ. He bought a beer and he was sitting there. These were the old-time, intimate joints where the bar was built around the stage. So he heard us play something, and he had this big grin on his face. He really loved what we were doing, and he looked up at me after the first song and I’ll never forget these exact words. He says, ‘Can I get that Yodel with y’all?’ I says, ‘Of course!’”

So his majesty could fight back. He could remember. He could take a compliment. And he could never turn down an opportunity to play the music he loved. But one reality persisted. His name was George Benson.

12 The Final Comedown The Mid- to Late 1970s

"He was somebody that was just kinda tired of a lot of stuff."

The song that took George Benson over the top was "Masquerade." What this meant to Grant Green is mere speculation. One thing is certain, however; Grant was provoked. In 1975, he decided to get a new manager to help manage his career and his life—Jay Glover. Jay, who had previously worked with Larry Young, saw Grant at a nightclub on the East Coast and decided to introduce himself. "The musicians retired to the dressing rooms, and I was invited into the back room to meet [Grant]," Jay recalls. "I had asked to be introduced to him because I had always liked his music. We instantly became friends because Grant was an independent person and very outspoken about how blacks were ripped off in the music industry, especially jazz musicians. And he was specific about that. He had complained strongly about how jazz musicians—the black ones—were ripped off and held back by white managers, producers, record company executives, what have you. And because I was a young black American working as a manager with artists who were equally as famous as Grant, Grant thought it was great. In fact, he said to me, 'We need people like you in the business because your being a black American, you can be trusted.'"

Grant hired Jay, who moved to Detroit. He says he was not only there to look after Grant, but to help with Grant's children, particularly Grant Jr., who was just a teenager. My husband has a vague memory about Jay's presence in the house. He doesn't recall Jay living there full-time. However, Jay insists, "Whenever Grant would go traveling, I would not go. I would stay there in the house because he'd ask me to. He wanted me to look out for Junior."

Jay says he saw firsthand how the business was affecting Grant's mind and his music. Others began to see things that concerned them, too. The most puzzling thing was Grant's growing paranoia. "A lot of times he was kind of paranoid, saying, '*They* were out to get' him," says Shelton Laster, who performed on the *Lighthouse* album. "He'd want to move here. 'Let's drive here. Let's go this way, let's go that way'—different things."

Who "they" were, and why they were "after him" was unclear. The easiest guess is that "they" were white music industry executives, who had serious problems with Grant's being a black Muslim. St. Louis percussionist Percy James passionately confirms the troubles facing black musicians, particularly the ones who were Muslim. "I bear witness! I bear witness!" says Percy one afternoon when my husband and I visited his home in St. Louis. "There were letters sent out, my brother, letters sent out! And here I am breaking record attendance at the Lighthouse. I have broken records at the London House. I broke the record in the Detroit arena, you know what I'm saying? I remember Ahmad Jamal came over to talk with us and called us downstairs to read the letter that says, 'Do not hire these brothers because they are black Muslims.' We were making money, but he was showing us what was out there."

Percy James, St. Louis–based percussionist and member of Quartet Trés Bien, recalled the difficulties facing the black musician. Photo by Sharony A. Green.

Jay says he is also certain who "they" are. "The white American Jews who run the record industry," he says. "And I know who they are because whenever

Grant wanted to negotiate a contract, he sent me to talk to them, and they'd tell me to go back and tell him to give up his religion. And they didn't know that I was a Muslim because I never told anybody. They wanted to get Grant because Grant was an organizer. A lot of musicians looked up to Grant because Grant would say, before they'd give him a ham sandwich, he would go and dig ditches. Do you know why Grant did not get everything that was due him? Because Grant was devout Muslim. Do you know that Grant Green was Elijah Muhammad's favorite musician? Louis Farrakhan and all of them knew him because many times when Louis Farrakhan, Muhammad Ali, and others had a wedding, a rally of some type or whatever, Grant would be invited to play the music because Grant would attract a lot of people. And then they'd start trying to convert them."

Deanetta James, Percy's wife, says that many of the world's greatest jazz musicians were practicing

Seeing the cover of **Born to Be Blue**, *which laid among other CDs on her mother-in-law's floor, first piqued the author's interest in Grant Green's life. Courtesy of Blue Note Records, a division of Capitol Records.*

With its alternately soothing and majestic playing, **Idle Moments**, *recorded in 1963, is considered an essential Grant Green recording. Courtesy of Blue Note Records, a division of Capitol Records.*

Joshua Breakstone, guitarist who recorded *Remembering Grant Green* (Paddlewheel and Evidence Records)

This is pretty much the story about me and Grant. I'll read from what I had previously prepared for a radio interview. It says, "The first time I heard jazz was about 1970. I'm not certain of the date, but I do remember that I was riding on Route 22 in Union, New Jersey, U.S.A. in my friend Ralph Douglas's Volkswagen Beetle at the time. The music was Lee Morgan's **Search for the New Land**. *Even though it was the excitement generated by Lee Morgan's fiery trumpet-playing that sparked my initial interest in jazz, Grant Green's playing was by no means lost on me that day either. Despite being a very young guitarist with only a small amount of experience playing rock, I was impressed by the fact that Grant was right there playing the melodies with the horns, and just like the horn players, playing single-note melodies. Many years elapsed however before I truly came to appreciate and admire the guitar playing of Grant Green. Early on I listened exclusively to horn players, and when my attention did finally turn to guitarists I gravitated toward those who exhibited more apparent technical muscle than Grant. Over a time though, my values changed as I came to understand and appreciate the music more, and Grant came to be the guitarist I've listened to more than any other."*

Muslims, and their spiritual beliefs came out in the music. She recalls seeing Sonny Stitt during her days at La Casa in St. Louis. "When Gene Ammons passed, it left Sonny in a terrible state because they were very good friends," Deanetta says. "And he was just drinking and drinking because at that time he had lost his best friend, Gene. One day at a matinee, before he went onstage, he prayed. I said Sonny, 'What is it?' Sonny said, 'I always pray to my God before I make my appearances.' Plus he said, 'I am praying for my best friend, Gene Ammons, who has passed and left me.' Sonny was a Muslim. Most of your jazz musicians were Muslims. They were peaceful people. They played peaceful music. The music would just grab you, and it would just put you in a peaceful state. I remember people saying, 'If we couldn't pray together, we can all play together.' Jazz was like that."

Grant Green was clearly a man looking for answers, and his dedication to some, if not all, the tenants of the Muslim faith reflected this. He also went to others for advice, for feedback, and for clues on how to get through what were evidently hard times. Herbie Holland, the Prestige promoter, recalls getting a phone call from Grant one evening. "One night I was in Jersey, and I got this call real late," Herbie says. "It was Grant, and he said, 'Hey, look. I've got this opportunity to go with CTI, and what do you think about it?' It kind of impressed me because, wow, the guy was asking me. I told him I thought it was a pretty good idea because I knew at the time CTI was real popular. I told him I thought it would be a good move because he would at least get the promotion, but he would have to take care of the business end."

While Grant would work with Creed Taylor and others, for the second half of his career he never settled anywhere too long. Why he didn't isn't clear. Was it that the music was changing? Was it in fact his religion? Was it his drug habit? Was it his lifetime struggle between his art and home life?

The one constant, besides his guitar, seemed to be a woman by his side. By 1977, his marriage to Karen Wallace, the nurse, had gone sour and he had begun dating a woman named Dorothy Malone. Malone would be the woman by his side on the fateful day he died two years later. Like Karen, Dorothy was light-skinned. An alright-looking woman, people said. Kinda feisty though. She took care of business.

Pete Gazes, a guitar player who befriended Grant around that time, recalls that Dorothy always accompanied Grant to his gigs in Charleston, South Carolina, a city in which Grant was becoming as much a fixture as he had in Detroit. By this time, however, he was not playing with the same intensity and seemed to be on his last legs. But the friendship, and even the compassion, he extended toward Peter, then a troubled young white college kid, offers an indication that while Grant may have been angry at the white executives at the helm of the music industry, he had not dismissed the entire race. "I was in college, and it had real strange effects on me. I just became a little too academic for a while," says Peter, who hung out at a local club where he saw Grant play. He overheard that Grant needed a lift back to his motel. Peter volunteered to be his chauffeur.

Besides his guitar, Grant Green, pictured here in the 1962 Nigeria *session, had another love—women. "He'd drive the girls crazy," St. Louis drummer Joe Charles recalled. Photo by Francis Wolff, courtesy of Mosaic Images.*

"I heard that he needed a ride to the West Ashley part of Charleston. That's like a borough of Charleston that had motels, and these club owners, especially back then, always tried to cut corners, not showing musicians the respect that they deserved," he says. "They would stick them way out. I think this was a Motel 6. That would have discouraged anybody. Someone had told him that I lived in the West Ashley area of Charleston and so I gave him a ride. He left his guitar in the back of my car, a D'Aquisto, and he didn't know me from Adam. I had an old AMC Hornet back then." Peter chuckles.

The next morning, Peter discovered the guitar and returned it. From then on, whenever Grant came to town, he asked Peter to be his personal driver. "He had a good sense of humor, and certainly he was a fine person, but I tell you I had a lot of talks with him about his disillusionment," says Peter. "I think that was something that was reflected when you saw him. He was somebody that was just kinda tired of a lot of stuff. He talked about the music business in particular. He just really thought that they were pirates, and he told me at one point that George Benson had just signed the contract with Warner Brothers, and he [said] that George wasn't going to be making that money, that someone else was making it."

Peter says he never saw any signs of drug use, but he had his suspicions. "There had been some indications that maybe he was using something, but I'll tell you he never, ever would let me see that side of him. He was a protective person, very protective of people he cared about. He didn't want to influence anybody. There was a resignation to him, but there was a lot of dignity and respect for other people. For instance, I mean, I was a lousy bass player then, and he had me audition for him. He told me to come to his motel room, and I came over with a bass guitar and a little amplifier, and he sat at the edge of his bed in his underwear and he said, 'Play me something.' And you know, I played some lines and stuff very badly 'cause I was just starting and didn't have any concept of what I was supposed to do, but he never told me how bad I was. We just never talked about it after that. That was the type of person he was. But I was a little better blues harmonica player—and this was another gift or act of kindness—he would let me sit in with the band and play the blues, whether it was 'Stormy Monday' or something like that."

Peter says Dorothy was always around, always by Grant's side. "They appeared to be very close and she was a nice person. She seemed to take care of his affairs, and she seemed very loving and caring with him. I remember one time we went to Western Sizzlin' Restaurant, and she would just kind of tease him a lot. You know, like give him a hard time about losing his hair, rubbing his head and stuff like that."

Her attention and love were not enough. Grant's spirit and whole body seemed to be breaking down. The last time Grant came to town, Peter says he complained of having a toothache and really needing a doctor.

"I didn't even see him when he was in town that time and now, of course, I regret it," says Peter. "He called me about a toothache, and I have a cousin [who's] a dentist and I made arrangements at the last minute, which you know with a dentist isn't easy. So anyway I was going to pick him up and take him to the dentist, but he said to give him another half hour, so I called my cousin back and said, 'Look, can you push this back a half hour?' Well, you know he wasn't nuts about it, but he went on with it. So anyway, when it was time to go again, Grant asked me to put it back another half hour, which I couldn't. I think his health was getting bad at that point."

So was his will to live.

Jay, his manager, says he and Grant would take long drives from his Detroit home and just talk. "Many times, like on a weekend when he was off, he would just pull the car out and we'd drive down to Ohio somewhere. Just to be out on the highway for two or three hours, just talking and planning. Grant was always a cheerful guy, like a comedian. It would be nonstop laughing. And then he started to complain about how he didn't feel well, and I noticed that his movements were slow. I think he knew he was going to die because one day when we were riding in the car, just the two of us, he reached over and he grabbed my hand. And I said, 'Well, Grant, what's the matter?' And he said, 'Jay, I want you to promise me that if something should happen to me, you'll see that my body gets back to St. Louis.' We were in New York. And I said, 'Why are you talking like that? Nothing's going to happen to you.' And he said, 'I'm thinking about putting this guitar down, and I probably won't pick it up again.' Grant was saying to me, 'Jay, you're my friend, you're my brother, you're my manager. And you understand Islam. You know me. The worst nightmare I have is that once I die and close my eyes, these people are going to give me a Christian funeral. I don't want that.' He stopped the car and grabbed me and said, 'Jay, promise me that you'll see that my body gets back home and that they don't do no Christian ceremony over me, because they'll do it. Those St. Louis people, they're like that because they don't understand.' And I said, 'Okay Grant, I promise.' He said, 'No. Promise me that if something happens to me, you're not going to just run away and act like you don't know me.' I said, 'No, Grant. I give you my word.' And I did it because then it dawned on me that Grant knew that he was dying. What person talks about going to the cemetery but a dying person? No person who's living even wants to think about the cemetery, right?

"But because of my experience in the military, being around dying men, I knew that Grant was on his way out. And I started to tell his children, especially his sons, that they'd better start getting their act together. See, being a musician of his caliber, Grant made a lot of money. And of course he wanted to compensate for being away by giving the children everything they asked him for. Being a father, I knew that a father can be a father, but he can't be a mother. And he was trying to be both. Their mother was in Jamaica, and he was making a mess of it. But he was trying, and I admired him for that because you know what they say about black men who have children and don't take care of them. Grant could have been in Las Vegas or anywhere he wanted to be. But when he finished working, he rushed back home like a mother. Toward the end, Grant was not playing up to his best. The club owners knew this and they started to pay Grant less and less. Sometimes they didn't even pay him."

Mark Whitfield, guitarist who participated on the Japanese CD *A Tribute to Grant Green* (Paddlewheel and Evidence Records)

I didn't really discover Grant's music until after I had gotten into college. A fellow student of mine, someone that lived in the dormitory, said, "Man, you haven't heard Grant Green? Well, you need to check this out." He put it on, and that was my introduction to Grant's playing. I had already been listening to George Benson, and I was sort of familiar with Grant's music via George Benson because there's so much of Grant's playing in George's playing, and when I finally heard Grant it was amazing. I realized he was the source of a lot of things that George was playing, and since then I've gone about collecting his records and learning his music, and most of all I'm listening to his recordings and talking to people that knew him. The most important thing about Grant was his feel and how he made the notes dance.

13 Over a Caddy Carrying a U-haul, He Fell

"He was the happiest man you ever saw."

In the middle of April 1978, Grant went into Opal Recording Studio in New York to record what would be his last album, *Easy*. Released on Versatile Records, the album featured quite a respectable assembly of musicians: Hank Crawford on alto and baritone saxophone; Jorge Dalto on piano; Buster Williams on acoustic and electric bass; Karen Joseph on piccolo, flute, and alto flute; Mario Sprouse on piano; Doug Wilson on drums; Wayne Morrison on electric guitar; a man called Shanimba on percussion; John Faddis and Lew Soloff on trombone; Mark Shuman on cello; and Anahid Ajemian, W. Sanford Allen, Paul Gershman, and Matthew Raimondi on violin.

Many of the songs on the album, especially the Commodore tunes like "Easy" and "Three Times a Lady," are eerily sorrowful, almost prophetic. The album appeared to be Grant's last gasp for air. It was unequivocally commercial.

"That was the secret of his success," Jay says, though many would question his view. "Grant would listen to the radio. He would listen to Top 40 radio, and he would listen for the ballad that made No. 1. I recall we were sitting in the house one day after Billy Joel had just done the song "Just the Way You Are." And we were listening to it, and Grant turned the radio up and said, 'Hey Jay. Listen to this.' He said, 'It's a winner, ain't it?' And within a few months, Grant recorded it and it became a hit. He did other Top 40 songs like "Love on a Two-Way Street" and "Never Can Say Goodbye."

During our interview, Jay gave the impression that the more commercial sound Grant had in his last days was a goal, something to celebrate and not a downfall. He called the commercial tunes Grant performed "hits." I have often wondered what makes a jazz song a hit. Certainly jazz songs will never, at least in my lifetime, be hits the way "Thriller" was for Michael Jackson. The music that we

In his happier days, Grant Green performs with ease in the 1962 **Oleo** *session. Photo by Francis Wolff, courtesy of Mosaic Images.*

call jazz, while powerful, does not have that kind of widespread acceptance.

Defining what "jazz" is could ruffle many feathers. I recall the most passionate campaign against the word came from Rama Lomax, the woman who deejayed at the Palm Cafe. "Have you ever seen a little thumb piano?" Rama asks in a whisper. "That's where the piano originated. I have one. It's about this size. It came from Africa."

I nod.

"And have you seen the wooden flutes that the brothers play over there?" she asks. "Well, it influenced other flutes. I know this because I grew up in Canada. I'm an African-Canadian, and everybody was in Canada. The Scots, Irish, and everybody. We were the only black family in the immediate area. On holiday we would dance with the kilts and stuff. But I didn't get my education until after I left school, and it was then I realized that the Scots got the bagpipe from Africa. So it's all related. Let's face it, even this country became enamored with the only original music created in America—because everything else was imported, the classics and what not—which was put together by African Americans. It's that which they call jazz! I prefer to call it the black experience in sound, as opposed to jazz. Some people think it's a misnomer just like the word Negro was a misnomer for us. How enamored they are and how impressed those people—Europeans—are with our music and the improvisational aspect of it, like a Grant Green who'll sit down and play just whatever comes in his head. Some people think you can't play unless you have notes in front of you. Listen, when the brothers started playing music in Africa, they didn't have any European lines in front of them did they? They didn't have nothing. They just played what came to their head. If you watch television, you still see them sometimes in the villages. They don't have any notes in front of them. Give me a break, for heaven's sake. Everything is innate. It's inherent. Jazz comes from the mind, comes from the head. Erroll Garner told me—he was a good friend of mine—that he refused to learn how to read music. He didn't want to learn how to read because he was afraid he was going to upset whatever it is that he had that was so unique and phenomenal as far as his style is concerned. He didn't want anybody messing with him. He could play anything he wanted to play. Same thing with Thelonious Monk. I remember one time watching Thelonious. He played the same melody over and over. And some European American finally said to him, 'How do you do that?' He said, 'How the hell do I know? I just do it.' So, am I bragging?"

I laugh. She looks away, resigned to one reality: "There's nothing we can do about it in terms of changing the word though. *Jazz*."

I ask her if she had a choice, which word she would prefer.

She pauses. "I don't know." After thinking for a moment, she says, "OK, I'll tell you what the word is. It's *classic*! Any music that lasts, anything that lasts, is a *classic*. *Classic music* is what I would call it. But there would have to be a differentiation because of what we now call classical music. We'd have to say *African American classical* if you really want to get specific."

I ask her whether she has heard of the term "acid jazz."

"Acid jazz?" she says. "Acid jazz? My dear, acid will burn your brain out!"

Grant, too, had much impatience with how people defined jazz. In the interview with Patricia Sweeting, the young college woman, he was asked to define his music.

"How would you classify your music? Modern jazz, or what would you call it?" she asked him.

"Music."

"Music?"

"Yeah, man. I don't like to put titles on it because I...might play some jazz, some rock, or whatever."

"So you don't limit yourself?"

"Yeah, so if I don't limit myself then—"

"It appeals to more people?"

"That's right. That's right," said Grant.

Whether he actually liked doing commercial songs, and whether those songs showed his best skills, may be a moot debate. Those in the industry, if no one else, knew what he was made of long before his body gave out.

Says Wendell Harrison, "Everybody was talking about Grant Green was a bebopper. But he made a lot of money doing the crossover thing, and it wasn't too far from the straightahead stuff...he tried to do something in his later years...but it was damn near too late because his career had gone down...he was up in age. See, when you're in the music business, if you don't make your impression and take care of business when you're young, you can forget about it."

Shortly after recording *Easy*, Grant suffered a stroke that left him temporarily paralyzed on the left side of his body. My husband says he will never forget the fall of 1978, when his father became ill. "I was about sixteen. He was in New York because he had just made an album, *Easy*. Me, him, and Greg were in New York together. Someone called my Aunt Helen's house and [said] he'd a stroke, and I was petrified. I didn't know much about strokes, and I thought a stroke meant that he was going to die. I thought that he really wasn't going to make it."

When he got to the hospital, his father was conscious, but very afraid. "He was more scared than I was," my husband says. "He was

George Benson, singer-guitarist

You know, everybody started dropping like flies, you know. We lost everybody. Wes died in '68. John Coltrane died in '68. Bits and pieces of people started keeling over, you know what I'm saying? All the big-name people. Those guys came from a very strange era. We didn't know that cigarettes killed. Nobody was telling us that. And all that liquor every night and eating before you go to bed. We'd eat dinner at three and four o'clock in the morning. We would go to a place like Wells and eat chicken and waffles, and Wes and them cats would eat grits with sausages and pork chops and go to sleep on that every night. We really abused our bodies, you know. But we didn't know any better. Nobody ever told us that you shouldn't eat like a horse and then go to sleep. The thing about Grant is that he wasn't recognized as a genius when he was alive except by people who experienced him, who knew him. A select few recognized his genius. In white circles, they didn't think of him at all. They didn't give him any respect at all. Now they do. It's amazing. They have gone back and discovered how great he was. If they had known what they know now about Grant Green, he would have been a wealthy man today. He was a great teacher. He was an unsophisticated man except on the guitar. On the guitar, he was a master and a genius, although his education was not obvious when you spoke to him. Everybody misses him. But to me, he's not dead, because I still remember the essence of the man. I play his records all the time here. We were playing them the other night. A friend of mine and I were putting them on and listening to how lyrical he was and how beautiful the phrasing was. I think I'm going to go back and restudy them again, because every time I do that, I pick up something different that I didn't pick up the first time.

really down and out. He had IVs in him. He was partially paralyzed on his left side, so he was worried about playing again. But he was more scared of being in the hospital itself than he was scared of dying."

I tell him that most people are afraid of death.

"Yeah, yeah, but he was really, really scared. And I was there most of the time, and he would ask me not to leave him and to stay there with him and stuff like that. He was real depressed and real sad and real weak, and he just told me don't leave him."

Some believe Grant's attempts to satisfy the marketplace by recording those kinds of albums did more harm than good. "[I] remember reading interviews and things; he seemed a little bit bitter toward the end," says Adrian Ingram, the London jazz professor. "There was one interview in particular where somebody said, 'Well, do you play any octaves like Wes Montgomery?' and he said, 'Correction. I play octaves like Grant Green.' But again, it depends on what you read into that. I mean that can be taken on many levels, can't it? He could be saying, 'I played the way I played,' in a humble sort of way, 'That's me.' On another level, he could say, 'Well, who's Wes Montgomery? I'm equally as good, and I'm Grant Green, you know?'"

The extent of Grant's inner pain and how he dealt with it during his last years is difficult to know. Some friends insist he was doing drugs until the very end. Others say emphatically that he was not. "From August 1975 up until I saw them put him in the ground, I was with him all the time. I knew everything that he was doing because I was the only person that he confided in. He was not messing with anything," maintains Jay Glover, his manager.

Lou Donaldson offers another view. He remembered going to Harlem Hospital in 1978, shortly after Grant had the stroke. He was reportedly hospitalized for ten weeks. "He had a girl—she was supposed to be one of the best doctors, and she would say, 'Ooh, I don't know what's wrong with Grant. We can't figure out what's wrong with him.' I started to tell her, 'Shit, I know what's wrong with him.' But I didn't have nothing to do with it. It was pitiful. I said, 'Grant, are you sure these guys aren't bringing some stuff in here to you?' and he'd be like, 'No, baby.' I used to go and see him every day. But man, I'm pretty sure he was. I didn't see him actually using it. But shit, didn't they still make it? If they still made it, he was probably still using it," says Lou. "Same way with Miles. All them cats used to say, 'You know, Miles straightened up,' and I said, 'I doubt that.'"

While Grant was recovering from his stroke, the doctors discovered something—a blood clot near his heart. They ordered a triple bypass. Grant refused.

Says Jay, "He was told he would not live thirty days. When the doctor said this, Grant looked at the doctor and looked at me and said, 'Jay, tell these people to give me my clothes.' And he left the hospital that day. But he could barely make it. The doctor also came to Grant's hotel room and told him the same thing. George Benson was standing right there. It was George, his wife, and me. George Benson, by then, had become rich. But he was saying to Grant, 'Grant, this is not right. You're a better guitar player than me. But they have made me greater than you. It's not right, Grant.' He said, 'I can't go around saying I'm the No. 1 jazz guitar player and I know that you're the No. 1.' George was telling Grant, 'Anything you need, man. I'll spend all my money to help you to get up out of here because it pains me to see you here.'"

George honored his word. Shortly after Grant got up from his hospital bed, he made the infamous long trip to California for yet another gig at the Lighthouse. *Easy* had some success on the East Coast and was getting lots of airplay on the West Coast, so he thought it was a good business move. Money was tight. All of the money the band was making was going to food and lodging. To top it off, Grant was behind on his car payments. George recalls, "We were out in Hollywood at the Holiday Inn when I saw him. They had confiscated his car. He owed a couple of car notes and he asked me to loan him the money. He had been very ill so he hadn't been working a lot, and they came and took his car back. So I said, 'Well man, come on. Let's go over and get it.' I went to the pound and got it out. He was the happiest man you ever saw. And we could have bought two cars with the money to get that old raggedy Cadillac out of the pound."

George said that Grant was in no shape to be performing. "He was very tired. He had been very ill. He had no business [being] out of the hospital. He didn't look well at all," he says. "I went to see him play. And even when he was at half mast—I call it—he still was great. His fingers were so weak they could just barely touch the strings when he was playing, and he still sounded great."

Ed Hansberry, Grant's brother-in-law, who had moved from St. Louis to the West Coast, also noticed Grant's fatigue. "Grant was supposed to be in bed, and when he called me and told me he was on his way out here, I said, 'Good, you should be out here soon.' He said, 'Yeah, I'll see you in two or three days.' I said, 'Two or three days?' He said, 'I'm driving.' I said, 'Man, you just had an operation and you're going to drive to California!' He said, 'Yeah.'

Lou Donaldson, saxophonist credited with discovering Grant Green

When Grant was in the hospital, I used to go down there, and I'd see this Muslim with him. Grant was Muslim then, but he had to have this soul food shit. I said, "Wait a minute. You aren't supposed to be eating that in the hospital." And he always said, "Ah, baby!"

"And when he arrived and got settled, he was three hours late to the club. He was rushing and he was sweating, and I could tell he was under pressure. He obviously needed some money or something, and he was really pushing himself to get it because he mentioned something to me about how he had some kind of money problem or something and that's why he didn't fly here."

When his gig at the Lighthouse ended, Grant headed back east to New York. The story was he didn't even have the money to pay for the U-haul trailer that carried his organ, but he needed to get the organ back to the East Coast. Still owing for the trailer, he left with it attached to the back of his Cadillac. It was a long and rough trip back across many states and many weather conditions. It was icy January 1979 and it was freezing cold. Percy James, the St. Louis conga and bongo player, remembers the weather conditions because he had had a gig at a different club in southern California that same month. "We both were in California, and I started to go over to see him the last few days, but California kicked my butt," says Percy. "So I left, and Grant came out right behind me. And I know what he came through because I came through the same snowdrift. I almost ran off a mountain."

In a long Caddy with a U-haul in tow and his woman by his side, Grant continued across the states. Dorothy drove most of the way. Family and friends all agree that Grant was never a good driver. There have been different accounts of exactly what happened when they arrived in New York, but all say it was in that car that Grant heaved over from a heart attack and died en route to Harlem Hospital on January 31, 1979. He was forty-three.

"That trip was really what killed him because it was too much stress and strain on him," says Ed Hansberry.

"He made a mistake," George Benson says. "He rented a trailer that he wasn't supposed to leave California with. He wasn't supposed to leave the state of California, but he had to get that organ back to

New York. That's what he was doing when he died. He fell over in the seat of his car. His woman was driving him, and they had a detective that had been looking for the trailer. And the guy was coming towards him, and Grant told her, 'Drive! Take off! Drive!' She says, 'Why? What's wrong?'' And he fell over and died. Right there. That's the way I heard it. My manager, Jimmy Boyd, told me that."

Grant apparently was headed to Boyd's Breezin' Lounge for yet another gig. George says he will never forget when Grant Green died. "He died the same time my father died. My father was killed in early '79," George says.

My husband had been summoned by his mother to Jamaica shortly after his father's stroke and was not in the States when his father died. He says he had just gotten home from school on the Caribbean island when she gave him the news. He says he will never forgive himself for leaving New York. "I kinda feel like if I woulda been with him, that maybe I could've prevented his death," he says. "I kinda looked out [for him] more than Greg. Greg was more like running around, kinda crazy. If I was sixteen, he had to be about twenty-two or something like that. He wasn't really doing nothing. He was just following my dad around and learning more about becoming a musician. He wasn't in school. He had no ambitions to go to school or nothing like that. He just wanted to be a musician. I figured if I could've stayed there, I coulda talked to him and told him, 'Dad, you know, don't take this trip to L.A. right now. It's the wrong time. Just take it easy. Take a month off, you know, and get your thoughts back together and let your body recuperate from the stroke.'"

Greg has another view. "Well, first of all, he should've never drove out there," says Greg. "But you know what it was? That was what he had done all his life. He couldn't do anything else, y'know what I mean? On that last date at the Lighthouse, the reviews weren't good because he'd had a stroke. I remember talkin' to him once on the phone, and I could hear his speech was slurred, 'cause that's what happens when you have a stroke. But he needed the money. He should've tried to stay home and get himself back in order. But he didn't know how to do anything else. He probably would've died anyway if he couldn't have played. I mean, there was nothing I could really do at that point. You can always sit back and say, 'Oh, I wished I could have done this. I wish I could've done that.' But unfortunately I wasn't in the position to do anything. I mean, if I could've I would've."

Greg pauses and says with a certain finality, "He was a very stubborn person. I couldn't have talked him out of not going there. He wouldn't listen to me anyway."

In a 1988 interview, Carlos Santana spoke about how playing music is more than just a job. His thoughts may provide insight on Grant Green's commitment to his instrument even while facing death. Santana said, "I'm not a weekend musician. I'm not a person who plays music just to deodorize—it's not a job. In other words, it's more like a way of life...Music is not a fad, it's a very serious lingo, a universal language."

When asked whether there was a time when he didn't want to play music ever again, Santana replied, "No, but I have met a few people who have come to that realization. For me, I haven't been there yet. I'm too much involved with discovering notes everyday. There's only so many notes, but to me, each one is like an ocean, there's so much to them. I don't measure my life according to *Rolling Stone* or the Pope or *Billboard* or anything like that." Perhaps Grant struggled more with such notions.

News of his death reached his friends in different ways. Some heard about it right away. Others didn't realize he had gone until they read *Down Beat* a couple of months later. "It was a sad day in St. Louis [for] me," says Deanetta James, who knew Grant from her days waitressing in St. Louis clubs in the 1970s. Today, she works in family services for the state of Missouri. "I think I was at work, and I think somebody told me that they had just heard it on the radio. When I got home I asked Percy, 'Did you hear that Grant had passed?' I think they said he was en route somewhere and had a heart attack, and everybody started putting it together—how blacks have such a rough time as musicians, trying to make a life out of it. Naturally, we called Sarah and Albert and we all got together and talked about Grant because we all knew Grant and we all loved Grant, and Grant's wife, Annie. So it was a great loss. It was a great blow to a lot of people here in St. Louis."

Barbara Morris, who had started a Nation of Islam chapter with Grant, was living in California at the time and recalls how disappointed she was when she got the news. Ironically, she had been trying to get to the Lighthouse to see him because she didn't know if she'd ever have another opportunity. She asked her second husband to take her, but he refused. "I had been living in California since 1967. So Grant was at the Lighthouse and I told my husband, 'Claude, I want to go hear Grant. I want to hear Grant!' and he told me, 'Oh, Barbara, I just don't feel like it. I'll buy you a record.' He was sickly then. So he bought me all of these records. But I told him, 'Claude, we're all getting up in age.' I said, 'You never know when you gon' see a friend for the last time.' And sure enough, Grant left there, had that heart attack, and left us," Barbara says.

Greg remembers exactly how he found out. "Somebody called me and said, 'Hey, man, I got some bad news for you.' I was like, 'What?' He said, 'Your father passed away.' And I was just—I was devastated, y'know. I was just crushed. That was, ah, man—that was really, really, really, really, out there."

Thomas Basir, the drummer who knew firsthand about Grant's love for James Brown, says he read the news in a magazine. "I had no idea. Nobody called me. Nobody told me." But then he chuckles, "You know, me and Grant had [gone] to Paul Chambers's funeral. I mean, we had been to all kinds of funerals. But I had no idea. It was very disappointing to me that I didn't know, because we were that close. It hadn't been too long since I [had seen] him. He was too young to die as far as I'm concerned, because he was full of life. Trust me. Full of life. He was not slow under no circumstances. He was always pop, pop, pop. Let's go. Let's do this, let's do that. Just like he was with his playing."

In an obituary, Jimmy Boyd told one reporter, "He opened my club for me back in the summer. Things seemed to [fall] into place for him on the East Coast, so he stuck around. Then, when his record hit big on the West Coast, he went there to play. But the mistake was in driving that distance. That's too long a trip."

Added Vic Chirumbolo, a producer at Versatile Records, "We were all anticipating working on his new release. Green was certainly one of the best."

Jay, Grant's manager, says he was in Detroit when he got the phone call about Grant's death. "I think it was from Dorothy Malone. She said, 'Jay, Grant is dead.'"

He says he didn't bother to ask for details. "I didn't want to know. I expected to hear it any day after what the doctors told him in the hospital," says Jay, who rushed to New York to a relative's apartment, where Kim, John, and Greg were staying. "Kim was almost hysterical," Jay says. "And I don't know whether John and Junior were there. I walked back in the bedroom, and Greg was sitting there on the bed with the guitar on his lap, just staring at it. And I had my camera and I took a picture of him. I have a copy of the picture."

A memorial service was held for Grant in New York. Lou Donaldson, Hank Crawford, and Harold Vick were among the musicians in attendance. Blue Note sent wreaths. A minister, known as the Jazz Priest, presided. "There is a ritual in New York when a famous jazz musician dies. They have a priest there who is called the Jazz Priest, and he will always do the eulogy," says Jay.

After Grant's last praises were played and sung, his body was taken from New York and shipped back to the city where it all began: St. Louis, Missouri.

My husband has never cared much for St. Louis. Neither did his oldest brother, Greg. I have heard my mother-in-law and her sister, Ardis, express similar sentiments. "It's too country," Greg says. "Too small. Ain't nothin' happening there."

Maybe. Maybe not. But on the day Grant Green was buried, something happened.

14 An Unusual Good-bye

"I heard what sounded like soldiers marching—Thrump! Thrump! Thrump!"

Grant Green's funeral had the makings of a motion picture. That is, depending on whom you asked. There were various accounts of what exactly happened the day he was buried. Or whether he was even buried at all.

Some say a Christian minister oversaw the ceremony. Others say black Muslims were at the helm of the service. Strangely, one relative says there were no religious overtones to the service at all.

Some say the funeral hall was packed with visitors paying their respects. Others say no one came.

Some say the body ended up in a certain cemetery. Others say they don't know where the body is.

When the minister asked for the wife of the deceased to stand, three women were said to have stood. Others say not one wife showed up.

On one thing everyone agrees: it was a very, very cold day. "On the day of the funeral, they had the biggest snowstorm in St. Louis history," says Jay. "But the funeral home was packed with people, and what happened during that funeral ceremony would make a wonderful movie. As the preacher was talking about Grant, he mentioned another famous St. Louis son [who] had died and been brought home two weeks before and buried. He was talking about Donnie Hathaway. I was so sad. I couldn't think. I was standing at the back of the room just looking at everybody. And the minister said, 'Grant was one of our famous sons. His father still lives here and he made a contribution to St. Louis and to the black people of St. Louis. He had a wife and some beautiful children.' And then he said, 'Will his lovely wife and children please stand up?' And guess what happened. Three women stood up with some children. In

Edmund Hansberry, Grant Green's brother-in-law

Grant was one of the first guys that I played with when I got to St. Louis, and I was his drummer for I think like two or three years. I was in Chicago with Muddy Waters. I was with Muddy Waters for about three or four years. Then my sister told me that somebody was looking for a drummer and to come to St. Louis, but I didn't hurry. When I got to St. Louis, the group had left town, so consequently I was stuck there, and after I joined the union, I began to inquire about jobs. That's when I began to work with Grant. Grant was a very mild-mannered guy. I liked him very much. He had a great demeanor. He was always in a hurry, but he never seemed to get there on time.

different places in the room! There was like surely one hundred to two hundred people in this room, and there was like one wife sitting in the center, one on the left, and one on the right. There was almost a riot there. They got those women up out of there.

"Somehow the minister cooled it out, and they went on with the service. The minister had brought one of those Holy Roller women to play the organ, and she started playing this depressing funeral music. And they started to give Grant a Christian funeral. I said, 'Oh my God! This is what Grant said he didn't want to happen.' So I shouted from the back of the room, 'Hey, wait a minute! Wait a minute!' And just as I said that, I heard what sounded like soldiers marching—*Thrump! Thrump! Thrump!* But you could tell it was footsteps. And the door just burst open. And I think it was a Muslim minister from the mosque in Cleveland. He burst into the room and he had six—do you know what the FOI is? They're the Muslim soldiers. He had six of them with him. They were acting like soldiers. As he walked in, one of them grabbed the woman who was playing her organ and just lifted her up out of the chair. The Muslim minister walked over to the Christian minister and just pushed him out of the way. The guy almost fell down. Then the Muslim minister walked to the rostrum and he said, 'My name is Minister so-and-so. Brother Grant Green was my good friend, and he was a devout Muslim. And he had made me promise, like his manager in the back there, that we would see that his body got home and he got the proper burial.' He said, 'So the manager has brought the body here, and I must do the rest. I don't want to offend anyone. But Grant, being a Muslim, is supposed to have an Islamic funeral, which is done only in Arabic. I apologize for those of you who do not understand the Arabic language. But this ceremony cannot be performed in English. So please forgive me.' He went on and performed the ceremony, which was like saying a prayer to God to forgive this man and accept this person. Oh, he must have spoken for about fifteen or twenty minutes. These six brothers were standing next to him, three on each side of him. When he finished, he said, 'That concludes the ceremony.' And when he closed the Koran, these six brothers snapped it together. They were like soldiers. *Thrump! Thrump! Thrump!* They went over and picked up the coffin and took it outside and put it in the hearse. By now, it was snowing like crazy. And the hearse was stuck in the snow. But they pushed the hearse until it started moving, and people were all running behind the hearse. So I walk outside and I said, 'Thank you God. Grant really must have been one of your favorite people because they were about to do to him the one thing he says he didn't want done. And at the last moment you saved him.' So I followed the hearse to the cemetery. I walked as far as the gate. I saw them lowering Grant's body into the ground. I stood there and it was snowing like hell. I'm telling you it was snowing so heavy I could hardly see. And I said, 'Well, Grant. I've done what you asked me to do. I brought your body home. I saw to it that you got the proper funeral, and now they're putting you in the ground. But I cannot stand here and watch them put dirt on top of you.' And I turned around and I walked away."

Greg, my brother-in-law, says he doesn't remember much about the funeral, but when asked about whether three wives stood and whether the Muslim soldiers showed up, he says, "No! And no! And no! I would've remember that. *That* didn't happen."

Greg's cousin, Ann Moody, smiled when hearing of the three wives and marching soldiers. But she admits her memory may be faulty. "Okay, let's make it plain that this was a long time ago, and I don't remember precisely what happened, but I vaguely remember Kim making the preparations for the funeral, and I remember distinctly thinking that it was very sad that she had to do that all alone. I think she was in her late teens, early twenties," says Ann, from her bedroom in the family house on Clara Street. "We were here in this very room, too, when she got the call. I ain't gon' never forget it. It was something like one o'clock in the morning when the call came. I distinctly remember that there was snow on the ground that day because John had just got these new shoes, right? He and Buster [Ann's brother] had got into this argument about them. They used to always argue about shoes because they had relatively good taste. Buster had bought these really expensive shoes. They were alligator boots, and they were buff now. I mean they were 'boof'! And John always [had] this thing that his shoes had to go boof, too, especially when he was on the dance floor. His shoes were always nice and shiny, and that was the thing, because John can't dance. But the thing I remember is John and Buster arguing because John wanted to wear these burgundy alligator boots that Buster had just bought. And Kim wanted to wear heels, but I told Kim, 'You know, it's snowing out there. You really don't need to wear those heels. You know it's going to really be slipping and sliding,' but you know Kim got to tip, right? So Kim put on her heels and I put on my heels, too, and I remember that they were all in black that day and they had on really sharp, cashmere black overcoats."

She continued, "It was a very small procession. It was basically just family. And the family consisted of just his children and myself. Now don't ask me how I got in the mix, but you know as close as me and Kim were, we were in there like that. I remember when we were in the funeral car, we were kind of joking around. Whenever we gathered, jokes will fly because that's just the kind of

Tracy Byrd with her cousin, April Moody. Tracy takes her name from her father, John Tracy, Grant's second son—who incidentally, inspired his father's tune "Tracin' Tracy." Photo by Sharony A. Green.

Tracy Byrd, Grant Green's granddaughter (interview)

SAG: Tracy, what's your last name?
TB: It's Byrd, but you can call me Green.
SAG: Tracy, what kind of instrument did your grandfather play?
TB: Guitar.
SAG: Is there anything special about him that you know?
TB: I heard that he was famous.
SAG: You told me something about him the other day—what was it? You mentioned something he did being named after you.
TB: A song.
SAG: What was the name of it?
TB: "Tracin' Tracy."
SAG: Who else has Tracy in their name?
TB: My dad.
SAG: What's your daddy's name?
TB: John Tracy Green.
SAG: Tell me about your dad.
TB: Well, he's nice and he's intelligent, and he's fun to be with.
SAG: What's the best thing about having a daddy?
TB: He's there with you when you have troubles.
SAG: What kind of troubles do you have when you're ten?
TB: If like, I tell a story or do something that I wasn't supposed to do.
SAG: What do you then talk to your daddy about?
TB: Well, I tell him that I'm sorry.

family we are. Regardless of the situation, there will be some levity somewhere, okay? John was kind of cracking jokes in his kind of offhanded way, which he usually does, and Gregory was being insulting like he usually is, and I remember Kim was rather quiet for Kim. She would jump in there every now and then, but for Kim she was really quiet. And I was just like taking it all in as I usually do because they just crack me up.

"I was moved by the scarcity of this funeral because in the black community large funerals dictate how well a person is loved—not to say that Grant was not loved, but in my mind there were a lot of circumstances that would have led to that sparse funeral. It was in February, and it was extremely cold that day. I believe it was also on a weekday, which was probably something else that would've added, too. And there had not been a lot of publicity as to his death that I had seen in the St. Louis area. That may have also contributed to the small turnout. So we took our seats in the funeral home, and there were a few people, a scattering of people, in the funeral home. They had it in the regular funeral home. And the casket—if I remember correctly—the casket was closed. I don't remember ever seeing the body. The funeral took place at Eddie Randall, over on Natural Bridge. I believe one of the officials at the funeral home officiated. There were a scattering of people behind us, but not very many, and I remember thinking how sad it was because I know in some realm this man was very well known, even though he didn't have that impact on me personally. It didn't seem to have that kind of impact on St. Louis at large. I knew he had been away from St. Louis for quite a number of years, and I remember thinking that may have had an impact on the turnout at the funeral.

"The service was relatively short. I wouldn't even call it a religious service at all, okay? Muslim, Christian, either way, it wasn't that. It was sorta like a let's-get-it-over-and-done-with, you know what I'm saying? And as far as music is concerned, there may have been organ music, kind of like piped-in music. You know how they pipe in music? But it didn't have any particular religious slant.

"When we got to the cemetery...it was freezing, and I remember shaking like a leaf. I mean when I think about it, I get cold. That's how cold it was out there. And it had stopped snowing, but we had to walk across the cemetery, and there was like a kind of yellowish parchment where they placed the casket in order to raise it up and put it into the ground. And one of the officials from the funeral home said a few words and that was it. There was nobody else at the grave site, but us—his sons, his daughter, and myself.

"And again, there were no religious implications to this funeral whatsoever. None whatsoever. I went to a Muslim funeral once, and they come in like hordes and they're all dressed in the Muslim garb, and you can tell Muslims when they walk into a place, and I didn't see any Muslims there. I'm sorry, I can't help it, but he watched the wrong funeral. That was not Grant Green's funeral. That was Malcolm X's funeral. With the Muslims marching in and stuff, I saw that on film somewhere, but it didn't happen in real life," Ann concludes.

Richard Henderson, a jazz historian in the city, says he recalls that the funeral was "very, very short. It was about five minutes. I will never forget that day because it snowed. I mean, it was snowing. It was Muslim all the way through. And...it didn't last but five or ten minutes." I asked him whether anything unusual occurred during the service. He pauses. "Not that I could think of," he finally says.

Ed Hansberry, Grant's brother-in-law, agreed that it was snowing and that the service was short, and one thing in particular was most unusual. "I remember the whole procession left, but the Muslims went one way and everybody else went the other way, and when we got to the cemetery there was no Grant there to be buried," Ed says. "They buried him somewhere else. I don't know what happened."

My husband was sixteen when his father died. He says he has no recollection of the funeral. "I never even looked in the coffin."

There may never be a consensus on what exactly happened at Grant Green's funeral. What may be more important is what happened during the man's lifetime. Who was he? What did he represent in jazz as a whole?

Jazz is an improvisational kind of music, meant for stretching out. It is a playground for the creative mind. And Grant played well on it. What he did with the guitar while he played will be remembered. He was a quaint storyteller who never completely lost his touch. Perhaps he did collude in his own marketing and paid the ultimate price. But, he understood his own power, how he could make each note and each phrase coalesce into a language that was uniquely his own. When he plucked a wrong note, it still had value. Wrong notes mimic life in all its imperfections. Grant Green loved his instrument. He loved music. He loved his family and he loved life. But given the years of his drug abuse and other unhealthy habits, one wonders how much Grant loved Grant. Was all that talkin' trash on the bandstand and naming songs after himself enough to suggest he fully understood his own worth? Maybe. Maybe not. One thing is certain, though: the muses did dance with Grant Green. Even at the end, they smiled on him and left us in wonder.

Jay Glover has a few other words to say about that funeral. "You know, Grant was a very, very lucky man," he says. "He used to brag about his name, Green. He wore green clothes. He drove a green car. He lived on Greenlawn. And you know when he died, they buried him in Greenhill Cemetery."

They might have. But on a visit to the cemetery in 1995, my husband and I never found the tombstone.

15 Moving On to the Color Purple
(bo-do-deh-yuldeh-deh-dul-dat)

"I think about it all of the time, because the music I'm listening to was made by black people, you know. There's no way around that."

Much has happened to make jazz cool again in the twenty years since Grant Green has been away. The rebirth of this particular music is due in part to young people. They sparked a movement, or a revival of a movement, which is not a new happening, however. Think of boogie-woogie in its day. And rock 'n' roll in its day. Young people are typically at the vanguard of trends. Unsettled spirits are always on the prowl. What's interesting about the young cats listening to, co-opting, and spinning and sampling jazz today is that they know how to call a spade a spade, and in doing so, they keep the music and the revival real.

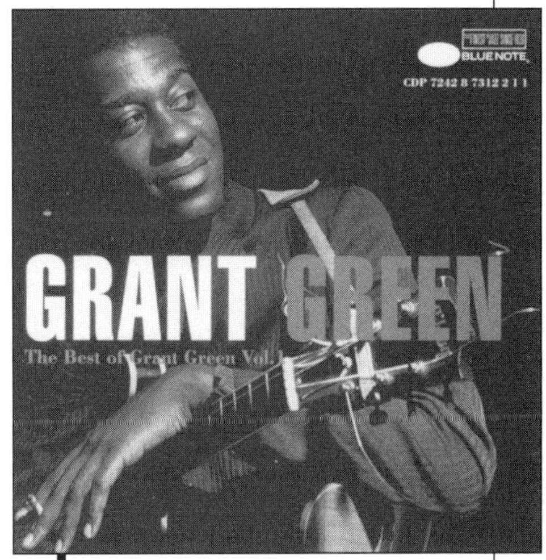

The Best of Grant Green Vol. I *features work from Grant's early, more straightahead beginnings. Courtesy of Blue Note Records, a division of Capitol Records.*

One young man's thoughts in particular are telling of where we are with jazz guitar, and jazz music in general, as we close this century. His name is Sam Miller. At the time of our interview, which took place on May 18, 1995, Sam was a jazz guitar student at Cabrillo College in Santa Cruz, California. He was working at a record store in the center of town. I asked him if I could speak with him at some length about Grant, a musician he seemed to admire. The following interview took place in Sam's home a few days later. My husband, Grant Green Jr., sat in. What we heard speaks to the days we're living in, where reaching into the bins for the old-school music may simply be a desire for less complicated times.

SAG: *How far back does your interest in music go?*

SM: I would say my whole life, really...I remember having classical music when I was a li'l kid. But when I was about fourteen or fifteen, I really got into [guitar] seriously, and I learned all of my scales and all kinds of theory that surely everybody studies at some point. A lot of guys teach fairly high-level theory at Cabrillo. I got into it for fun when I started. I was like, 'Hmm, playing guitar. That sounds really interesting.' When I was in third grade I wanted to play the saxophone.

SAG: *Was there ever a turning point when you said, "This is what I want to do with my life?"*

SM: I've said that many times now. I would say it was really after I started hearing jazz music and meeting a lot of people and that's what they did with their life.

SAG: *When was this?*

SM: I'd say when I was about fifteen or sixteen I started meeting these people. One of my best friends is a young drummer. His dad is a wonderful piano player who's played with Bobby Hutcherson. In fact, I met Bobby.

SAG: *What was it like meeting Bobby Hutcherson?*

SM: I was aware that he was a renowned vibraphonist. I don't think I'd heard *Idle Moments* or *Street of Dreams* yet. I'd heard a record he had made with Eric Dolphy called *Out to Lunch.*

SAG: *You mentioned earlier that there's been a resurgence in interest in hard bop. Why do you think that's happening?*

SM: I think people my age, those in their late teens and early twenties, are into some kind of nostalgia. Everyone I've met, they have '80s nostalgia or '70s nostalgia or '60s nostalgia, or whatever. I know a bunch of people that go around greasing their hair back and wearing leather jackets. I know people that, y'know, dress like they are in a disco all of the time, and I think a lot of them are kinda looking back into simpler... times, different periods, because I think our generation is really facing some new problems that others didn't have, like AIDS. We grew up with AIDs, you know what I mean? I knew about AIDs way before I was old enough to be having sex or anything like that, and that is different than the generation before us, and really different than two generations before. And so I think everyone is looking back at simpler times. Me, personally, I just got into hard bop and jazz or whatever you want to call it 'cause I'm always looking for good music to listen to. There's a lot of integrity in the music.

Q-tip, rapper in A Tribe Called Quest, on using Grant Green's "Down Here on the Ground" on the group's tune "Vibes and Stuff"

It was something that I stumbled upon. I was looking at the personnel that was on it—the guitar. Like that wasn't my first Grant Green, but it was sorta like boom—check that out—you know? It was funky.

SAG: *Who had you heard before you heard Grant Green?*

SM: I loved Kenny Burrell. I still do. I just love Kenny Burrell, and that was like the first jazz guitar player that really just hit me and made me go, "Oh, wow. Maybe I should be checking more of this stuff out."

SAG: *How does Kenny Burrell's style differ from Grant's style?*

SM: Grant was much more rhythmic about everything. It was where he put the note, how he played the phrase, and he was swinging really hard. I mean, I had never heard a guitar swing like that before. A lot of guitar players don't swing. I know a lot of people who don't like playing with guitar players for just that reason. Because of the nature of the instrument, you can't swing it like you can a horn or drums or even a piano or bass. It's harder for guitar players to get that swing feel. It has something to do with the instrument.

SAG: *The stuff that seems to be what the kids are into now, seems to be the funkier stuff, the later '60s and early '70s stuff.*

Dave Stryker, guitarist who participated on the 1996 Japanese CD *A Tribute to Grant Green* (Paddlewheel KICJ 282)

I've always been a Grant Green fan, but I don't rank people. I mean, once you reach the level of guys like this, everybody has something beautiful to offer. How could you compare Grant and Wes Montgomery? One sounds like Grant Green and one sounds like Wes Montgomery. And George Benson, the same way. Kenny Burrell, Joe Pass, Jim Hall, Pat Martino, all these guys—if you've listened to them enough you can tell who they are in one note. That's what all musicians strive for, I think...to have that individuality, and Grant certainly had that.

SM: That's not my main interest. I've heard of 'em. I've heard *Alive!* and stuff like that, but I like to hear to swing, and I like to hear the musicians that he was playing with.

SAG: *Tell me about your style and how you attempt to emulate him.*

SM: In every way. A lot of the times I usually try to play like Grant Green. His tone is unbelievable. I've never heard a tone like that. I'd love to be able to swing like that. There's this flowing to his playing that's like—I can't really describe it. It's so natural sounding. It's like it's a piece of cake for him.

GG: *I want to ask you one question. A lot of people have certain licks that [they] do, that they really practice a lot. Is there a certain Grant Green lick that you had trouble trying to do?*

SM: That sweep picking lick I've been practicing lately. It's like bleo-bleh-bu-blep-peh. That's one of 'em. That's a tricky lick to play right. And I'm getting pretty good at it. I don't know if I'll ever whip it out in the middle of a tune, but he really gets into [it] in "Nomad" from *Idle Moments.* There's like practically a whole chorus of him checking that sweep picking thing out, and I think that's the first time that anybody ever went about playing that technique like that.

SAG: *Is there a tune that you like more than others?*

SM: No, there's something great about all of them. I play "Blues in Maude's Flat" all the time. That's one of my favorite blues to play. I can't play it right. I don't know how he did that trill like that, but him and Yusef both pulled it off and I've never been able to play it like that.

SAG: *Sing it.*

SM: It's bo-do-deh-yuldeh-deh-dul-dat, you know what I mean? That's it! I can't do that. I have to go, bo-do-deh-ooh-doo-deh-doo-dat. Yuldeh-dul-dat. I can't do it. It's too weird.

SAG: *Where do you gig?*

SM: I played in a ska band for a long time, a ska and reggae band. I played...in every place in Santa Cruz with that band. I played in San Francisco, in a lot of places, like Paradise Lounge and the Great American Music Hall.

SAG: *Do you think this is something you will be doing professionally?*

SM: I think so. I mean, there's a lot of competition out there, and that makes me nervous. I think that in the long run what's going to make me last as a musician [is what made] all of the really great musicians that I listen to last, and that is to have a very clear voice. You can tell who they are right away. I can hear two bars of Grant Green and know, Grant Green!

SAG: *I don't want to define what the race issue is for you, but as a young white musician—*

SM: I think about it.

SAG: *You do?*

SM: I think about it all of the time because the music I'm listening to was made by black people, you know. There's no way around that. There's no way of changing that. People have tried. I think there was a time when white musicians were really getting pushed by the media to be more original than they were. This is really a hard subject to talk about, but people wanted to hear white people play it. White people wanted to hear white people play it, and the industry pushed certain musicians, and I think it's unfortunate.

SAG: *Now, your dad's an astronomy professor, and your mom?*

SM: She's mom. She's a quilter. That's what I would say. She makes some mean quilts.

SAG: *I see that pillow over there. Did she make that pillow?*

SM: Probably. And she, of course, was around in the '60s. I try to piece things together as best I can through the books, and obviously there was a pretty significant Civil Rights movement in the '60s and maybe it's going to happen again.

SAG: *Well, life is always evolving and society is always evolving. Is there anything you'd like to say that I haven't asked you about? Do you really want to play professional guitar?*

SM: Yeah, I think at this point I'm looking into going into—I don't want to say jazz per se, but I'm interested in stuff like Living Color. Have you heard of Living Color? I'm interested in playing that kind of style. I want to do something new. I think what would be hip is if the hip-hoppers and the rappers and the jazz musicians really did get together and collaborate on something instead of sampling or whatever, because with sampling all you get is this repetition of one thing again, again, and again...whereas jazz musicians improvise and they take something and they develop it again and again. I think everybody should get together and take it to the next step.

(Sam gets up to show us his Grant Green Street of Dreams *album. It has a photo of a street intersection of Grant Avenue and Green Street on the cover.)*

GG: *You're very lucky to have this one.*

SM: I know. I was flipping through the racks and I was like—

SAG: *Where is this street sign?*

SM: In San Francisco. My mom looked at that and said, "Oh, yeah. San Francisco."

There were other young people with whom I spoke. Most contacted me via the Internet. Tobias Jundt, a nineteen-year-old guitar player in Switzerland, was one of them. Tobias has a way of mixing words and sounds and beats that floor me. I was so impressed by a CD he single-handedly produced, arranged, recorded, and distributed titled *TJ's Spherelogy: Toddler Grooves, Chapter One (1996-1998)* that I asked him to do an essay on Grant's style and review some of his albums for this book. That he was able to assume the task speaks to the universality of music, despite things like race, geography, and age. Of course, jazz has no dibs on reaching the masses. How many videos have you seen of

Grant Green with Bobby Hutcherson during in the 1964 Street of Dreams *session; the cover of the album features a photo of a fitting intersection in San Francisco—Grant Avenue and Green Street. Photo by Francis Wolff, courtesy of Mosaic Images.*

Michael Jackson making Japanese and German girls faint? But TJ is pretty special. The back of his powder-blue CD has an in-your-face disclaimer that reads: "This product is not meant for the open market. You can get it where it draws its inspiration from...on the street." The arrangement of his music is innovative. His beats are way-funky and the shout-outs on the album from artists like Alice Day, Dee Dee Bridgewater, and Bluey of Incognito—people he's made a point of meeting—are telling of what could be ahead for a maverick like himself. I knew he was on to something when my mom, who knows nothing about jazz, heard me playing the CD and said, "Who's that? Grant's dad?"

My mama asking about Grant Green? As a world, we sho' nuff making progress. On all kinda levels. For jazz, this could mean a whole lot.

~

Today, I am no longer with Grant's son. We were married for a month short of five years. A lot happened in that time. Good and bad. What's beautiful is that today we both know more about his father's legacy. Research for this book required travel to many cities and even across country to California, where I had an artist residency to work on this manuscript. Looking back, I can say, despite the hurdles, it's been worth it. Often Grant's son was by my side, listening and learning with me. A novice photographer, I took many photos of him beside the people who knew his father long before he was born. As we traveled down the highway, we stopped the car every time we saw a city or county or street with the words "Grant" or "Green" in it. Our most memorable stop was the famous corner in San Francisco—Grant Avenue and Green Street, used many years before as the cover art for his dad's 1964 Street of Dreams *album. While in San Francisco we met Joe Henderson and Herbie Hancock at a tribute to the late Antonio Carlos Jobim. In other cities, we met Quincy Jones and P-funkster George Clinton. The names reflect the vast span of music and musicians with whom Grant came into contact. Each attested to his unique gifts. The last time we spoke, I was making plans to go overseas, and Grant Jr. was still working as a chef in Detroit. He was getting to know some well-known deejays on the techno front.*

Maybe we came together just for something like this to happen.

Maybe for other things, too.

I left my job at the Detroit Free Press. *Art had long been my first love, and I decided to give it my full attention. The difficulty of leaving a nine-to-five job helped me understand what a musician like Grant Green was up against. One can lose a lot in the process. Your health. Your family. Your faith. And more. I remember a time when I was having some sleepless nights over an artistic project gone bad. My husband, who does not remember many of his dreams, remembered one. I'll never forget it. He woke up early one morning and told me that he'd had a dream about his dad. He remembered it as clear as day. He said in the dream his father was sitting on a rooftop, playing a purple guitar. He showed him a few licks. And then his dad stopped playing and told him that he had a message. A message for his wife. He said his dad wanted me to know that things would get far worse before they got better, but that in time, everything was gon' be alright.*

A year later, a purple guitar pick ended up in our home. I'm not sure how it got there. I put it away for my husband, who by then had started fiddling around with a second-hand guitar. Somehow, the pick ended up in my purse. I took it out and put it away. Again, I found it in my purse. I took it out and put it away a second time.

Two years later, after his son and I had separated, I found it again in my purse. Maybe in some far away galaxy his dad has moved on to the color purple. In the book of the same name, Alice Walker wrote that it sure pisses God off when people walk by a field of purple flowers and don't notice them. Maybe it would do us equal harm to walk by a world of music and forget a man like Grant Green.

On Sound, Style, and Technique

Grant Green is one of those musicians you immediately recognize after hearing the very first note. He has a unique tone with a different timbre. A lot of guitarists tried to emulate it, but no one ever really could.

Green had one year of formal lessons back in St. Louis with a man named Forrest Alcorn, but he mostly considered himself a self-taught musician. "Sometimes that's better," he says. "You're not tied to any certain way of being taught... The guitar is a very personal instrument. Nothing is really wrong until you make it wrong."

Green's technique was somewhat unpredictable, depending on how he felt at the moment of the performance. His playing had a lucid, full, and singing tone that was brittle and bluesy, warm and relaxed, or clear as crystal. His phrasing—and the way he made love to melodies—was some of the best you could get. He used different articulations—like staccato slurs, glissandos, or tremolos—but he didn't rely on specific guitar techniques like string-bending, muting, harmonics (flageolettes), or hammer-ons and pull-offs (except for trills). He described his playing simply as "God's gift."

Green's main musical influences were Charlie Christian and Charlie "Bird" Parker. In a 1975 interview he said, "Listening to Charlie Parker was like listening to a different man every night."

Among guitarists, he liked Jimmy Raney. Said Green, "I liked [Raney's] style of improvising, and he gets a good sound. I also like Kenny Burrell very much and, of course, Charlie Christian. You can't get around him. But I don't listen to guitar players a lot. I dig horn players."

That's probably one thing that sets Grant apart from many other guitarists. He didn't think like a guitarist when it came to creating a melodic idea. He had a hornlike approach to improvisation and phrasing. His style was one of single notes. He sometimes swept arpeggios, but he used octaves sparingly (which was Wes Montgomery's main thing).

In the second half of his career, Green often used fourth, fifth, and minor sixth, which he would repeat over and over again to get the joints jumping. When it came to playing chords, he liked to use cluster-type and closed chords, which had harmonic value. On his own dates he used chords more in a compositional context, as in his originals "Grant's Dimension" and "Green with Envy" (both are on *Green Street*) or on the intros to "The Things We Did Last Summer" and "Little Girl Blue" (both of which can be found on *The Complete Quartets with Sonny Clark*). To hear him comp behind a soloist you have to check his sideman dates, like *Blue and Sentimental* by Ike Quebec, *Stop and Listen* by Babyface Willette, or Reuben Wilson's *Love Bug.*

For improvising, Green used the bebop shapes introduced by people like Bird and other bebop players, but more than anything, he was a true blues player. This was perfect for Blue Note's hard bop sound of the '60s. Green played in a strong, flowing lyrical vein, but he was very rhythmic and groovy at the same time.

Another characteristic of Green's style is the repetition of a single phrase with slight, but subtle, shifts in accent. The most important thing may have been that he seemed to be more concerned about sound and feeling than anything else. He wasn't a hell of a technician, but he could talk. He could really tell a story on his instrument, and he was a ballad player of the first rank.

A lot of musicians who worked with Green said he must have had a tremendous ear. They said you could play him any phrase and he'd play it right back. He wasn't that great of a reader, but he was versatile and quite astute in any setting. He played some of everything—boogie-woogie, spirituals, and rock 'n' roll. But as he puts it himself, "It's all just the blues anyhow." It doesn't matter where a song comes from. What's important is what's being done with it. Very often Green had a number on his records that was from a different musical corner than where he was at the time. He did Bacharach–David ("Wives and Lovers" on *Matador* or "I'll Never Fall in Love again" on *Green Is Beautiful*), W.A. Mozart ("Symphony No. 40 in G-minor" on *Visions*), Kool & the

Gang ("Let the Music Take Your Mind" on *Grant Green Alive!*), Bell-Creed ("Betcha by Golly Wow" on *Live at the Lighthouse*), or James Brown ("Ain't It Funky Now" on *Green Is Beautiful* and "I Don't Want Nobody..." on *Carryin' On*).

Some of his most well-regarded covers are his takes on songs by the Beatles ("A Day in the Life" on *Green Is Beautiful* or "I Want to Hold Your Hand" from the record of the same title). These performances show how most vocal standards can be rearranged, and thus reborn as jazz standards. Let's not forget that Grant Green was a true entertainer. He followed a particular program to suit the demands of his audience. At least toward the end of his career, he really tried to take care of that business. He also planned to write a book about his approach to modern jazz guitar and expressed the wish to cut a record with strings as Charlie Parker once did.

One thing that also defines a musician's sound is his equipment. Green's first axe was an old Harmony guitar along with a little amp. Early in his career Green mainly played Gibson guitars, although he wasn't a huge fan of the Gibsons they made at that time. Possibly among others, he played an Epiphone "Emperor," a Gibson "ES-330," and a Gibson "L-7." There is also an early picture where Green's rocking a Fender Stratocaster. In 1973, he had a dream come true when he acquired a hand-carved guitar by the famous New York luthier Jimmy D'Acquisto (now owned by George Benson). It was an arched acoustic D'Acquisto "New Yorker Deluxe" with a single cutaway, a medium-wide neck, and a mother-of-pearl inlay in the fingerboard reading "GG." Instead of the normal DeArmond pickup, the guitar had a specially made low-impendance pickup Bill Lawrence made for him (as he had done for Wes Montgomery earlier).

At that time Green used a Gibson Les Paul-LP-12 amplifier (which contained four 12-inch speakers and two 10-inch horns). George Benson says that Green had the bass and treble knobs turned down to zero and the middle all the way up (it sounds funny, but try it). Even when playing blues, Green never used distortion. He occasionally turned up the vibrola knob on his amp (an effect combining tremolo and vibrato). The strings he used at that time were light gauge, flat-wound by D'Acquisto, and he seemed to be pretty conscientious about changing them every six weeks to two months. He played with a small, stiff pick and never used his bare fingers or finger picks. He also had in his possession a classical concert guitar, but he never really used it. But when talking about guitars and equipment, this is all just peripheral details. The soul of a musician's sound is still in his fingers.

—Tobias "TJ" Jundt, Berne, Switzerland

For further study, try to get a copy of the following interviews:
Dan Morgenstern, "GG—New Guitar in Town," *Down Beat,* Jul. 1962
G.N. Bourland, "Grant Green," *Guitar Player,* Jan. 1975
"Grant Green Discusses His Approach to Modern Jazz Guitar," *Crescendo Int.,* Sept. 1971

Selected Reviews

These reviews, written by Tobias Jundt, of Berne, Switzerland, represent but a fraction of Grant Green's work.

Title: ***Up at Minton's*** **(Stanley Turrentine)**
Date: February 23, 1961
Label: Blue Note
Producer/Engineer: Alfred Lion/Rudy Van Gelder

This session from the legendary Minton's Playhouse is the first recording capturing Green live in action in New York City. Led by a huge and booming toned Stanley Turrentine, it features a trio with high empathy known as "Us Three"—Horace Parlan on piano, George Tucker on bass, and Al Harewood on drums. (And yes, the British acid jazz group's name is a take on this group's name.) The album features standards such as "But Not for Me," "Broadway," and an exciting rendition of "Love for Sale." Turrentine wrote two originals of which "Later at Minton's" opens the second set. It's a very slow improvised blues. Starting with bass and drums only, Turrentine and Green join in, blowing some relaxed heart-grabbing lines. Most tracks are over ten minutes in length and leave space for Green to stretch out. His lines on fast-tempo songs are very long and fluent, probably some of the most comparable to Charlie Parker. While he sometimes seems uncertain on how to end a phrase, his playing is lively, direct, and at a high level. *Up at Minton's* was originally released on vinyl and is now available on an affordable two-compact-disc set. It is an important recording because it captures a young Green blowing free from studio time limits with total ease in the very club where Charlie Christian laid his own foundation for jazz guitar two decades before.

Title: ***Reaching Out***
Date: March 15, 1961
Label: Black Lion
Producer/Engineer: Fred Northsworthy/Tom Nola

This is an uncomplicated straightahead date put together by drummer Dave Bailey, but it was released under Green's name on the Black

Lion label. The album features a solid Ben Tucker on bass, an immature and shaky Billy Gardner on piano, and a firm and soulful Frank Haynes on tenor saxophone. The motor of the band is the tight and swinging teamwork of Bailey and Tucker. They kept everything together so Haynes and Green could blow. The material consists mainly of originals by band members or fellow musicians including a modal title track and a standard. These bouncy cuts feature some bluesy playing, although Green has his most adventurous solo during the bright rendition of Rodger and Hart's "When I Fall in Love." *Reaching Out* is not the strongest Green recording. It sounds kind of like a taped jam session. Sadly, the sound quality is not on the level of Green's sessions recorded by Rudy Van Gelder. The drums are too loud in certain spots and the guitar sounds muffled.

Title: *Workout* (Hank Mobley)
Date: March 26, 1961
Label: Blue Note
Producer/Engineer: Alfred Lion/Rudy Van Gelder

Still profiting from being the new man in town, Green was joined on this project by two of Miles Davis's sidemen and drummer Philly Joe Jones, a Davis alumnus. The tight-running team of Paul Chambers and tenor saxophonist Hank Mobley with Wynton Kelly on piano worked together perfectly with Green on *Workout,* one of the better known Blue Note records. Although Green only functions as a sideman, this album shows how he could play with a hard-grooving band. The opener "Workout" is brought home by Jones, who maintains an incredibly fiery groove all through the record. The way Mobley smolders through the changes, he probably surprised his then-boss Miles Davis. Green gently soars on top of the rhythm section and does a great job swinging. Green's unique sound and soul give this rhythm section a special timbre and groove. He seems to be particularly at home on the funky blues "Greasin' Easy." Here, Jones tries to push him into double-time. The blowing of these young modernists is definitely happening.

Title: *Green Street*
Date: April 1, 1961
Label: Blue Note
Producer/Engineer: Alfred Lion/Rudy Van Gelder

Green Street is an early straightahead date featuring the swinging drummer Dave Bailey, who reacts immediately to Green and the very inventive and melodious Ben Tucker on bass. The trio format leaves a lot of space for Green to stretch out and play, shifting motives in pitch while making rhythmic variations, using fingered tremolos and double stops in his lines. His compositions "Green with Envy" and "Grant's Dimension" both feature a steadily walking solo by Tucker and, as another highlight, an interchange of phrases between Green and Bailey. The other Green original "No. 1 Green Street" is a bouncy and humorous 12-bar blues. The two featured standards are a blues-driven version of "Alone Together" and a simply amazing version of Monk's "'Round Midnight." Here, Green speaks with all the accents that make his musical voice what it is, pulling the ballad in refreshing directions. The CD is reissued in the Connoisseur Series and includes three rare photographs and two bonus tracks. One of them, "Green with Envy," stops abruptly with Bailey saying "my fault..."

Title: ***Stop and Listen*** **(Baby Face Willette)**
Date: May 22, 1961
Label: Blue Note
Producer/Engineer: Alfred Lion/Rudy Van Gelder

Willette's second and last recording for Blue Note is pure groove music with deep roots in the blues. It's an organ trio date with Ben Dixon shuffling a backbeat that swings hard. The interplay on the simple and direct date is very tight and the musicians are listening and reacting to one another. All of the tunes are concerned with the blues in one way or the other. Even the way that the artists approach the three standards "They Can't Take That Away from Me," "At Last," and "Willow Weep for Me" is blues-oriented.

One of the great things here is that Green does a lot of comping such as strumming triplets, sliding chords, playing four to the bar, sometimes even on the upbeat. His solos incorporate classic blues techniques like riffing behind the soloist or string bending, which he didn't do often elsewhere. This is an important date because it shows that he was focused on three things that he had mastered: the blues, the blues, and the blues.

Title: ***Sunday Mornin'***
Date: June 4, 1961
Label: Blue Note
Producer/Engineer: Alfred Lion/Rudy Van Gelder

When this recording came out, a Blue Note advertisement in *Down Beat* read, "The Record with the Sunday Morning Feeling." It's a quartet date with a very adventurous Kenny Drew on piano, Ben Dixon on drums, and Ben Tucker on bass, who was often Green's main bassist at the time. This straightahead session has a lot of gospel influence, which perfectly suits the Sunday morning context. Green's playing over the changes is lucid and clear as always, only the mood of the record is even more relaxed. It is somewhat of a predecessor to the *Feelin' the Spirit* session although there aren't any real "spirituals" included here.

The record features soulful renditions of "Exodus," Billie Holiday's "God Bless the Child," and a simplified version of Miles Davis's "So What." Dixon and Tucker also get some spots to solo. Four of the tracks are penned by Green, of which "Tracin' Tracy" is one that hadn't been released previously. The title track is a bouncy spiritual-influenced track with a triple feel. The other three originals are blues. *Sunday Mornin'* used to be difficult to find, but it's now available as part of the Blue Note Connoisseur CD series.

Title: *Grantstand*
Date: August 1, 1961
Label: Blue Note
Producer/Engineer: Alfred Lion/Rudy Van Gelder

In his fourth Blue Note recording under his own name, Green met legendary organist Jack McDuff, with Yusef Lateef on tenor sax and flute. Al Harewood completes the quartet with his discreet and supportive style of drumming. It's a soulful date with Green playing interesting straightahead solos, both on uptempo tunes and ballads. It showcases his strong lyrical bent beside his better known swinging blues side. Lateef impresses with a full sound and great technique while McDuff delivers all of the harmonies behind Green, playing bass and organ simultaneously. The hard-swinging Green original "Grantstand" opens the session. It was previously issued in the UK on the sampler *Street Funk & Jazz Grooves.* The fifteen-minute soliloquy "Blues in Maude's Flat" featured on *The Best of Grant Green, Vol. 1* is an original blues in B♭. In certain choruses, McDuff holds the chords for their full length. This produces a lot of space for the soloist to stretch out and have a good time.

The standards on this date are the two all-time favorites, "My Funny Valentine" and "Old Folks." The first one, taken at a very slow and challenging tempo, is one of the most impressive ballad performances recorded by Green. He plays very carefully, choosing his notes, showing that less can be more. Lateef on flute dialogues with him. They are truly two of the most unique stylists in the history of jazz.

The CD contains the first track from the session, which is an original tune called "Green's Greenery" that had not been released before. Most impressive is McDuff's bass pushing Green and Lateef into some hot blowing. As Nat Hentoff aptly stated in the original liner notes: "These performances are in the vintage jazz vein of straightforward story-telling, and accordingly they are refreshingly and durably enjoyable."

Title: ***Standards***
Date: August 29, 1961
Label: Blue Note
Producer/Engineer: Alfred Lion/Rudy Van Gelder

Once he arrived in New York, Green was a very prolific recording artist. He recorded far more music then Blue Note could release. One of those records is *Standards,* which was previously released only in Japan. The spotlight is on Green's mastery of interpreting well-known melodies. The chosen songs include "You Stepped Out of a Dream," a painfully slow "If I Had You," and an inhibited rendition of "You and the Night and the Music." Al Harewood on drums and Wilbur Ware on bass offer a good trio format for Green, whose playing is somewhat more reserved than on other dates. It is an interesting recording for the collector, but not one of the essential dates.

Title: ***Born to Be Blue***
Date: December 11, 1961
Label: Blue Note Records
Producer/Engineer: Alfred Lion/Rudy Van Gelder

Born to Bebop could also be the title of this quintet date with Sonny Clark, Sam Jones, Louis Hayes, and the late Ike Quebec. The record mostly includes standards (such as "Someday My Prince Will Come," "If I Should Lose You," and "My One and Only Love"), which have always been Green's strong point. He approaches the changes on this date using bebop shapes and scales, sometimes incorporating chords or arps in his lines. Although this is vintage Green, the star of the show is Quebec, whose interpretation of the title tune is a definite heart grabber of a ballad. He develops his ideas straight from the melody of the tune with an intense yet sentimental sound that brings to mind great saxophonists like Coleman Hawkins and Ben Webster. "In My Own Backyard" features Green and Quebec soloing at the same time. The only Green original, "Outer Space," has Green on rhythm guitar and could composition-wise join the row of the other standards. "Cool Blues," the bonus track, is one of the few Charlie Parker compositions Green has recorded and the only pure blues here. This classic date has a light-as-a-feather swing. It's a very ear-catching jazz record because both heads and solos flow so easy you feel like singing along with every note.

Title: ***Blue and Sentimental*** **(Ike Quebec)**
Date: December 16, 1961
Label: Blue Note Records
Producer/Engineer: Alfred Lion/Rudy Van Gelder

The great thing about this quartet date is that there is neither an organ nor a piano, and therefore Green has to use his whole arsenal of chords and comping techniques. Back in the studio as a leader, Quebec blows his big breathy old-school tenor backed up only by the harmonies of Green's guitar. The band's engine is the tight, but flexible duo, Miles's sidemen Paul Chambers and Philly Joe Jones. Quebec's originals "Like" and "Minor Impulse" are hard-swinging numbers with Green pulling his bebop registers. He puts himself to the test, delivering some sparkling runs. The most memorable renditions are the rarely played ballads "Don't Take Your Love from Me" (with a funny change in sound after about five minutes) and the mood-setter "Blue and Sentimental." Quebec's sensitive sound is squealing and whining at the same time while Green is moving some nice chords behind his lines. His solo work here is strong and rooted in the blues, often sliding up to a specific note he goes on to accentuate. Green's use of repetition is more shifted rhythmically. His sound is dry, somewhat metallic but nevertheless warm. Green pays tribute to his idol Charlie Parker, with the blues "Blues for Charlie." From time to time Quebec is sparsely comping on the piano, which was originally his instrument when he started out. But it is somewhat distracting and does not add to the overall sound. The CD reissue offers two mid-tempo bonus tracks from the session, "That Old Black Magic" and "It's All Right with Me," along with "Count Every Star" from the Nigeria sessions. This is the ultimate record to get if you want to hear Green comp in all kinds of styles.

Title: ***The Complete Quartets with Sonny Clark***
Date: December 23, 1961; January 13, 1962; January 31, 1962
Label: Blue Note
Producer/Engineer: Alfred Lion/Rudy Van Gelder

The Complete Quartets with Sonny Clark combines the three hard-bop albums *Nigeria, Gooden's Corner,* and *Oleo,* all of which have the solid and very melodious Sam Jones on bass. Green and Clark, both somewhat underrated players, are in very good shape here, playing inspiring material consisting mostly of standards plus three originals by Green. *Nigeria* is Green's only collaboration with Art Blakey, whose hard-swinging drums push Green into some virtuoso bop lines using arps and staccato motives. It is particularly interesting how they remodeled "It Ain't Necessarily So," almost making it a new composition. This is an all-standards date that includes Sonny Rollins's "Airegin" and the ballad "The Things We Did Last Summer" (the latter has a rather bizarre waltz intro). *Gooden's Corner* and *Oleo* both feature Louis Hayes on drums, whose empathy toward Jones is clearly evident. Their playing offers a solid base for Green to explore his material. The deluxe set has additional bonus tracks and alternate takes, and it features the original liner notes.

Title: *The Latin Bit*
Date: April 26, 1962
Label: Blue Note (CD 37645)
Producer/Engineer: Alfred Lion/Rudy Van Gelder

This is the first in a series of three recordings honoring a certain style of music. As the title reveals, Green collaborates with a Latin rhythm section consisting of Johnny Acea on piano, Wendell Marshall on bass, Willie Bobo on drums, Carlos "Potato" Valdez on congas, and Garvin Masseaux on chekere. He delivers some of the best known Latin tunes but as usual, in his own sweet way. The interesting thing is that they're not just playing straightahead while adding percussion as is very often done. They switch back and forth between Latin grooves and swing. The head might be played as a mambo while the solo section has a swing feel for Green's bopping solos. The percussion section always offers the Latin flavor.

The album is anchored by two mambos, "Mambo Inn" and "Besame Mucho," the latter having a more African rhythm. "Mama Inez" is actually performed in an uplifting hybrid of mambo and calypso. They swing "Brazil," but add a little bossa in the mix, too. "My Little Suede Shoes," which also appears on the album, is one of the Charlie Parker compositions Green recorded. The CD version contains three bonus tracks. The first one, an original blues in B♭ by Green, is the only one from the original session. It was probably recorded when the percussionists went for a tequila since it is the only pure straightahead cut in a quartet setting.

Title: ***Goin' West***
Date: November 30, 1962
Label: Blue Note
Producer/Engineer: Alfred Lion/Rudy Van Gelder

The second in a trilogy of albums dedicated entirely to a particular style of music, *Goin' West* features country western songs. This isn't new to the jazz world if you remember Sonny Rollins' "Way Out West" and others that were to follow, such as Gary Burton's "Tennessee Firebird" or Bill Frisell's chart-topping "Nashville." On his country outing Green does jazz takes on cowboy songs such as "On Top of Old Smokey," "Red River Valley," and "Tumbling Tumbleweeds." Recorded a month earlier than "Feelin' the Spirit," the date features a soulful Herbie Hancock on piano, a lively Billy Higgins on drums, and bassist Reggie Workman. It is in many ways similar to the spiritual date, offering songs in simple form with easy chord changes underlaid with light Latin grooves. Green is very cautious, playing only what really needs to be played. His measured delivery produce no forced emotions, but a sunny mood. His improvisations are not his best on record, but the production is very amusing and at times has a real good swing. This one is a collector's item and very hard to find.

Title: ***Feelin' the Spirit***
Date: December 21, 1962
Label: Blue Note
Producer/Engineer: Alfred Lion/Rudy Van Gelder

This is a classic as well as a collector's item. In early 1962, Green recorded both a Latin date and a country-western flavored session. On this album, he takes on the gospel format. As on *Goin' West,* the album features Herbie Hancock on acoustic piano and Billy Higgins on drums. Butch Warren is playing bass, and Garvin Masseaux reduces his percussion set down to the tambourine, which is the main church instrument besides the organ and the human voice.

These songs are famous spirituals known throughout the world. On them, Green is very bluesy and uses a great deal of repetition, which suits the mood of the tunes. At certain points the playing gathers an intensity that is almost unbearable. The rendition of "Just a Closer Walk with Thee" is very uplifting. Higgins's drum rhythms sound like early break-beat with a swinging ride cymbal.

"Nobody Knows the Trouble I've Seen" starts out with a rubato introduction, and Higgins joins in with brushes for the solo section.

Green is the only one taking the lead but Hancock responds beautifully to his ideas. One chorus features him repeating line after line from Green. Sometimes it seems as if Hancock is comping the question to Green's single-note answer. "Sometimes I Feel like a Motherless Child" is one of the saddest, most beautiful songs. The rhythm section lays down an ostinato over the whole form that creates a melancholy mood that makes one sway softly. Green's bluesy motifs and Hancock's sparkling lines are very different in style, but both fit into the same piece without breaking the mood. The bonus track is the only song not in the public domain. It's a very sweet version of Burleigh's "Deep River," and it sounds different from any other track on the record. This is probably because it is interpreted more as a song than a standard, which means that Green is singing on that one.

More attention could have been paid to the tambourine, which sounds a little lost and lonely in the background. If you feel like church on a weekday, then this is the record to listen to. Just spin it and let the music say the prayer for once.

Title: *Good Gracious* (Lou Donaldson)
Date: January 24, 1963
Label: Blue Note
Producer/Engineer: Alfred Lion/Rudy Van Gelder

Released as part of the Rare Groove series, Lou Donaldson's *Good Gracious* is a jam-oriented rhythm & blues album, probably reminiscent of what Green played in his hometown when Donaldson discovered him half a decade earlier. Donaldson's band at the time featured Ben Dixon on drums and John Patton on organ, who would both stick with Green for most of his career. Green's guitar is given much attention in the mix, not just for his bluesy solos, but also when he strums chords. He's pretty much up front throughout the date. The material is mostly rhythm & blues or spiritual-influenced groove music, four of the six coming from altoist Donaldson's pen. His sound is full and singing. His playing is not as close to Bird's as usual, except on "Cherry." The men to watch here are Patton and Green, who deliver fiery down-home solos. Check Green's intro to "Caracas." His guitar is miked directly and offers an unplugged sound you won't get anywhere else. He strums eighth-notes on a simple four-chord vamp, but shifts the accents, creating some kind of Latin rhythm. Green's short solos here and on the title track are of interest too, although the strongest one is on the closing number, a beautiful ballad made famous by Billie Holiday, "Don't Worry 'Bout Me."

Title: ***I'm Movin' On*** **(Jimmy Smith)**
Date: January 31, 1963
Label: Blue Note
Producer/Engineer: Alfred Lion/Rudy Van Gelder

I'm Movin' On is Green's only recorded collaboration with the father of the Hammond organ, Jimmy Smith. The album also features Donald Bailey on drums. The material is not surprising for a Smith session. It's soul-jazz with a shade of gospel, mostly blues with a light backbeat and some slow standards also, including Smith's swinging "Back Talk," which is probably the most cooking tune with Green and Smith trading choruses. Green's playing is not extraordinary on this date, but he is in good form. The CD reissue includes two bonus tracks, including a Smith original called "Organic Greenery" that might have been written for Green since it serves as an improvisational showcase for him.

Title: ***Idle Moments***
Date: November 4 + 11, 1963
Label: Blue Note
Producer/Engineer: Alfred Lion/Rudy Van Gelder

This is a classic recording featuring Green with an all-star band. A hot Joe Henderson is backed up by a cautious but lyrical Duke Pearson on piano, who donated the painfully lazy title track "Idle Moments" plus the Eastern-toned "Nomad." Even with the hard-swinging and sensual pulse of bassist Bob Cranshaw and drummer Al Harewood, the album owns a mellow, toned-down, after-hours ambience, due to the presence of Bobby Hutcherson's toned-in vibes.

The selections show Green's versatility and flexibility covering somber ballads and swiftly moving changes. All of the tracks have a very distinctive mood. "Jean de Fleur" demonstrates the soloist's ability to create an enormous excitement in a short amount of time while reading the mood of these tunes with great sensitivity.

Interestingly enough, the date reveals a problem that doesn't happen with the technical advantages we have today. Some of the tracks were too long to fit the vinyl and two had to be redone on a later date. The CD version includes the longer versions of "Django" and "Jean de Fleur" along with some very amusing liner notes by Duke Pearson on why the fellas played so long. They just got carried away! It has been recommended by the *All Music Guide to Jazz* as a first purchase and as part of any essential Grant Green collection.

Title: *Search for the New Land* **(Lee Morgan)**
Date: February 15, 1964
Label: Blue Note
Producer/Engineer: Alfred Lion/Rudy Van Gelder

Green figures as a sideman with an all-star lineup (including Herbie Hancock, Wayne Shorter, Billy Higgins, and Reggie Workman) for one of trumpeter Lee Morgan's most sophisticated modal outings. This album showcases Morgan as a great composer. He wrote and arranged all five selections. The title track is a cruise in 6/8 meter, played hip by Higgins, followed by sections with no distinctive time-measure. The modal progression is an F-minor and a G-flat-major chord alternating all the way through. The head is somewhat adventurous with a slight spiritual touch and long sustained notes creating a very airy mood. Green's repetitive solo is not the most interesting one on the record. His role is more in the background, adding soft little motives or trills as he does on "The Joker," a song which demonstrates how the music was carefully and beautifully arranged to fit the musicians on the date. Jointly responsible for the tasteful, modern sound is Hancock's harmonic conception on piano. The record sounds like a voyage and rewards repeated listening.

Title: ***Matador***
Date: May 1965
Label: Blue Note
Producer/Engineer: Alfred Lion/Rudy Van Gelder

In May of 1964 Green teamed up with McCoy Tyner and Elvin Jones, who had just finished recording *Crescent* with John Coltrane. Alfred Lion added Bob Cranshaw on bass, and the end result was a hard-swinging rhythm section that would push any musician to excel. Take the guitarist's playing on "My Favorite Things." As Michael Cuscuna puts it in the liner notes: "Green deserves a medal for doing Trane's hit in the same setting." They approach it with a similar rhythmic feel, but don't simplify the harmonic structure as radically as Trane did. Nevertheless you won't miss Tyner's left-hand pedal-bass, and you know how Elvin Jones can treat those 6/8 grooves.

Green recorded the song before in 1962 with Sonny Clark. But here he delivers a more beautiful solo, alternating bright staccato phrases with bebop lines and repetitive legato motives.

Another track that had been previously recorded by Green is Duke Pearson's "Bedouin." It takes you all the way to North Africa on a polyrhythmic trip, crossing the desert with a caravan. Jones is most remarkable here, contributing his only solo on this date. He maintains the mood of the tune by making it a real drum solo, using mainly toms and snare. Tyner's solo is typical because of his use of pentatonics and the interval of the fourth.

Green penned two originals for this date. The title track, "Matador," has an AAB structure with an interesting total of 28 bars that is repeated throughout. The melody is somewhat syncopated, and his solo is very bluesy. Writes Cuscuna, "It typifies Greens ability to be completely rhythmic and lyrical simultaneously."

Bob Cranshaw doesn't get a chance to solo on the date, but he supports all the way through. The CD contains a previously unissued bonus track with a 6/8 feel. It's a mellow but groovy version of Bacharach/David's "Wives and Lovers." No clue why this hasn't been released before since it is a true classic.

Title: ***Solid***
Date: June 12, 1964
Label: Blue Note
Producer/Engineer: Alfred Lion/Rudy Van Gelder

The follow-up to *Matador, Solid* is one of Green's most significant straightahead dates. He was obviously inspired by the presence of McCoy Tyner, Elvin Jones, Bob Cranshaw, James Spaulding, and Joe Henderson. Duke Pearson's "Minor League" and George Russell's "Ezz-Thetic" both have strong and modern-sounding horn arrangements, complete with Tynerish harmonies driven by Jones's hard-pushing swing. Henderson and Spaulding are hot and blow some earthy phrases. But it is especially interesting to hear what these guys do with a Green composition such as "Grant's Tune." Tyner stimulates the harmonies while Jones's triplet-pulls go all the way through. Also featured is an early version of Henderson's "The Kicker" before it became a hit with Horace Silver. The CD was released as part of the Connoisseur series and contains the bonus track "Wives and Lovers," also a bonus track on the *Matador* reissue. This is an exceptional album not just for guitarists, but for all jazz fans.

Title: ***Talkin' About***
Date: September 11, 1964
Label: Blue Note
Producer/Engineer: Alfred Lion/Rudy Van Gelder

This is the first recording of the legendary trio of Grant Green, drummer Elvin Jones, and organist Larry Young. The album is vintage Green and features some of his most fluid straightahead jazz. Both his sound and conception are clear and his improvisations are adventurous. Young's solo excursions are simply amazing backed up with some nice ostinatos and chord-playing by Green. Jones is kept in the background, but grooves hard and complex, with a fierce cymbal swinging straight through the whole date, yet he answers every little twist from the soloists. Some strong spots include Green's stretching out on the ballad "People" and the up-tempo title marathon "Talking About JC" (John Coltrane).

Title: ***Into Something*** **(Larry Young)**
Date: November 12, 1964
Label: Blue Note
Producer/Engineer: Alfred Lion/Rudy Van Gelder

On his debut for Blue Note, organist Larry Young takes a big step away from Jimmy Smith, fashioning a distinctive modal approach to the Hammond. His trio with Green and Elvin Jones is joined for four tracks by earthy-toned Sam Rivers on tenor. All of the tunes are originals, quite complex and adventurous, reminiscent of Coltrane's modal period. One of them is Green's refreshingly Latin "Plaza de Toros."

Only the Jimmy Smith-like blues "Backup" is more traditional and therefore suitable for Green to pull apart. His classic solo on this cut is a transcendent outburst of beboppish blues lines that show his total command of the roots. The fact that we have four totally different stylists makes this recording very exciting. The groove on the date is strong and the harmonies are larkish, but there is a strong connection to tradition.

Title: ***I Want to Hold Your Hand***
Date: March 31, 1965
Label: Blue Note
Producer/Engineer: Alfred Lion/Rudy Van Gelder

This is a blue-toned, totally relaxed date that features both bossa nova and straightahead playing. The legendary trio of Green, Larry Young, and Elvin Jones is joined by the "middleweight champion of the tenors," Hank Mobley. While Young is experimenting with modern harmonies, Green's sound is full and singing as usual. The material is very well chosen and features two bossa novas, two ballads, and a pair of uptempo numbers. The title Beatles track turns Latin just as the following "Corcovado." Straightahead numbers like Kurt Weill's cooking "Speak Low" or Steve Allen's "This Could Be the Start of Something Big" are also highlights, due partly to the vibrant rhythms of Jones. Slow songs include a groovy "Stella by Starlight" and a very bluesy "At Long Last Love," which has some nice question-and-answer playing by Mobley and Green at the end. This moody date was Green's last recording for Blue Note until he signed for a second time in 1969.

Title: ***His Majesty King Funk***
Date: May 26, 1965
Label: Verve
Producer/Engineer: Creed Taylor

His Majesty King Funk is a significant Green recording because it shows his first attempt at using boogalooish beats along with bluesy tunes and it is his only recording for Verve. But it is a rather disappointing date compared to his later excursions with Idris Muhammad and Claude Bartee. The tempos are slow and uninspiringly lazy while the selection of tunes and their renditions are rather questionable.

The only originals, "The Selma March" and "The Cantaloupe Woman," are the funky tracks, and they feature Green's classic shouts and crispy double stops. Ben Dixon lays a resilient boogaloo rhythm with Candido Cameron spicing it up on congas. Larry Young gets his B-3-feature on "Willow Weep for Me" with Green at times strumming unsuitable chords but then delivering a coherent down-home statement. Harold Vick has a few good moments on tenor but doesn't satisfy on flute, playing off-key behind Green on the bossa "That Lucky Old Sun." The CD was reissued with the unrelated and equally weak "Up with Donald Byrd" session which doesn't make it much more valuable.

Title: ***Let 'Em Roll***
Date: December 11, 1965
Label: Blue Note
Producer/Engineer: Alfred Lion/Rudy Van Gelder

John Patton and Grant Green go together like bread and butter. This was Patton's fifth recording for Blue Note and also the fifth with Green at his side. The group is completed by Otis Finch on drums and Bobby Hutcherson on vibes. While vibes is not the usual instrument for soul-jazz sessions, it works fine here and gives this fiery session a relaxed overtone. The basslines are provided by Patton's incredibly swinging organ pedalwork. The record also showcases Patton as a very gifted and soulful composer. Four of the six tracks are his originals with catchy heads and well-established grooves falling somewhere between boogaloo and R&B. Green throws in funky chords and an occasional melodic outburst behind Patton's solos.

The one standard of the date, "The Shadow of Your Smile," is done in a bossa vein and is kicked off at the smooth tempo of 104 bpm. The other cover on the session is the Hank Mobley composition "The Turnaround" from the recording with the same title released earlier that year.

Title: ***Iron City***
Date: 1967
Label: 32 Jazz (32048)
Producer/Engineer: Joel Dorn

This trio date with Big John Patton and Ben Dixon was recorded in 1967 while Green was on an extended recording hiatus. Besides *Live at the Lighthouse,* this is the hottest Grant Green album you can get (with the only difference being we have just three and not seven people cooking here). Ben Dixon's twisted boogaloo beats roll deft and strong. His press rolls hit one like thunder while Green is fighting on top, bursting his famous, slightly distorted sound that is just as tense and crisp as Patton's roaring Hammond organ. It all trudges over a swampy low bass right into the opener, "Iron City." The only original here, the title song has Green burning right away, showing some of the techniques that would become famous a few years later such as slided double stops, tremoloed intervals, insistent trills, and his own approach to pentatonics. The Latin-embraced "Samba de Orpheus" keeps Green busier than normal, rocking on adjacent-string duplicate notes, using chromatic pull-offs, tremolos shifted in pitch, and even some string bending. His renditions of the spirituals "Old Man Moses (Let My People Go)" and "Motherless Child" are the grooviest versions one has ever heard. Originally issued on the Cobblestone and Muse labels, this date is now available as a reissue. The original cover showed Green behind the whole of his guitar with the strings figuring in as the iron bars he got to know well. The cover of the reissue therefore is somewhat corny, but eye-catching and up-to-date. *Iron City* is a true textbook of soul-jazz guitar.

Title: *Rusty Bryant Returns*
Date: February 17, 1969
Label: Prestige
Producer/Engineer: Bob Porter/Rudy Van Gelder

While not the most famous, this is one of the best of all boogaloo recordings with Green handling a hot axe. He fits perfectly into the new group of Rusty Bryant, who had been away from the recording business for several years too. But he is still squealing notes and taking advantage of new technologies by electrifying his alto horn with a Conn Multi-Vider. Green is in great form here, fresh and fast, his conception very clear, his lines hip. His chords are strong, in tune and in place. Sometimes it would appear that Green was much more relaxed as a sideman since some of his landmark performances are on other people's dates. Most tunes on this album were composed by Bryant. The strongest and most electrifying songs are "Zoo Boogaloo" and "Streak o' Lean," which has a firm boogaloo beat by Herbie Lovelle with Sonny Phillips punching on Hammond organ. Green shines on all of the songs, but brings the last one back home by himself, playing some deep sensitive blues on Kenny Burrell's "All Day Long."

Title: *Love Bug*
Date: March 21, 1969
Label: Blue Note
Producer/Engineer: Francis Wolff/Rudy Van Gelder

This is one of those records that makes people like Reuben Wilson and Grant Green get respected as "Godfathers of Acid Jazz" by a younger generation. I'm always skeptical of those kinds of titles, but let's look at the facts. The lineup for this date almost speaks for itself: Lee Morgan and George Coleman figure in the horn section. Green and Wilson funk it up with the right chords while Jimmy Lewis lays the harmonic base and Idris Muhammad (then known as Leo Morris) bangs his drums. The last two both grooved with Green earlier that month on the *Carryin' On* date.

The material is exceptional. "Hot Rod," "Love Bug," and "Back Out" (also on *The Best of GG—Vol. II*) are originals by Wilson. They are groovy boogaloos with blowing passages typical for that Blue Note period. "Stormy" is played as a bossa nova that moves the soloist like a soft breeze moves a wave on a Brazilian sea. The other three tracks were originally vocal tunes associated with soul music: "I'm Gonna Make You Love Me" (made famous by the Temptations), the Supremes' "Takin' Care of Business," and the Sam and Dave hit

"Hold On, I'm Coming." Added in the mix is another Top 40 hit, the Bacharach standard "I Say a Little Prayer."

The soloists do not get a whole lot of space to really stretch out, but the record features some very nice blowing by Green. It's an interesting date because Green is comping even though the band is pretty big.

Title: *Carryin' On*
Date: October 3, 1969
Label: Blue Note
Producer/Engineer: Francis Wolff/Rudy Van Gelder

Carryin' On is aptly named since it was the start of Green's second stint with Blue Note Records after being out of the recording business for awhile. His sound and phrasing are still the same, although the music has been changed to match the changing sound of the music industry. It's laidback and easy listening with a funky sound. The material consists of two pop songs, an original by Green, and the James Brown hit "I Don't Want Nobody to Give Me Nothing." While the arrangements are simple and melodious, the material doesn't really seem to keep the band busy. The most impressive track is Earl Neal Creque's "Cease the Bombing," which is based on a C-pedal bass with C and B♭ chords alternating above and a harmonically complex bridge. It also became a classic due to William Biven's typical vibes-and-voice solo, Clarence Palmer's inventive and most sophisticated solo, and Claude Bartee's dying notes thrown in behind the guitar melody on the second go 'round. The mood the players create on the album is quite relaxed.

Title: *Alive!/Green Is Beautiful*
Date: January 30, 1970/August 15, 1970
Label: Blue Note
Producer/Engineer: Francis Wolff/Rudy Van Gelder

Spurned by critics as music that is "churned out R&B with one eye on the clock and the other on the dollar pouring into the cash till," these two recordings include some of the most electrifying and funky sounds Blue Note has to offer. *Alive!* was recorded live at the Cliche Lounge in Newark and features solid Ronnie Foster keyboard work, Earl Neal Creque on organ, a laidback William Bivens on vibes, the squeezing trademark tenor sax of Claude Bartee, Joseph Armstrong on congas, and Idris Muhammad on drums. "Let the Music Take Your Mind" is a pop song that features some slided double stops, insistent trills and tremolos along with a shuddering melody interpretation.

"Time to Remember," a classic mysterious Earl Neal Creque original and the chill-out number of the night, offers Bivens singing along with his only stand-out on the date. Bartee riffs effectively behind Green. The sparkling break-beats of Muhammad help make "Sookie, Sookie" and "Down Here on the Ground" the most sampled of all Grant Green songs.

Green Is Beautiful consists of similar material but is a nontet studio date. Besides the hardcore playing of Emmanuel Riggins and Earl Neal Creque on organs, Jimmy Lewis on Fender bass, and Claude Bartee on tenor, the album features special guest Blue Mitchell on trumpet and the percussion of Candido Cameron and Richard Landrum. The beat is tight and rolling with the ensemble playing being inventive and on fire. "Ain't It Funky Now" is Green's bow to James Brown, whom he admired a lot. The Bacharach-David ballad "I'll Never Fall in Love Again" is a heartbreaking classic with the guitar singing the song the way a human voice probably never could. Green's crying guitar over the organ chords is funky and lyrically blues drenched.

Both records have been reissiued on vinyl and have a good balance of slow-tempo numbers and uplifting funk-vamps. There is a little less excitement and fire on the studio date, but the arrangements are more mature and sophisticated than on the earthy live session. However, both records have a dense groove.

Title: *Visions*
Date: May 21, 1971
Label: Blue Note
Producer/Engineer: George Butler and W. Marcus/ Rudy Van Gelder

This is easy-listening from the first rank and could be described as an homage to nice melodies. A decade earlier Green had made records featuring country and Latin music; the spotlight here is on popular music of the era. That includes the Top 40 hits of those days, film music, classical music, and some blues.

"Does Anybody Really Know What Time It Is" was penned by Robert Lamm from the band Chicago. The following tune, "Maybe Tomorrow," was originally used in the movie *John and Mary.* It is mellow and beautifully arranged as is every other selection on this date. The most unexpected title is an adaption of Wolfgang Amadeus Mozart's "Symphony No. 40 in G minor." This sounds like a little joke, but it is quite funky, particularly when they squeeze in a bridge consisting of a II-V vamp. I'm sure Amadeus would be groovin' in his grave if he had a chance to hear how Green tears apart this composition. "Love on a Two Way Street," "We've Only Just Begun," and "Never Can Say Goodbye" are all Top 40 hits, the latter written for the Jackson 5 and later recorded by singers like Gloria Gaynor and Roberta Flack. "Cantaloupe Woman" by Ben Dixon (previously recorded on *His Majesty King Funk*) and "Blues for Abraham" by Emmanuel Riggins (the only original composition of the date) are the exceptions of the set. They're both blues and blowing numbers with the main focus on soloing rather than on arrangement.

Visions gives Green a chance to show something he'd mastered—the ability to uniquely state a simple melody. It is not the record to buy if you're looking for a whole lot of improvisation. It's mainly about interpretation and arrangement.

Title: *The Final Comedown*
Date: December 13, 1971
Label: Blue Note

In the '70s, it was a good marketing move for an artist to have a soundtrack album and a live record in addition to his studio recordings. So Green teamed up with the "creme de la creme" of the current studio scene, an all-star lineup featuring Richard Tee on keys, Cornell Dupree on wah-wah guitar, Gordon Edwards on electric bass, Grady Tate on drums, Ralph McDonald on percussion, Marvin Stamm and Irv Markowitz on trumpets, Harold Vicks on soprano, and Phil Bodner on woodwinds. This is different from any recording that Green had ever made. It is without question the most experimental record, "avant-guardistic funk," with marching drums, Latin percussion, light and sweet strings, horn arrangements, wah-wah guitars, and rolling thunder effects, but unfortunately a not always present Grant Green. He has a few nasty spots but often figures in the background since this is film music and probably arranged that way. His playing has a light touch of country-blues, probably because the material is different and because his normal licks wouldn't work here. The sound quality of the whole recording is amazing. Green's guitar sound is one of the best on record, warm and clear with a subtle reverb making it bigger and a little more modern. The disco-burner and turntable-killer is the title track, "The Final Comedown," a driving one-chord vamp with Green's archtop guitar bursting on top like a rocket. The R&B ballad "Father's Lament" is arranged for silky strings, underlaid by a whiney Hammond. Green's bluesy, country-touched talking is so sweet, it's a sure heart-winner. "Slight Fear and Terror" is very modern, ahead of its time, and easily a forerunner of the recent hip-hop-meets-jazz movement. Unfortunately, it's a very short cut.

Other titles include "Afro Party," "Battle Scene," or "Past, Present and Future." The conception and production differ from a conventional studio date. One wonders whether Green shouldn't have been given more space to go for new ways in his playing, for example, taking over the wah-wah parts of Dupree. But this is definitely one of the guitarist's recordings that needs to be reissued since it is unique.

Title: ***Live at the Lighthouse***
Date: April 21, 1972
Label: Blue Note (BN LA 037/CDP 93381)
Producer: George Butler

This album captures Green in a live performance at the Lighthouse with one of his hottest working bands. Hank Stewart preaches love and introduces the band members: the regular Grant Green Quartet featuring Shelton Laster on Hammond organ, Greg Williams on drums, and Claude Bartee on tenor and soprano saxophones—plus three guests: Gary Coleman on vibes, Wilton Felder on electric bass, and Bobbye Hall on percussion. The latter three are famous for recordings with artists such as Barry White, Joni Mitchell, or the Jazz Crusaders. Now you know what that means. Get your dancing shoes down from the attic...push play or set the needle in the groove.

They start it off with "Windjammer" by organ player Earl Neal Creque. It's a funky bass ostinato based on a B♭ dominant chord spiced up by Williams's syncopated hi-hat. Grant takes the first turn and burns right away, playing some of his most typical motives of his so-called nonstraightahead period. The joint is definitely jumping when he gets hold of that fifth (B♭ and E♭) at the end of his solo. (If you're not dancing by then, you probably bought the wrong record.) After Bartee's soprano sax solo Williams gets a turn for some four minutes of polyrhythmic cooking (with drums and whistle), an early highlight of this session.

Green usually had a tune on his records that came from another musical genre, in this case the pop ballad "Betcha by Golly Wow." He probably chose this song for its beautiful melody or because it is a sure crowd-pleaser. Green loved to please an audience. Bartee plays a wonderful intro on the soprano, and when Green comes in with the melody the people are hollering. Listen to his phrasing, his articulation, and how he uses slurs and tremolos. He's making love to the melody. Those of you who know the original words know that his guitar is definitely singing.

On Donald Byrd's "Fancy Free" from the 1969 Blue Note record with the same title, one should listen to how Bartee's sound seems to be an extension of Green on the head. When the guitar fades, it trips into a horn sound. "Flood in Franklin Park" is an original by organist Laster, and definitely a highlight of the date. Green, Bartee, and Laster play some of their nicest solo work on record. Green's solo builds up gradually, and there comes an intense point when he holds that fourth and strikes it hard for some time, just like someone who's screaming for help in a flood. (When it comes to soloing, Bartee seems more comfortable on tenor than on soprano.) Laster himself takes an unbelievable funky solo using a lot of repetition. At the end the music gets softer as if the flood took it all!

One reason why reissues are important is that younger listeners can discover that it's all been there before. Take "Jan Jan" and spin it at a slightly faster tempo and you'll get a pure drum 'n' bass/jungle groove. They were a good twenty years ahead of their time even though they were not aware of it. Hall's vibrant congas and Williams' consistent pulse push Green, Laster, and Bartee into some burning blowing. This take of "A Walk in the Night" was previously used on a *Best of Grant Green* compilation in the UK (*Street Funk & Jazz Grooves*). Perhaps Green chose to perform this tune because Junior Walker & the All Stars' version was on the charts and folks were familiar with it. Green's version is much more relaxed, with a beautiful question-and-answer playing style. Bobbye Hall's percussion and Gary Coleman's vibes could have used more attention throughout, although they add a certain something to the overall sound. You have to listen carefully in order to hear how they support the music, but you can definitely feel them. The original double-LP version (BN LA 037; containing four introductions more than the reissue) was hard to find for a long time. It was Grant's last recording for Blue Note. The recording is now available on a single compact disc and ready for a younger generation that wants to go back to the roots of their own music. Check it out.

Title: ***The Main Attraction***
Date: March 1976
Label: KUDU (LP: KU-29; CD: KICJ 8102)
Producer: Creed Taylor

The Main Attraction, released on CTI's subsidiary KUDU (at that time, also home for such musicians as Idris Muhammad, Grover Washington Jr., and Hank Crawford), is the most uninspiring Grant

Green record currently available. With all of the efforts to have his never-before released work out, somebody must have really been hurting for money when they reissued this. The lineup reads like a who's who list of studio musicians, including Ron Cuber, Jon Faddis, Don Grolnick, Hubert Laws, and Michael Brecker. But good musicians don't necessarily mean good music, and such is the case here. The record consists of three lengthy pieces that are probably supposed to be funky. The title track is a nineteen-minute march to the gas chambers, kicked off at 75 beats per minute. You wait more than a minute until Green plays his very first note. His sound and feel are still intact, but the interaction of musicians playing together in the moment is missing, and the material is too poor to push him to play an inspiring solo.

"Future Feature" makes you hope you get a nice little samba, but it turns out to be something like the title melody of a '70s beach party. At least it's the only track with something like a head melody. The last cut is an original by Green, a blues in E entitled "Creature." The chosen tempo is 49 bpm, which makes you think that B.B. King might be somewhere around the corner. It's the best track of the record with some bluesy playing by Laws, Brecker, and Green.

This is a notable recording only because it is different from every other Green record and it uses effects like flanger and reverb. In a 1972 interview, Green says that he would like to produce his own records. I wish he could have done so.

Title: ***Street Funk & Jazz Grooves***
Date: Released in 1993
Label: Blue Note (CD: 0777 7 89622 2 9/UK: BNZ317)
Compiler: Kevin Beadle

This compilation is highly recommended as an introduction to the funkier side of Grant Green. Compiled by deejay Kevin Beadle, it focuses on groove (and danceability). But it features some beautiful mellow cuts, too. This sampler might be hard to find outside of Europe. The tunes on it are "Grantstand," "Lazy Afternoon," "Sookie, Sookie," "Talking About JC," "Windjammer," "A Walk in the Night," "I Won't Want Nobody," "Cease the Bombing," "The Final Comedown," and "In the Middle."

Title: ***The Best of Grant Green—Vols. I & II***
Date: Vol. I: 1993/Vol. II: 1996
Label: Blue Note
Compiler: Vol. I: Michael Cuscuna/Vol. II: Bob Belden

Volume I focuses on the first and straighter half of the Blue Note years, while Volume II combines some of the funkier, boogalooish tracks from the second half. All of the tunes have been previously released, although a few are hard to get. If you purchase these two samplers, you will get a very good sense of what Grant Green sounded like throughout his career as one of the main recording artists for Blue Note. The songs on Volume I are "Miss Ann's Tempo," "'Round Midnight," "Blues in Maude's Flat," "Speak Low," "Idle Moments," and "Ezz-thetic." The tunes on Volume II are "Back Out," "Cease the Bombing," "Ain't Funky Now," "Sookie, Sookie," "Cantaloupe Woman," "California Green," "The Final Comedown," and "Windjammer."

Title: ***Jazz Profile—No.11***
Date: Released in 1997
Label: Blue Note
Compiler: Bob Belden

This sampler compiled by Bob Belden is part of a series launched by Blue Note for a new and younger audience interested in getting to know some masters of the label. I recommend this as an introduction to the straighter and jazzier side of Grant Green. The tunes on it are "Baby's Minor Lope," "My Little Suede Shoes," "Go Down Moses," "Talkin' About JC," "Somewhere in the Night," and "My Favorite Things."

—Tobias "TJ" Jundt

Discography

***All the Gin Is Gone*/Jimmy Forrest (Delmark)**
Dec. 10, 1959; with Jimmy Forrest, Harold Mabern, Gene Ramey, and Elvin Jones
Caravan, All the Gin Is Gone, Sunkenfoal, Myra, Laura

***Black Forrest*/Jimmy Forrest (Delmark)**
Dec. 10, 1959; with Jimmy Forrest, Harold Mabern, Gene Ramey, and Elvin Jones
All the Gin Is Gone (alt. take), Sunkenfoal (alt. take), These Foolish Things, Dog It, But Beautiful

***Sam Lazar* (Chess) Germany**
Jun. 1, 1960; with Sam Lazar, Willie Dixon, and Chauncey Williams
Blues

***Space Flight*/Sam Lazar (Argo)**
Jun. 1, 1960; with Sam Lazar, Willie Dixon, and Chauncey Williams
Funky Blues, Big Willie, Space Flight, Dig a Little Deeper, Gigi Blues, Caramu, Mad Lad, We Don't Know, Ruby, Put Your Old Grey Bonnet, My Baby, All or Nothing at All

***Here 'Tis*/Lou Donaldson (Blue Note)**
Jan. 23, 1961; with Lou Donaldson, Baby Face Willette, and Dave Bailey
Watusi Jump, Here 'Tis, Cool Blues, Walk with Me, A Foggy Day

***Grant's First Stand*/Grant Green (Blue Note)**
Jan. 28, 1961; with Baby Face Willette and Ben Dixon
A Wee Bit o' Green, Miss Ann's Tempo, T'ain't Nobody's Business If I Do, Baby's Minor Lope, Lullaby of the Leaves, Blues for Willarene

***Face to Face*/Baby Face Willette (Blue Note)**
Jan. 30, 1961; with Fred Jackson, Baby Face Willette, and Ben Dixon
Face to Face, Something Strange, Whatever Lola Wants, Goin' Down, Swingin' at Sugar Ray's, High 'n' Low

***The Honeydripper*/Jack McDuff (Prestige)**
Feb. 3, 1961; with Jimmy Forrest, Jack McDuff, and Ben Dixon
Blues and Tonic, Whap!, The Honeydripper, I Want a Little Girl, Mr. Lucky, Dink's Blues

***Up at Minton's Vol. 1*/Stanley Turrentine (Blue Note)**
Feb. 23, 1961; with Stanley Turrentine, Horace Parlan, George Tucker, and Al Harewood
But Not for Me, Stanley's Time, Broadway, Yesterdays

***Up at Minton's Vol. 2*/Stanley Turrentine (Blue Note)**
Feb. 23, 1961; with Stanley Turrentine, Horace Parlan, George Tucker, and Al Harewood
Love for Sale, Come Rain or Shine, Later at Minton's, Summertime

***Reaching Out*/Grant Green (Black Lion) Japan**
Mar. 15, 1961; (also released as *Green Blues,* Muse) with Frank Haynes, Billy Gardner, Ben Tucker, and Dave Bailey
Reaching Out (take 4), Our Miss Brooks (take 4), A Flick of a Trick (take 1), One for Elena (take 5), Baby You Should Know It (take 3), Falling Is Low with Love (take 1), Our Miss Brooks (take 1), One for Elena (take 4)

***Workout*/Hank Mobley (Blue Note)**
Mar. 26, 1961; with Hank Mobley, Wynton Kelly, Paul Chambers, and Philly Joe Jones
Smokin', Uh Huh, The Best Things in Life Are Free, Workout, Greasin' Easy, Three Coins in a Fountain

***Green Street*/Grant Green (Blue Note)**
Apr. 1, 1961; with Ben Tucker and Dave Bailey

Green with Envy, Grant's Dimensions, Alone Together, 'Round About Midnight, No. 1 Green Street

***Stop and Listen*/Baby Face Willette (Blue Note)**
May 22, 1961; with Baby Face Willette and Ben Dixon
Jumpin' Jupiter, Work Song, Stop and Listen, Chances Are Few, Soul Walk, At Last, Willow Weep for Me

***Sunday Mornin'*/Grant Green (Blue Note)**
Jun. 4, 1961; with Kenny Drew, Ben Tucker, and Ben Dixon
Come Sunrise, Freedom March, Sunday Morning, Exodus, God Bless the Child, So What

***Up and Down*/Horace Parlan (Blue Note)**
Jun. 18, 1961; with Booker Ervin, Horace Parlan, George Tucker, and Al Harewood
Light Blue, Up and Down, The Book's Beat, Fugee, Lonely One, The Other Part of Town

***Goodnight It's Time to Go*/Jack McDuff (Prestige)**
Jul. 14, 1961; with Harold Vick, Jack McDuff, and Joe Dukes
Sanctified Waltz, Goodnight It's Time to Go, McDuff Speaking, I'll Be Seeing You, A Smooth One

***Steppin' Out*/Brother Jack McDuff (Prestige)**
Jul. 14, 1961; with Harold Vick, Jack McDuff, and Joe Dukes
Godiva Brown

***Sanctified*/Brother Jack McDuff (Prestige)**
Jul. 14, 1961; with Harold Vick, Jack McDuff, and Joe Dukes
Godiva Brown

***Grantstand*/Grant Green (Blue Note)**
Aug. 1, 1961; with Yusef Lateef, Jack McDuff, and Al Harewood
Green's Greenery, Blues in Maude's Flat, My Funny Valentine, Grantstand, Old Folks

***Remembering*/Grant Green (Blue Note) Japan**
Aug. 29, 1961; with Wilbur Ware and Al Harewood
I'll Remember April, You and the Night and the Music, All the Things You Are, If I Had You, I Remember You, Love Walked In

***Z.T.'s Blues*/Stanley Turrentine (Blue Note)**
Sep. 13, 1961; Stanley Turrentine, Tommy Flanagan, Paul Chambers, and Art Taylor
For Heaven's Sake, The Lamp Is Low, More than You Know, I Wish I Knew, Z.T.'s Blues, Be My Love, The Way You Look Tonight

***Sonny Red Quintet* (Jazzland)**
Dec. 14, 1961; with Sonny Red, Barry Harris, George Tucker, and Jimmy Cobb
Moon River, Super 20, The Mode

***Blue and Sentimental*/Ike Quebec (Blue Note)**
Dec. 16, 1961; with Ike Quebec, Paul Chambers, and Philly Joe Jones
Like, Don't Take Your Love from Me, Minor Impulse, Blues for Charlie, That Old Magic, It's Alright with Me, Blue and Sentimental
Dec. 23, 1961; with Ike Quebec, Sonny Clark, Sam Jones, and Louis Hayes
Count Every Star

***Gooden's Corner*/Grant Green (Blue Note) Japan**
Dec. 23, 1961; with Sonny Clark, Sam Jones, and Louis Hayes
Moon River, On Green Dolphin Street, What Is This Thing Called Love, Shadrack, Gooden's Corner, Two for One

***Nigeria*/Grant Green (Blue Note)**
Jan. 13, 1962; with Sonny Clark, Sam Jones, and Art Blakey
Airegin, I Concentrate on You, The Things We Did Last Summer, The Song Is You, It Ain't Necessarily So

***The Complete Blue Note Recordings of Grant Green with Sonny Clark* (Mosaic Records)**

Jan. 13, 1962; with Sonny Clark, Sam Jones, and Art Blakey
Airegin (alt. take), Nancy
Jan. 31, 1962; with Louis Hayes, replaces Blakey
Oleo (alt. take)
Sep. 7, 1962; with Ike Quebec, Sonny Clark, Wendell Marshall, Willie Bobo, and Carlos "Potato" Valdez
Grenada, Hey There

***Oleo*/Grant Green (Blue Note) Japan**

Jan. 31, 1962; with Sonny Clark, Sam Jones, and Louis Hayes
My Favorite Things, Hip Funk, Oleo, Little Girl Blue, Tune Up

***Born to Be Blue*/Grant Green (Blue Note)**

Mar. 1, 1962; with Ike Quebec, Sonny Clark, Sam Jones, and Louis Hayes
Someday My Prince Will Come, If I Should Lose You, My One and Only Love, Back in Your Own Backyard, Born to Be Blue, Born to Be Blue (alt. take), Cool Blues

***My House of Need*/Dodo Green (Blue Note)**

Apr. 2, 1962; with Ike Quebec, Sir Charles Thompson, Milt Hinton, Al Harewood, and Dodo Green, vocalist
Little Things Mean a Lot, Down by the Riverside, Trouble in Mind, Let There Be Love,
Apr. 17, 1962; with Herbie Lewis, Billy Higgins, replaces Hinton, Harewood
I Won't Cry Anymore, Lonesome Road, There Must Be a Way, You Are My Sunshine, My Hour of Need, I'll Never Stop Loving

***The Latin Bit*/Grant Green (Blue Note)**

Apr. 26, 1962; with Johnny Acea, Wendell Marshall, Willie Bobo, Carlos Valdez, and Garvin Masseaux
Mambo, My Little Suede Shoes, Brazil, Besame Mucho, Tico, Tico, Maza Inez
Without Valdez, Masseux
Blues for Juanita

***Elder Don*/Don Wilkerson (Blue Note)**
May 3, 1962; with Don Wilkerson, John Acea, Lloyd Trotman, and Willie Bobo
Drawin' a Tip, Senorita Eula, Poor Butterfly, Scrappy, San Antonio Rose, Naughty Neenie, Lone Star Shuffle

***The Natural Soul*/Lou Donaldson (Blue Note)**
May 9, 1962; with Tommy Turrentine, Lou Donaldson, John Patton, and Ben Dixon
Spaceman Twist, People Will Say We're in Love, That's All, Funky Mama, Love Walked In, Sow Belly Blues, Nice 'n Greasy

***Preach Brother*/Don Wilkerson (Blue Note)**
Jun. 18, 1962; with Don Wilkerson, Butch Warren, and Billy Higgins
Jeanie-Weenie, Pigeon Peas, Eldorado Shuffle, Homesick Blues, Camp Meetin', Dem Tambourines

***Images*/Sonny Red (Jazzland)**
July 1962; with Blue Mitchell, Barry Harris, George Tucker, and Jimmy Cobb
Blue Sonny, The Rhythm Thing, Bewitched, Bothered and Bewildered

***Goin' West*/Grant Green (Blue Note)**
Nov. 30, 1962; with Herbie Hancock, Reggie Workman, and Billy Higgins
Wagon Wheels, Tumbling Tumbleweeds, Red River Valley, On Top of Old Smokey, I Can't Stop Lovin' You

***Feelin' the Spirit*/Grant Green (Blue Note)**
Dec. 21, 1962; with Herbie Hancock, Butch Warren, Billy Higgins, and Garvin Masseaux
Go Down Moses, Just a Closer Walk with Thee, Joshua Fit the Battle of Jericho, Sometimes I Feel Like a Motherless Child, Nobody Knows the Troubles I've Seen
Without Masseaux
Deep River

***Good Gracious*/Lou Donaldson (Blue Note)**
Jan. 24, 1963; with Lou Donaldson, John Patton, and Ben Dixon
The Holy Ghost, Good Gracious, Caracas, Cherry, Bad John, Don't Worry about Me

***I'm Movin' On*/Jimmy Smith (Blue Note)**
Jan. 31, 1963; Jimmy Smith and Donald Bailey
Hotel Happiness, Cherry, T'ain't No Use, I'm Movin' On, Back Talk, What Kind of Fool Am I

***Jimmy Smith—Special Guests* (Blue Note) Japan**
Jan. 31, 1963; with Jimmy Smith and Donald Bailey
Organic Greenery, Day In Day Out

***Happy Frame of Mind*/Horace Parlan (Blue Note)**
Feb. 15, 1963; Johnny Coles, Booker Ervin, Horace Parlan, Butch Warren, and Billy Higgins
Happy Frame of Mind, A Tune for Richard, Home Is Africa, Dexi, Back from the Gig, Kucheza Blues

***Oh, Baby!*/Big John Patton (Blue Note)**
Mar. 8, 1963; with Blue Mitchell, Harold Vick, John Patton, and Ben Dixon
One to Twelve, Night Flight, Oh, Baby, Each Time, Good Juice, Fat Judy

***My Point of View*/Herbie Hancock (Blue Note)**
Mar. 19, 1963; with Donald Byrd, Hank Mobley, Herbie Hancock, Chuck Israel, and Anthony Williams
Blind Man, Blind Man
Along with Grachan Moncur III
And What If I Don't Know

***Along Came John*/Big John Patton (Blue Note)**
Apr. 5, 1963; with Fred Jackson, Harold Vick, John Patton, and Ben Dixon
The Silver Meter, Spiffy Diffy, Gee, Along Came John, Pig Foot, I'll Never Be Free

***Soul Sisters*/Gloria Coleman Quartet (Blue Note)**
May 21, 1963; with Leo Wright, Gloria Coleman, and Pola Roberts
Que Baby, Sadi Green, Hey Sonny Red, Melba's Minor, Funky Bob, My Lady's Waltz

***Steppin' Out*/Harold Vick (Blue Note)**
May 27, 1963; with Blue Mitchell, Harold Vick, John Patton, and Ben Dixon
Trimmed in Blue, Vicksville, Steppin' Out, Our Miss Brooks, Dotty's Dream, Laura

***Am I Blue*/Grant Green (Blue Note)**
May 16, 1963; with Johnny Coles, Joe Henderson, John Patton, and Ben Dixon
Am I Blue, Take These Chains from My Heart, I Wanna Be Love, For All We Know

***Blue John*/John Patton (Blue Note)**
Jul. 11, 1963; with George Braith, John Patton, and Ben Dixon
Blue John
Along with Tommy Turrentine
Nicety
Aug. 2, 1963; with George Braith, John Patton, and Ben Dixon
Hot Sauce, Bermuda Clay House, Dem Dirty Blues, Country Girl

***Shoutin'*/Don Wilkerson (Blue Note)**
Jul. 29, 1963; with Don Wilkerson, John Patton, and Ben Dixon
Sweet Cake, Cookin' with Clarence, Movin' Out, Happy Johnny, Easy Living, Blues for J

***Two Souls in One*/George Braith (Blue Note)**
Sep. 4, 1963, with George Braith, Billy Gardner, and Donald Bailey
Mary Had a Little Lamb, Poinciana, Mary Ann, Home Street, Braith-A-Way

***Idle Moments*/Grant Green (Blue Note)**
Nov. 4, 1963; with Joe Henderson, Bobby Hutcherson, Duke Pearson, Bob Cranshaw, and Al Harewood

Idle Moments, Nomad
Nov. 15, 1963; with same personnel
Django, Django (alt. take), Jean de Fleur, Jean de Fleur (alt. take)

***Soul Stream*/George Braith (Blue Note)**
Dec. 16, 1963; with George Braith, Billy Gardner, and Hugh Walker
The Man I Love, Boop Bop Bing Bash, Billy Told, Outside Around the Corner, Soul Stream, Jo Anne

***Search for the New Land*/Lee Morgan (Blue Note)**
Feb. 15, 1964; with Lee Morgan, Wayne Shorter, Herbie Hancock, Reggie Workman, and Billy Higgins
Mr. Kenyatta, Search for the New Land, The Joker, Morgan, The Pirate, Melancholee

***Extension*/George Braith (Blue Note)**
Mar. 27, 1964; with George Braith, Billy Garner, and Clarence Johnson
Nut City, Sweetville, Ethyln's Love, Out Here, Extension, Ev'rytime We Say Goodbye

***Solid*/Grant Green (Blue Note)**
Jun. 12, 1964; with James Spaulding, Joe Henderson, McCoy Tyner, Bob Cranshaw, and Ervin Jones
Grant's Tune, Minor League, The Kicker, Ezz-thetic

***The Way I Feel*/Big John Patton (Blue Note)**
Jun. 19, 1964; with Richard Williams, Fred Jackson, John Patton, and Ben Dixon
Jerry, The Rock, The Way I Feel, Just 3/5
Without Williams, Jackson
Davene

***Talkin' About*/Grant Green (Blue Note)**
Sep. 11, 1964; with Larry Young and Elvin Jones
Talkin' About JC, People, Luny Tune, I'm an Old Cow Hand, You Don't Know What Love Is

***Into Something'*/Larry Young (Blue Note)**
Nov. 12, 1964; Sam Rivers, Larry Young, and Elvin Jones
Plaza de Toros, Tyrone, Back Up, Paris Eyes
Without Rivers
Ritha

***Street of Dreams*/Grant Green (Blue Note)**
Nov. 16, 1964; with Bobby Hutcherson, Larry Young, and Elvin Jones
Lazy Afternoon, I Wish You Love, Somewhere in the Night, Street of Dreams

***I'm Tryin' to Get Home*/Donald Byrd (Blue Note)**
Dec. 17, 1964; with Ernie Royal, Snooky Young, Jimmy Owens, Clark Terry, Donald Byrd, J.J. Johnson, Jimmy Cleveland, Henry Coker, Benny Powell, Jim Buffington, Bob Northern, Don Butterfield, Stanley Turrentine, Freddie Roach, Herbie Hancock, Bob Cranshaw, Grady Tate, and vocal choir voices conducted by Coleridge Perkinson, Duke Pearson, arr.
I'm Tryin to Get Home, March Children, Brother Isaac

***Joe's Blues*/Johnny Hodges—Wild Bill Davis (Verve)**
Jan. 6, 1965; with Lawrence Brown, Johnny Hodges, Wild Bill Davis, Bob Cranshaw, and Grady Tate
Harmony in Harlem, Warm Valley, Joe's Blues, Solitude
Jan. 7, 1965; same personnel
I'll Walk Alone, Someday Loves Me, Wild Bill Blues, Clementine

***I Want to Hold Your Hand*/Grant Green (Blue Note)**
Mar. 31, 1965; with Hank Mobley, Larry Young, and Elvin Jones
Corcovado (Quiet Nights), At Long Last Love, Speak Low, I Want to Hold Your Hand, Stella
Without Mobley:
This Could Be the Start of Something Big

***Matador*/Grant Green (Blue Note) Japan**
May 20, 1965; with Elvin Jones, McCoy Tyner, and Bob Cranshaw
Matador, Green Jeans, My Favorite Things, Bedouin, Wives and Lovers

***His Majesty King Funk*/Grant Green (Verve)**
May 26, 1965; with Harold Vick, Larry Young, Ben Dixon, and Candido Camero, bongo, conga
The Cantaloupe Woman, That Lucky Old Sun, Daddy Grapes, The Selma March, Willow Weep for Me

***Musty Rusty*/Lou Donaldson (Cadet)**
Jun. 3, 1965; with Ben Dixon, Bill Hardman, Lou Donaldson, and Bill Gardner
The Space Walk, Musty Rusty, Hippity Hop, Cherry Pink and Apple Blossom White, Hav' Mercy, Midnight Sun

***Wings and Things*/Johnny Hodges—Wild Bill Davis (Verve)**
Jul. 26, 1965; with Lawrence Brown, Johnny Hodges, Hank Jones, Richard Davis, and Ben Dixon
Take the A Train, Imbo
Jul. 26, or 27, 1965; Wild Bill Davis replacing Jones
Wings and Things, Spotted Dog, Casanova, Dow De Dow Dow, Peg o' My Heart

***Let 'Em Roll*/ Big John Patton (Blue Note)**
Dec. 11, 1965; with Bobby Hutcherson, John Patton, and Otis Finch
The Shadow of Your Smile, The Turnaround, Latuna (Latona), Jakey, Let 'Em Roll, One Step Ahead

***Grasella Oliphant* (Atlantic)**
Mar. 1, 1966; with Clark Terry, Harold Ousley, John Patton, Major Holley, and Oliphant
Get Out of My Life Woman, Later Day, Ain't That Peculiar, Valerie, The Yodel, Peaches Are Better Down the Road, Rapid Shave
Without Terry, Ousley, Holley
Soul Sister, Cantaloupe Woman

***Laughing Souls*/George Braith (Prestige)**
Mar. 1, 1966; with George Braith, John Patton, Eddie Dieghl, Victor Sproles, Ben Dixon, and Richard Landrum
Hot Sauce, Chop Sticks, Chunky Cheeks, Crenshaw West,

Cooleodge (Collage), With Malice Toward None, Little Flame, Cantaloupe Woman, Please Let Me Do

***Got A Good Thing Goin'*/Big John Patton (Blue Note)**
Apr. 29, 1966; with John Patton, Richard Landrum, and Hugh Walker
Soul Woman, Amanda, The Shake, Ain't that Peculiar, The Yodel

***Hold On I'm Coming*/Art Blakey (Limelight)**
May 27, 1966; with Chuck Mangione, Tom McIntosh, Garnett Brown, Frank Mitchell, Malcolm Base, Reggie Johnson, Art Blakey, and John Rodriguez
I Can't Grow Peaches on a Cherry Tree, Walking My Cat Named Dog, Hold on I'm Coming, Skakeena
Melba Liston, replacing McIntosh
She Blew a Good Thing, Day Dream, Mame
without Brown
Got My Mojo Working, Secret Agent Man, Monday, Monday

***Rough 'n' Tumble*/Stanley Turrentine (Blue Note)**
Jul. 1, 1966; with Blue Mitchell, James Spaulding, Stanley Turrentine, Pepper Adams, McCoy Tyner, Bob Cranshaw, and Mickey Roker
What Could I Do Without You?, The Shake, Walk on By, And Satisfy, Baptismal, Feeling Good

***Iron City*/Grant Green (Cobblestone)**
1967; with John Patton and Ben Dixon
Iron City, Sama De Orfeu, (Black Opheus), Old Man Moses, Put on Your High Heel Sneakers (High Heeled Sneakers), Sometimes I Feel like a Motherless Child, Work Song

***Rusty Bryant Returns* (Prestige)**
February 1968; with Rusty Bryant, Sonny Phillips, Bob Bushnell, and Herbie Lovell
Zoo Boogaloo, The Cat, Ready, Rusty, Streak o' Lean, Night Flight, All Day Long

***The Soul Brotherhood*/Charles Kynard (Prestige)**
Mar. 10, 1969; with Blue Mitchell, David Newman, Charles Kynard, Jimmy Lewis, and Mickey Roker
The Soul Brotherhood, Jealjon, Piece o' Pisces, Big City, Blue Farouk

***Love Bug*/Reuben Wilson (Blue Note)**
Mar. 21, 1969; with Lee Morgan, George Coleman, Reuben Wilson, and Leo Morris (Idris Muhummad)
Love Bug, Back Out, Stormy Hot Rod, Say a Little Prayer, I'm Gonna Make You Love Me

***Brother 4*/Don Patterson (Prestige)**
Sep. 15, 1969; with Sonny Stitt, Don Patterson, and Billy James
Alexander's Ragtime Band, Creepin' Home, Brothers D, Walk On By

***Donnybrook*/Don Patterson (Prestige)**
Sep. 15, 1969; with Sonny Stitt, Don Patterson, and Billy James
Good Bait, Starry Night, Donnybrook, St. Thomas, Mud Turtle

***Tune Up*/Don Patterson (Prestige)**
Sep. 15, 1969; with Sonny Stitt, Don Patterson, and Billy James
Tune Up

***Carryin' On*/Grant Green (Blue Note)**
Oct. 3, 1969; with Claude Bartee, Clarence Palmer, Earl Creque, Willie Bivens, Jimmy Lewis, and Idris Muhummad
Ease Back, Hurt So Bad, I Don't Want Nobody to Give Me Nothing (Open Up the Door I'll Get It Myself), Upshot, Cease the Bombing

***Green Is Beautiful*/Grant Green (Blue Note)**
Jan. 30, 1970; with Blue Mitchell, Claude Bartee, Emmanuel Riggins, Jimmy Lewis, Idris Muhummad, Candido Camero, and Richard Landrum
Ain't It Funky Now, A Day in the Life, Dracula, I'll Never Fall in Love Again
Neal Creque, organ replacing Emmanuel Riggins
Windjammer

***Afro Disiac*/Charles Kynard (Prestige)**
Apr. 6, 1970; with Houston Person, Charles Kynard, Jimmy Lewis, and Bernard Purdie
Afro-Disiac, Chanson du Nuit, Sweetheart, Odds On, Belladonna, Trippin'

***Black Out*/Fats Theus (CTI)**
Jul. 16, 22, 1970; with Fats Theus, Wilton Felder, Jimmy Lewis, Chuck Rainey, Idris Muhummad, and Eddie Moore, vocals
Light Sings, Bed of Nails, Stone Flower, Moonlight in Vermont, Check It Out
Clarence Palmer, organ, replacing Felder
Black Out

***Alive!*/Grant Green (Blue Note)**
Aug. 15, 1970; with Claude Bartee, Williams Bivens, Ronnie Foster, Idris Muhummad, and Joseph Armstrong
Let the Music Take Your Mind, Sookie Sookie
Neal Creque, organ, replacing Foster
Time to Remember, Down Here on the Ground

***Person to Person* (Prestige)**
Oct. 12, 1970; with Virgil Jones, Houston Person, Sonny Phillips, Jimmy Lewis, Idris Muhummad, and Buddy Caldwell
Teardrops; The Son of My Man; Close to You; Yesterday Me, Yesterday You, Yesterday Drown in My Own Tears; Up at Jones—Down at Jim

***Visions*/Grant Green (Blue Note)**
May 21, 1971; with Billy Wooten, Emmanuel Riggins, Chuck Rainey, Idris Muhummad, and Ray Armando
Cantaloupe Woman, Never Can Say Goodbye, Maybe Tomorrow, Mozart Symphony No. 40 in G Minor K 550 Ist Movement, We've Only Just Begun, Does Anybody Really Know What Time It Is, Love on a Two Way Street
Along with Harold Cardwell, percussion
Blues for Abraham

***Shades of Green*/Grant Green (Blue Note)**
Nov. 23, 1971; with Billy Wooten, Emmanuel Riggins, Wilton Felder, Stix Hooper, King Erison, Harold Caldwell, Joe Newman, Joe Wilder, Victor Paz, Jimmy Sedlar, Harry DiVito, Dick Hickson, Jimmy Buffington, Phil Bodner, Romeo Penque, George Marge, John Leon, and Wade Marcus
Overdubbed on Dec. 16–17, 1971
California Green, In the Middle Medley, I Don't Want Nobody to Give Me Nothing (Open up the Door, I'll Get It Myself), Cold Sweat
Nov. 24, 1971; same personnel
Overdubbed on Dec. 16–17, 1971
If You Really Love Me, Cast Your Fate to the Wind, Sunrise Sunset, Never My Love, Got to Be There

***The Final Comedown*/Grant Green (Blue Note)**
Dec. 13, 1971; with Marvin Stamm, Irving Markowitz, Harold Vick, Phil Bodner, Richard Tee, Cornell Dupree, Gordon Edwards, Grady Tate, Warren Smith, Ralph McDonald, Eugene Bianco, Charles McCracken, Seymour Barab, Julian Barber, Harry Zaratzian, and Wade Marcus, composer and conductor
Past Present and Future, Fountain Scene, Soul Food-Africa, Shop, Slight Fear and Terror, Luanna's Theme
Without Smith
The Final Comedown, Afro Party, Traveling to Get to Doc, One Death
Dec. 14, 1971; Burt Collins, Romeo Penque, replacing Markowitz, Bodner, along with Warren Smith, tympani
Father's Lament, Battle Scene

***Live at the Lighthouse*/Grant Green (Blue Note)**
Apr. 21, 1972; with Claude Bartee, Gady Coleman, Shelton Laster, Grant Green, Wilton Felder, Greg Williams, and Bobby Hall Porter
Windjammer; Betcha by Golly Wow; Flood in Franklin Park; Fancy Free; Jan, Jan; Walk in the Night

The Real Thing (Eastbound)

1973; with Marcus Belgrave, Donald Towns, Eli Fountaine, Houston Person, Wild Bill Moore, Jimmy Watson, Jack McDuff, Sonny Phillips, Robert Lowe, James Jamieson, Idris Muhummad, Hank Brown, Buddy Caldwell, Etta Hones, and Spanky Wilson, vocalist

You Are the Sunshine of My Life, Since I Fell for You, Until It's Time for You to Go, Angel Eyes, Easy Walker, Kittian Carnival, Couldn't Be I'm Falling in Love, Where Is the Love, Don't Go to Strangers, Crazy Legs

The Main Attraction/Grant Green (KUDU)

March 1976; with Jon Faddis, Burt Collins, Sam Burtis, Hubert Laws, Mike Brecker, Joe Farrell, Ronnie Cuber, Don Groinick, Steve Khan, Will Lee, Andy Newmark, and Carlos Charles

The Main Attraction, Future Feature, Creature

Easy/Grant Green (Versatile)

Apr. 17–20, 1978; with Jon Faddis, Lew Soloff, Janice Robinson, Kiani Zawadi, Karen Joseph, Hank Crawford, Jorge Dalto, Wayne Morrison, Buster Williams, Doug Wilson, and Shanimba

Easy, Just the Way You Are, Wave, Empanada, Nighttime in the Switching Yard

Along with Mario E. Sprouse

Three Times a Lady

The Best of Grant Green Vol. 1 (Blue Note)

1995; Miss Ann's Tempo, 'Round Midnight, Blues in Maude's Flat, Speak Low, Idle Moments, Ezz-thetic

The Best of Grant Green Vol. 2 (Blue Note)

1996

Back Out; Cease the Bombing; Ain't It Funky Now; Sookie, Sookie; Cantaloupe Woman; California Green; The Final Comedown; Windjammer

Produced for release by Bob Belden

Videos

Grant Green, Kenny Burrell, and Barney Kessel performing Kessel's "Blue Mist" in Ronnie Scott's Jazz Club on *Jazz Scene,* a British TV show, Dec. 26, 1969

Album Projects with Tributes to Grant Green

***Remembering Grant Green*/Joshua Breakstone (King Record Co.) Japan**
Jan. 29 and Mar. 5, 1996; Joshua Breakstone with Jack McDuff, Al Harewood, Kenny Barron, Ray Drummond, and Keith Copeland
Street of Dreams, Grantstand, Moon River, Green's Greenery, Idle Moments, Falling in Love with Love, Remember
Produced for release by Jim Eigo and Dave Stryker

***The Lost Grooves, 67–70* (Blue Note)**
1995
Reuben Wilson, Hold On I'm Comin'; Grant Green, It's Your Thing; Lou Donaldson, The Scorpion; Grant Green, Hey Western Union Man; Lou Donaldson, Brother Soul (alt. take); John Patton, Village Lee (alt. take); Stanley Turrentine, Spooky; Lonnie Smith, Dancin' in an Easy Groove; and Stanley Turrentine, You Want Me to Stop Loving
Produced for release by Bob Belden

***Street Funk & Jazz Grooves (The Best of Grant Green)* (Blue Note) United Kingdom**
1993
Grantstand, Lazy Afternoon, Sookie Sookie, Talkin' About, Windjammer, A Walk in the Night, I Don't Want Nobody, Cease the Bombin', The Final Comedown, In the Middle

***A Tribute to Grant Green* (King Records) Japan**
June 12 & 24, 1996

Gregory Green with Peter Bernstein, Ed Cherry, Russell Malone, Dave Stryker, Mark Whitfield, Larry Goldings, and Idris Muhummad
Matador, Green Jeans, Jean de Fleur, Gooden's Corner, Grantstand, Grant's Tune, A Wee Bit o' Green, Plaza de Toros, California Green

***'C' Breeze*/Calvin Brooks (C.B. Records)**
1996
Calvin Brooks with Emmanuel Riggins, Mike Ogorek, Greg "Vibrations" Williams, Charles T. Hokins, Melvin L. Maxwell Jr., and Eric W. Williams
Jan Jan; Bump 'N; Kiss of Life; Next Time; 'C' Breeze; Summertime; Cease the Bombing; Children of the Night; Bump 'N on Sunset; Miles

***Back to the Groove*/Gregory Green (King Records)**
Dec. 8, 1996
Gregory Green with Bobby Watson, Brian Charette, and Cindy Blackman
Blue Things, Naima, Back to the Groove, Send in the Clowns, Something She Said, How Insensitive, Blues in Maude's Flat, 'Round Midnight
Produced for release by Jim Eigo and Dave Stryker

***The New Groove, The Blue Note Remix Project* (Blue Note)**
1996
Donald Byrd, Kofi; Nat Adderly, Hummin'; Stevie Wonder, Living for the City; Eddie Harris, Listen Here (W. Jeffrey/D. Oliver/R. Robinson), Friends and Strangers (G. Garnett/L. Schifrin), Down Here on the Ground (Dianne Reeves with Grant Green's version); Ronnie Foster, Summer Song; Lonnie Smith, Move Your Hand; Horace Silver, The Sophisticated Hippie; Bobby Hutcherson, Montara; Jacky Terrasson/Angel C. Mixed Feelins, (The New Groove)
Executive Producer: Keith M. Thompson

***Grant Green: The Blue Breakbeats* (Blue Note)**
1998
Blue Mitchell, Claude Bartee, Emanuel Riggins, Jimmy Lewis, Idris Muhammad, Candido Camero, Richard Landrum, Billy Wooten,

Ray Armando, Chuck Rainey, Earl Neal Creque, Willie Bivens, Ronnie Foster, Joseph Armstrong, Clarence Palmer, Cornell Dupree, Grady Tate, Gordon Edwards, Ralph McDonald, Richard Tee, Phil Bodner, Harold Vick, Marvin Stamm, and Irv Markowitz
Ain't It Funky Now; Cantaloupe Woman; The Windjammer; Sookie, Sookie; Ease Back; The Final Comedown
Compiled by DJ Smash

Grant Green: Jazz Standards **(Blue Note)**
Aug. 29, 1961
Wilbur Ware, Al Harewood, and Grant Green
You Stepped Out of a Dream, Love Walked In, If I Had You, I'll Remember April, You and the Night and the Music, All the Things You Are, I Remember You, If I Had You (alt. take)

Artists Using Grant Green Samples

Artist Us3
Title *Tukka Yoot's Riddum*
Label Blue Note
Sample "Sookie, Sookie"
Year 1993

Artist Youngblood
Title *Thicker than Water*
Label Medley

Artist Public Enemy
Title *Gotta Do*
Label Def Jam
Sample "Ain't It Funky Now"

Artist May May
Title *Heey*
Label Scotti Bros
Sample "Windjammer"

Artist 3rd Bass
Title *Gladiator*
Label Columbia
Sample "Never My Love"

Artist Cypress Hill
Title *Stoned Is the Way of the Walk*
Label Columbia
Sample "Down Here on the Ground"

Artist A Tribe Called Quest
Title *Vibes and Stuff*
Label Jive
Sample "Down Here on the Ground"
Year 1991

Artist Madonna
Title "Forbidden Love" (*Bedtime Stories*)
Label Warner Bros.
Sample "Down Here on the Ground"
Year 1994

Artist Madonna
Title "Forbidden Love" (*Greatest Hits*)
Label Warner Bros.
Sample "Down Here on the Ground"
Year 1995

Sources

Let's Understand Islam, brochure published by Islamic Circle of North America, New York.

Leonard Feather, "Blindfold Test, Grant Green," *Down Beat.*

"Beatnik Poets' Bar on Downbeat over Liquor Law," St. Louis Post-Dispatch, Jan. 25, 1960.

Robert Levin, liner note, *Grant's First Stand,* Jan. 28, 1961.

Leonard Feather, liner notes, *Green Street,* Apr. 1, 1961.

Nat Hentoff, liner notes, *The Latin Bit,* Apr. 26, 1962.

Dan Morganstern, "New Guitar in Town," *Down Beat,* July 19, 1962.

Michael Cuscuna, liner notes, *Solid,* Jun. 12, 1964.

Stanley Dance, liner notes, *Carryin' On,* Oct. 3, 1969.

Laurie Henshaw, "Three guitar greats," *Melody Maker,* Nov. 8, 1969.

Patricia Sweeting, Interview with Grant Green, Detroit, sometime in early 1970s.

Bernard Comas, liner notes, *Visions,* May 21, 1971.

Gary N. Bourland, "Grant Green," *Guitar Player,* January 1975.

Rita Griffin, "Guitarist Grant Green Dies in NY, Rites in St. Louis," *Michigan Chronicle,* Feb. 10, 1979.

Paul DeMarinis, "Kind of Blue, Cool Jazz Blows Hot and Cold in St. Louis," *The Riverfront Times,* Dec. 16–22, 1987.

"Mixed Signals, WGPR, the Nation's First Black-Owned and Operated TV Station Never Fulfilled Potential," *Detroit Free Press,* November 27, 1994.

David Germain, "King of Boxed Sets Celebrates 10 Years in Business," *Associated Press,* Sep. 3, 1993.

Lars Bjorn and Michael G. Nastos, "Motor City Jazz, a Quick Critical Study," 1994 Montreux Jazz Festival guide.

Michael Erlewine, *All Music Guide to Jazz,* 1998.

Tom Evered, liner notes, *The Best of Grant Green, Vol. 2,* 1996.

Acknowledgments

Many people have helped me, in one way or another, in writing this book. I thank them all. But I would especially like to thank Sky Awamy, Bob Belden, Ed Benson, Joshua Breakstone, Gary Carner, Leo Chears, Bob Cranshaw, Michael Cuscuna, Patrick Dodd, *Down Beat,* James Edmonds, Jim Eigo, Michael Erlewine, Tom Evered, Pete Gazes, Grant Green Jr., Gregory Green, Ardis Hansberry, Jocelyn Heard, Richard Henderson, Nat Hentoff, Herbie Holland, Tobias "TJ" Jundt, Ruth Lion, Charlie Lourie, Bruce Lundvall, Jorge Martinez, Virgil Matheus, Coleman Mellett, Ann Moody, Alan Moss, Yoichi Nakao, Dan Ouellette, Tony Parker, Bob Porter, Dave Stryker, Patricia Sweeting, Kenny Washington, Lori Wood, Bob Yelin, and everyone who agreed to be interviewed. A very special thanks to the Villa Montalvo Artist Residency Program in Saratoga, California, and to Roy Zarruchi and Carolyn Page of the Potato Eyes Foundation in Troy, Maine, for their support during the transcribing stage of this manuscript. And, because I am not ashamed to say it, I would like to thank the Creator, who inspired a people, who inspired a man, and who inspired a music.

Index